Even as We Grieved

Journal of a Plague Year

*The Coronavirus Crisis of 2020-21
as experienced in small-town Ireland*

First published in Ireland in 2021
by Wordkern Media
wordkernmedia@gmail.com

Design and typesetting by Inspire.ie
Set in Adobe Caslon

Remembering the O'Donovans of Ahilnane
and the children of Queensfort

CONTENTS

PREFACE

These are my diaries for the months of the coronavirus crisis of 2020-21. They represent an account of the crisis from an Irish point of view but additionally offer a snapshot of the century as it comes of age, albeit the focus is on the North Atlantic world for the most part.

I did not set out to keep a 'pandemic diary,' the idea of so doing would have been unappealing. It's simply that I diary — diarizing regularly if not routinely — and out cycling one winter's day it occurred to me that maybe the virus diaries could be extracted and made into something, collected for the historical record if nothing else.

Maybe — maybe a print book, maybe an ebook, maybe a blog, maybe a podcast.

And maybe nothing at all because at the time I hadn't reread any of the diary files so I'd little sense of how they might read.

As I say, it was just an idea, a notion — one of those thought-bubbles that bubble up as one cycles meditatively in a churchyard on a frosted winter's morning — nevertheless I was sufficiently struck by the idea to make a note of it — see diary entry for Tuesday, 1 December 2020.

I didn't do anything about it then, or even think about it much so far as I'm aware, but, clearly, the conception had staying power for I returned to the subject in the new year, which is when I first began reading through the 2020 diary files — see entries for Monday, 4 January 2021, and Tuesday, 19 January 2021 — at that stage just seeking to get a sense of what I'd written and accumulated.

Unsurprisingly, during the pandemic I diaried more than I would do normally, particularly during the lockdown months. Generally, I don't diary every day; on average I do so maybe four or five times a month, it's not regularized. I'll write a thousand or two thousand words whenever I'm minded to do so. And sometimes I'll start something and spend a couple of days on it, or a whole week maybe — writing up a report on a trip, say, or going off on some expostulation or polemic — then other times I'll write but once or twice in the month.

The main thing about diary-writing for me is that it's a means by which I sidestep coming to my desk and dumbly staring at a winking cursor, a petty horror of mine. Once I come to my desk I like to start writing asap. It doesn't matter what to begin with, a few simple paragraphs to get the word-flow going, even if only about the look of the morning and the weather we're having, or have been having, or are about to have.

Often I'll use diary docs as a space wherein I sandbox stuff, so in the 'raw' files — the original diary files — will be drafts of things, letters and/ or emails, say, or a sketch-outline of an idea, or, most frequently of all, offcuts from something being composed in another document, cuts & clips I'm not willing to del just yet, but then all too often I forget about them so there they remain like post-glacial erratic boulders.

Or if I come across an essay or article (or part of one) that interests me and, if it's not obvious where it needs to be filed in my existing files, I'll copy and paste it into that month's diary pages, temporarily at least, with the result that there's an immense amount of accumulated in the raw files — same with poetry, song lyrics, recipes, bookmark-hyperlinks, scree from social media and Wikipedia, bits from books and/or movies which I'll sometimes transcribe if a particular section, speech or rally of dialogue resonates.

For want of copyright almost all such cuts & pastes and transcriptions have had to be deleted.

In fact, what I call the 'raw diary files' are partly diaries in the com-monly understood sense — qua journals — and partly what would more aptly be characterized as commonplace book material.

In addition I've a tendency to repeat myself, saying on Friday or Saturday something I already said Monday or Tuesday the preceding week but because something's still worming in my brain, or because I've simply forgotten that I've already had my say on the subject, I end up starting in on it again, oftentimes repeating myself. All of which is fine so far as my own private diary docs go but when putting together something like this — this publication — the like is repetitive and as a consequence has had to be deracinated and ruthlessly scissored.

Unedited the raw diaries amount to hundreds of thousands of words, which would come to well more than a thousand typeset pages! Firstly, no way I'd consider having a multi-volume production for something like this, and, secondly, as I say, the diaries needed a thorough sorting-through because unedited they're a bit of a nick-knack shed-in-the-yard mess.

There's no mention of the virus in the diaries until March 2020 therefore March 2020 is the month I begin with. And I got vaccinated in May 2021 so I end with that.

Nothing dramatic happens to me during these pandemic months: I didn't get Covid, I didn't have a crisis with my patched-up teeth, my house wasn't burgled, nor inundated with floodwater, nor fire- nor storm-damaged, I didn't enjoy a relationship start-up nor suffer one coming to a sad or bitter end, I encountered no celebrated personage perambulating in the church grounds, nor even an exotic egret or misguided booby alighting on the lawns or nesting in the adjoining scrubland... it's all been fairly low key, quotidian, mundane: we had three lockdowns in the space of 12 months, I complied with the regulations as thoroughly and as genuinely as I could, Fields delivered groceries to my front door, I did a bit of gardening, some cycling and walking, I wrote up these diaries, read a stack of books and watched the last year of Benito Trumpolini's clown-car term of office and (simultaneously) — the undercard — Alexander Boris de Piffle Johnson become a little MinneMe Trumpolini in England. This has been my life.

Perry O'Donovan
Skibbereen, August 2021

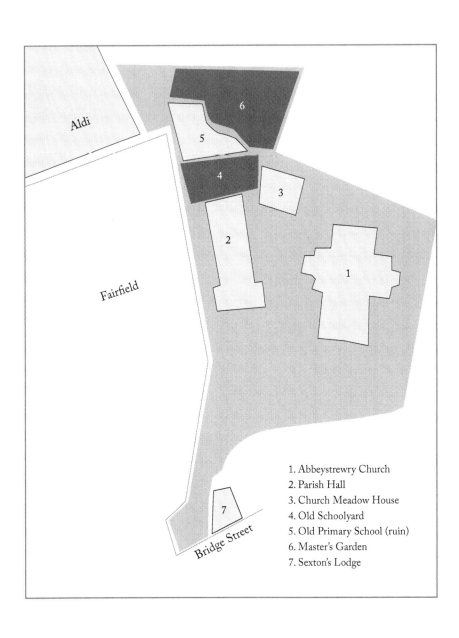

Aldi

6

5

4

3

2

1

Fairfield

7

Bridge Street

1. Abbeystrewry Church
2. Parish Hall
3. Church Meadow House
4. Old Schoolyard
5. Old Primary School (ruin)
6. Master's Garden
7. Sexton's Lodge

MARCH 2020

Been busy with stuff: videography course — not just attending the classes also doing stuff for the classes, or thinking about/planning for same, following up links to various related — I've done a fair amount of gardening too — this is the time of year for it, some things simply have to be done this time of year otherwise they cannot be done at all — and I've washed all the windows inside and out, including window frames and glass porch out front, and to be wholly honest I don't know how much more besides but I feel like I've been going non-stop.

Which is why, for instance, when that second meeting with Deirdre Walsh came round I was a little astonished because it didn't seem like 3 weeks had passed since the previous meeting. Time seems to have scudded by as if in a time-lapse sequence. And then it's been busy in the outer world too, lots happening at the minute. There's been a general election for one thing, in February, of course, but campaigning still ongoing because there's a game of musical chairs going on to do with government formation and at present everyone's a player, so they're all in continuing campaign mode as it's not out of the question that there will be another general election before matters resolve, there's been the ongoing funhouse-mirror farce with Clown-prince Trump — he was impeached before Christmas but acquitted in a farce trial in the Senate in January — and now the focus has moved on to who the Dems are going to select to go up against him in the election later this year (more on this in a section to come), and, most of all, there's been the Corona Virus scare which is causing serious chaos: Six Nations and Serie A fixtures postponed, for example, St Patrick's Day parades cancelled, and there's talk of postponing the Euro 2020 football tournament due to take place in 12 European cities in June and early July, and even this summer's Olympics in Tokyo.

In the U.S. the Indian Wells tennis tournament has been cancelled, as has Austin's SXSW, and there's a cruise ship with 3,000 passengers, 40 or 50 of whom have tested positive for the virus, due to dock at Oakland but the Prince of Orange won't let them because it'll double the infection numbers in the U.S. and it'll mean quarantining 3,000 people for a couple of weeks, so they remain out at sea, panicking increasingly, no doubt.

The U.S. is in a total mess with respect to this coronavirus thing, firstly because the tangerine buffoon refused to take it seriously early on, hoping he could deny/minimize it out of frame — fearing the impact of it on his re-election campaign — but also because for millions their health system is a shantytown mess; this is where their shitty inequitable system comes and gets them in the ass because in an situation such as this if you've got millions of people without any kind of health care it doesn't matter how gilt-edged your own individual policy is, the whole society is infected because you've got millions of people who aren't going to go and get tested, fearing the cost of the tests, say, or maybe they're in the country illegally or semi-legally, and because of the hopelessly fragmented nature of their healthcare system(s) there's no command and control levers to push or pull, at least none that'll work in an emerging emergency such as this.

And even if they do go for a test and they're 'positive' many will continue going to work anyway because six times out of ten your mean-spirited welfare system(s) doesn't pay sick-pay to the people who most need it. In a situation such as this your system is as strong as the strength of cover the weakest can command. And by this metric the bottom end of the American socio-economic ziggurat is a shambles, as they're likely to find out in the coming weeks and months. More on coronavirus and American politics in a little while, first, matters closer to home.

As I write — end of the first week in March — there's 20 cases in Ireland, including at least one in Cork, a patient in CUH which has caused alarm because this guy has not been abroad so it's not clear how he's come into contact with the virus — he's a patient in the hospital — and now everyone who has been in contact with him — an estimated 60 members of staff — are self-isolating for 14 days as a precautionary measure. There's about 200 cases in the UK (with 2 deaths so far), but, in Europe, Italy is worst hit: 200 dead at the minute and I don't know how many thousands infected. Large parts of northern Italy on lockdown, flights to and from cancelled. And some experts say the true situation in Italy — and all across Europe indeed — is much worse than official figures suggest, with hundreds of thousands infected maybe, however because most people suffer only fairly mild symptoms they're not presenting themselves for diagnosis. And of course if this is the case then millions will inevitably be infected and hundreds of thousands will die.

Since writing the above this morning I've come across some really dreadful figures: first of all, today (this evening), Sunday, 8 March, the authorities in Italy have announced that in the past 24 hours there have been 133 deaths — in just one day! Most of northern Italy now on lockdown with schools, universities, museums, swimming pools, sports centres, nightclubs — everything — closed until early April, 16 million people on lockdown apparently. Bars and cafés still open, I believe, but you're supposed to keep at least one metre distance from others!

Second update: Italy's figures continue to shock: in less than a week Italy has gone from 200 dead from coronavirus-related issues to over 800! Italy's important because it's part of Europe, obviously, but also in that it offers a picture of what's to come. People saying France and the UK about two or three weeks behind where Italy is right now, albeit Italy has managed things rather poorly, as the Italians are wont to do, so, for example, when they went to extend the lockdown areas mentioned above, extending it to take in an estimated 16 million people, news of this leaked before the authorities were ready to make the announcement with the result that thousands packed up a few essentials and took flight, planes, trains and automobiles in all directions — to holiday homes, presumably, or to their parents' place, or to far-flung cousins or wheresoever — not wanting to be confined in the quarantine. Which is precisely what you don't want in such a situation! That's thousands and maybe tens of thousands taking the virus out to all parts of the country, potentially, so that two or three days afterwards they had to extend the quarantine area again to take in the whole of the country.

Also, by the bye, I've seen several reports say that these Italian quarantines aren't worth a spit, they're just for PR purposes, B-roll for the evening news broadcasts.

Third update: and now they've had to take things a step further again — Italy — ordering everything, other than foodstores and pharmacies, to shut, effective immediately.

And — leading all the news broadcasts this morning — last night Trump addressed the nation in a White House address — sitting behind the Resolute desk in the Oval Office — in which he announced a 30-day ban on all traffic out of Europe; passengers anyhow it seems, in his address he said people *and cargo* but in a rushed supplementary briefing White House officials hastened to make clear the ban did *not* apply to cargo. This is a piece of clown politics as much as anything: now he wants to appear decisive, commanding, the great leader in a solemn crisis, however just a little while ago he was saying this whole 'coronavirus thing' was a hoax, Fake News, something designed to make him look bad, and that, even if you got it [the virus], most people would still be well enough to go to work as it's not much worse than regular flu. He said this even as his newly appointed chief-of-staff announced he was self-isolating for the recommended 14 days having been in contact with a confirmed case. It's a mess over there, a mess with a narcissistic clown in the wheelhouse.

Figures for Spain, France and Germany shooting up alarmingly too, especially France and Spain.

Tim & Laurence still down in Trabuco, panicking a little now, understandably. Rocked by the fact that everything sold out of pharmacies here in Skibbereen, I sent them an email towards the end of February advising them to secure whatever protective gear they could get hold of for their journey home (then due to be at the end of March) and at that time — judging by their response — they were fairly blasé about the situation, saying more or less 'Thanks very much for that, Perry; we'll certainly look into it.'

Since then things have escalated in a compound way, one day hard upon the heels of its predecessor. By 4 March they'd brought forward their return-home plans by 9 days. I would have come home sooner to be honest but I didn't say anything other than that I thought this wise. Yesterday evening Tim sent me a WhatsApp message saying that Laurence was packing for the return trip (now next week — the day after St Patrick's Day is when they get the [France-to-Ireland] ferry, so presumably they will start their journey this coming weekend: fully packed Sunday evening, leave Trabuco first thing Monday morning, stay somewhere near the Pyrenees that night — maybe sleeping in the van — then travel north through France on Patrick's Day, maybe sleeping in the van again that night, and catch the ferry the following day) and that her stress level was '7 out of 10'. I can imagine. If it's 7/10 now what the fuck will it be next week?

Look, I believe they'll be fine but they certainly wouldn't want to have left it any later than next week. France and Spain will go to total shut-downs earlier than Italy has done, and when they do so they will execute the thing more vigorously and comprehensively than the Italians have done. (In fairness, we're all learning from the situation in Italy, good things and bad.) By the end of next week I think we may well see borders close and maybe schools and workplaces too. Might even happen this weekend, it's certainly being discussed in the capitals of Europe right now, of that you may be sure. As I write (the most up-to-date information I can find — EU Centre for Disease Prevention and Control website — says) 48 dead in France (with 2,281 confirmed cases) and 47 in Spain (with 2,140 confirmed cases), my guess is that once France goes to 3 digits dead (100+ dead and, say, circa 5,000 confirmed cases) they'll push the emergency procedures button, that is to say, serious steps towards containment before things get out of hand altogether, because no health system could possibly cope with a situation in which you have 100,000 cases, which would mean circa 15,000 people seriously ill and thousands needing ventilators, not to mind a million or more, which is what they'll have to deal with if they don't go to emergency measures early and effectively.

China, where the outbreak began, did so swiftly, decisively and ruthlessly and — if you believe their figures — they appear to have the situation under control now: altogether 80,932 confirmed cases in China, so far, 3,172 deaths, however only 2,773 confirmed new cases in the past 14 days, a figure which is falling rapidly (i.e., the 14-day figure coming down rapidly), so they appear to have the thing corralled.

Meanwhile here in Ireland there's been another case in another hospital in Cork, in the Bons this time, apparently. Again this appears to be community transmission, which is to say, rather than the person having been to an infected area or having been in contact with someone who had been in an infected area (so far as we know). And according to an article on the RTE website posted this evening now 175 hospital staff in Cork and Limerick hospitals self-isolating for precautionary reasons.

Also at one point the same article says 'Earlier, the Health Service Executive said that it cannot dispute projections that 1.9 million people in the Republic of Ireland may contract the virus.'

And 'Minister for Health Simon Harris has said it is highly likely we will see many cases of Covid-19 in Ireland.'

'Around 80% of cases of Covid-19 are a mild to moderate illness, close to 14% have severe disease and around 6% are critical. The latest data from the World Health Organization is that Covid-19 has an estimated global mortality rate of 3.4%.'

Aside from the 80% figure these are much higher percentages than we've heard of hitherto: a couple of weeks ago they were saying that the mortality rate was just 1% to 2%.

Nor, obviously, do they know about the long term consequences of being infected with this virus.

'Generally, you need to be 15 minutes or more in the vicinity of an infected person, within 1-2 metres, to be considered at-risk or a close contact.'

6% of cases 'critical' is a lot of people: 6% of 1.9 million is 114,000! Especially in light of the closing paragraphs:

> Dr [Chris] Luke, a consultant in emergency medicine and a senior lecturer in public health at University College Cork, said that currently Ireland has only around 250 intensive care beds.
>
> He said we "probably don't" have the capacity to deal with an increased demand on intensive care facilities, if the numbers are stark.
>
> "We will have to triage accordingly and be creative in our use of intensive care unit facilities, but very hard decisions may have to be made about who gets intensive care and in what order of priority, so there will be tricky decisions ahead of us", he said.

Thursday, 12 March

Just drafted the following email to Dominic Casey [Videography for Beginners course at the College of Commerce's West Cork campus], however, I didn't press 'send', I thought I go and have lunch first then reread it and see how it reads:

> Dominic, I think I won't attend class this evening. I'm concerned about this corona virus thing, to be honest.

> I have COPD (Chronic Obstructive Pulmonary Disease) and so need to be extra careful. (Normal flu can be fatal for me.) The idea of sitting in a computer room with 15 or 16 people for two hours is freaking me out.

> Rationally, I know that the chances of someone in the class having the bug is low to moderate but I'm simply not willing to take chances at the present time. In addition to my actual condition I suffer from a level of paranoia about colds and flus and such like, psychosomatically getting flu-like symptoms if I'm anywhere near someone who coughs or snivels or sneezes. So it's best if I not go, I feel, because, aside from the risk of infection itself (which, as I say, I know to be not great), the whole thing is very likely to wreck my head and well-being for days afterwards, so much so it's just not worth it.

> This whole corona virus thing is no joke; even here in Ireland the HSE acknowledge that we might be looking at serious piles of corpses before we're finished. Respiratory failure is a seriously shitty way to go, which is what this is, essentially, it's a form of SARS (Severe Acute Respiratory Syndrome, SARSCoV2 to be precise), and I have no one to nurse me if I get it so it would be especially wretched and miserable.

> In the circumstances, I feel I cannot be too careful; or at least I feel that not attending your class this evening is not 'being too careful'.

> You'll send me the slides I trust and if I have any questions I'll email or WhatsApp you. In any event, this is what's best for me, I've concluded.

> Sincerely (and trusting you'll understand), Perry

At 1 o'clock I tuned in for the lunchtime news and the lead item was that Ireland's gone to emergency Level 1 — from 6 o'clock this evening all schools, colleges and childcare facilities to close until the end of the month. No gathering of more than 100 people indoors and no more than 500 outdoors (for the text of the Taoiseach's announcement, see following). Even before I'd finished my lunch my phone started pinging with emails and text messages saying the CoC would be closing up at 6 o'clock this evening and so therefore there would be no classes this evening (not that it matters too much, but this — the promptness of the College of Commerce — tells me this has all been coordinated and that the college authorities were ready to go with those emails and text messages as soon as Leo Varadkar made the announcement). Needless to say, I didn't send my email as all classes cancelled.

Taoiseach's statement:

> Good morning,
>
> I need to speak to you about Coronavirus and CoVid-19.
>
> For the past few weeks, the Government and our public services have been focused on the impact of the virus.
>
> In that time we have taken several important and unprecedented measures to protect public health.
>
> We have been preparing for all eventualities.
>
> Yesterday, the World Health Organisation formally described it as a pandemic and the European Centre for Disease Prevention and Control (ECDC) updated it guidelines advising us all to act early to be effective.
>
> Our own National Public Health Emergency Team met last night and has issued new advice to Government. We are acting on that advice today.
>
> There will be many more cases.
>
> More people will get sick and unfortunately, we must face the tragic reality that some people will die.
>
> The virus is all over the world. It will continue to spread but it can be slowed. Its impact can be reduced making it easier for our health service to cope and giving our scientists more time to develop better testing, treatments and a vaccine.
>
> It is important to remember that the disease effects will be mild for the majority of people especially the young and healthy.

We know that older people and those with chronic diseases are at real risk. We have a duty as a society to protect ourselves and above all to protect others – our parents and grandparents, our family and friends, co-workers and neighbours.

We have not witnessed a pandemic of this nature in living memory. This is unchartered territory.

We said we would take the right actions at the right time.

We have to move now to have the greatest impact.

So, from 6pm today, the following measures are being put in place. They will stay in place until March 29th.

Schools, colleges, and childcare facilities will close from tomorrow. Where possible, teaching will be done on-line or remotely. Cultural institutions will close.

Our advice is that all indoor mass gatherings of more than 100 people and outdoor mass gatherings of more than 500 people should be cancelled.

Arrangements are being made to ensure that everyone entering Ireland through our ports and airports is fully informed and self-isolates if they develop symptoms.

You should continue to go to work if you can but where possible work from home. In order to reduce unnecessary face to face interaction in the workplace, break times and working times should be staggered and meetings done remotely or by phone.

Public transport will continue to operate.

Shops will remain open and we have plans to ensure that supply chains will not be interrupted.

We need the public and businesses to take a sensible and level-headed responsible approach.

Restaurants, cafes and other businesses can stay open but should look at ways they can implement the public health advice on social distancing.

As a general rule, outside of work people should seek to reduce social interactions as much as possible.

You can play your part by hand-washing, coughing and sneezing into your elbow, and seeking medical advice if you develop symptoms. This is now more important than ever.

The Cabinet will meet later today.

Opposition party leaders and our counterparts in Northern Ireland and Britain will be briefed.

In the period ahead, the Government will deploy all the resources we can muster, human and financial, to tackle this threat head-on. Those resources are extensive but not unlimited.

Healthcare workers have been at the forefront of this crisis since it started. They will be at the frontline of the crisis in the time ahead. We must do all we can to help them, so they can help those who need help the most.

I know that some of this is coming as a real shock and it is going to involve big changes in the way we live our lives.

I know that I am asking people to make enormous sacrifices.

We're doing it for each other.

Together, we can slow the virus in its tracks and push it back.

Acting together, as one nation, we can save many lives.

Our economy will suffer. It will bounce back.

Lost time in school or college will be recovered. In time, our lives will go back to normal.

Above all, we need to look out for each other.

Ireland is a great nation. And we are great people. We have experienced hardship and struggle before. We have overcome many trials in the past with our determination and our spirit.

We will prevail.

This virus is believed to have jumped from bats to humans. The Chinese love eating and doing stupid backward (quasi-medieval) shite with exotic animals and bits of animals — snakes, beavers, badgers, peacocks, rhino tusks, monkey brains… — which they dignify with the OK-sounding umbrella term 'Traditional Medicine', and in these almost totally unregulated street markets you have traders trading these things, creatures in cages stacked on top of one another in confined unsanitary spaces, and, hop-step-and-jump, we've got a global pandemic which might yet result in premature deaths for millions, old people mostly but also the weak and the sick and the poor, the vulnerable, basically, one way or another.

Apparently the so-called 'Spanish flu' epidemic of 1918-20 was responsible for more deaths than any of the more infamous genocides in that genocidal century — an estimated 50 million people died in that pandemic (an estimated 500 million infected, 27% of the world's population at that time). 100,000 U.S. soldiers died in WWI; 40,000 of them as a result of that flu epidemic which is believed to have jumped from domesticated fowl to humans — ducks, it is thought — which soldiers had cooped-up in confined spaces in battle- and supply-line trenches.

I must say I'm a little freaked about it all. I've got COPD so that's one reason to be concerned (if not alarmed) right there, it's a real issue for me — I might not be so concerned otherwise — but also I'm concerned because I'm poor and am without good connections the way other people know doctors or pharmacists or the like.

I don't think I wrote about this in February but a couple of weeks ago I thought I'd be smart — be ahead of the curve — and get a few packets of surgical masks and any other kinds of protective masks I could get my hands on because one evening [on YouTube] I saw a Chanel 4 News report about how surgical masks were selling in Hong Kong for over $1,000 HK dollars a packet, normally *circa* $100 HK, and there were long queues of worried-looking people snaking out of places still selling them. Watching the report I thought to myself, 'We might be only a few weeks away from the like here' — at the time there were cases in Europe already. However, when I went to the pharmacy they'd totally sold out and they'd no date for when they'd have more. Same story in all 3 pharmacies in Skibbereen! Instead of being ahead of the curve turns out I was way behind it!

But my point here is that at least in Cleary's pharmacy for some reason I got the distinct impression that the woman I spoke to was not telling me the truth. I got the feeling that if I'd been someone more significant/prominent/local/likeable I would have gotten a different answer/

response. The woman seemed to be getting off on the gatekeeper power circumstances conferred on her.

In the end I went to Drinagh Hardware and got a few industrial type things; and even in the hardware store there were clear gaps on the racks where they stock these products. Altogether I spent €75 on stuff that day: I got a good P3 one [P3 is the top level of protection in our system of signification], not too big and bulky but fully sealed to the face by way of soft rubber lips, which was expensive, along with replacement filters, the replacement filters alone were €13.50 each [for each pair], I also got a couple of less prominent looking P2 level ones because I feared looking like a bit of a langer if I felt I ought to be wearing a mask and went out wearing something like you might see someone wearing in wartime,[1]

---

[1] In fairness, it's not a full WW2 type gasmask, it's more Bane in Batman. Also — just to report — I've seen the first person I've seen wearing a surgical mask in Skibbereen, a woman in Fields, earlier this week. People around here have them, clearly, but no one wants to risk being ridiculed, except that woman, obviously. In the aisles you could see people tittering and twittering about the silly woman in her surgical mask but, if I myself am any guide, while people may feel it's OTT at this stage, you kinda wondered whether we were at that stage already, i.e., if the woman wearing the mask was the wise one and we the smirking hayseeds. But that will change as soon as we get a story of someone in Clonakilty or Bantry or here in Skibbereen infected or in isolation. Which may already have happened, in fact, because we know about the guy in CUH and the person in the Bons but the authorities are being coy about where the infections are because they don't want to engender panic, so they say 'a new case in the south of the country' for example but they never say where specifically. The CUH thing different because it was all over the hospital within a couple of hours, presumably, with a crisis management team figuring out which members of staff needed to be sent home to self-isolate and then teams of people reassigned to cover for the staff sent home, in addition to which there is now a visitor ban in place in the hospital and all elective and non-essential procedures have been put on hold for the duration, so the story was all over the city before suppertime, and it doesn't suit the authorities to have a situation in which the real story about what's going on is passed along by word of mouth and official pronouncements are regarded as government PR guff. So the fact that there was a case of infection in CUH was reported out. (It may well be, for example, that one of the 60 staff members sent home lives in Clon or Bandon or Macroom or Dunmanway which, to an ever-growing extent, are dormitory towns for the fast-expanding city.) In addition to which all the staff in the Credit Union, for example, and in Fields, and in other shops too I imagine are wearing latex gloves already. And like with the SARS thing a few years ago there are hand sanitizers everywhere now, even in church porches. One of these days people working in pharmacies (for example) will start wearing surgical masks and that will light the fuse, then suddenly everyone will start wearing them. Or a couple of coronavirus-related deaths in the local area, anywhere in the west Cork area, and you may be sure within a couple of days you'll see people wearing protective masks. One last thing for now in this absurdly overburdened footnote: 'wartime' is a term we're hearing more and more in relation to this coronavirus business; in the UK, for example, where they're now saying an epidemic is not an 'if' but a 'when', emergency powers legislation designed

and subsequent to that I spent another €50 on cold & flu medicines — Lemsips, another bottle of Vit C tablets (90 days' worth), Day & Night tablets and so on. Also bought swimmer's goggles because apparently the infection can get into your system by way of your eyes too, which are connected to the top of the respiratory system.

Overreacting (with the masks and medicines) maybe — I could do without the expense you may be sure — but not altogether a waste of money insofar as I would need to get all these medicines later this year anyway before heading into winter again and, with the way things are, the respiratory masks will not go to waste either — this is about the fourth or fifth scare we've had in this wholly globalized century: SARS (Severe Acute Respiratory Syndrome), MERS (Middle East Respiratory Syndrome), Ebola, H1N1…, a century which began with the Foot & Mouth crisis in the UK which also involved strict quarantines (causing pile-ups and carnage in sporting and cultural schedules) and shooting all those animals — the whole national herd put down, burning their bodies in huge piles of animal corpses, like scenes in a disaster movie. At the time I remember wondering whether such dreadful sights were a harbinger of the century to come. It's a fairly safe bet that there will be another scare along after this one is what I'm saying.

It's not that I think I need these things right *now*, I ought to add, but if the whole thing turns really nasty and I feel I do need them I don't want to go into shops and be told that they're all sold out and that whatever it is I want or need cannot be got anymore by some smug fuck who has her own supply secured at home or under the counter.

Also I ought to add, this shit could continue for some time. As far as I understand things they expect the present crisis to peak in the next 6 to 8 weeks, after that we'll be into early summer wherein the health system will be in much better shape to cope and the weather conditions will help stay the spread to some extent, but come autumn and winter this thing could flare up again. They ain't gonna have a vaccine for this any time soon, if one is developed at all, not for 12 months at least, and

---

to facilitate dealing with the situation being fast-tracked through parliament, the like of which have not been invoked since wartime, apparently, including powers to put towns and cities on lockdown if necessary, put the army on the streets to maintain law and order, and to detain people who ought to self-isolate but refuse to do so and so on. Also measures to secure food and medical supplies &c &c &c.

probably 18 months by the time it's fully tested and trialled and licenced and manufactured and out into GP surgeries and high street pharmacies &c. So it's not just for now it's the winter to come as well. And as I say the next infectious crisis too, which, no doubt, is just a little way down the road we're travelling on.

This virus crisis is having a severe impact on the economy: stock markets have experienced the worst hit since the financial crash of 2008-10. And they continue to tumble. That's corporations and big businesses, big enough to be stock market-listed anyhow, but small businesses are going to be really badly hit. Restaurants, for example: if you're making widgets and there's some kind of crisis and you stop producing them (or you continue producing them but at a slower rate, stockpiling them), after the crisis pent-up demand will mean greater volume of business for six months or so. But the like is not the case with bars and restaurants. People aren't going to eat two meals at lunchtime or have 6 cups of mid-morning coffee after the crisis is over. If you have a serious crisis wherein markets are tanking and people are self-isolating and wearing surgical masks and not going out for 8 or 10 or 12 weeks many places will go out of business. Venice and other tourist honeypots (ski resorts, for example) like tumbleweed ghost towns apparently. And an airline (Flybe) has gone out of business, an airline that was struggling admittedly but this has been the final straw.

The only upside to this whole thing may be that it does for Trump's re-election bid. Along with the Federalist Society judges he's been appointing, the record stock market performance has been one of his main boasts. You can see him panicking about it all, and it's not that thousands may suffer horribly and die before their time that's concerning him, not a bit of it, it's the impact on the stock market and the impact that that in turn might have on his re-election prospects — because, believe me, if he doesn't get himself re-elected he's going to be caught up in so many legal tangles it wouldn't surprise me if he ends up getting cuffed. Normally someone at that level would never be cuffed but Trump has shown such contempt for the way things are done and for the people who know how to do things he will not now be able to claim establishment privileges, and even if he himself avoids detention, which I doubt — far too much bad blood at this stage — lots of people around him are going to get it, and, assuredly, unless they flip and become witnesses for the prosecution, they'll be joining his lawyer & fixer, Michael Cohen, his 2016 campaign manager, Paul Manafort, his first National Security Advisor, Michael Flynn, and his old pal and political mentor Roger Stone. As the old adage goes, show me your company and I'll tell you what you are.

And from a crisis management pov Trump is handling it all sooo badly — compare and contrast with the Obama administration's handling of the Ebola threat! — even saying the whole thing's 'a Democrat hoax' at one point! He said the Dems and their allies in the mainstream media are whipping up 'this corona virus thing' because they failed to take him down by way of Jim Comey, failed again with the Mueller probe, and failed yet again with the 'Impeachment hoax', and now this coronavirus thing is their latest ruse. The guy's a turd in the punch bowl. An incompetent, ludicrous fool. Stung by the criticism he has had he made a big deal of going to the CDC this week, but did so wearing a re-election campaign cap — 'Keep America Great' is the slogan this cycle; in 2016 it was 'Make America Great Again', same cap, same act, same guff but an updated slogan. He did a photo-op/press-avail at the CDC which was astonishing for its ignorance and bombast and foolish self-centredness, at one point saying that even top experts are amazed at how well he understands epidemiology; maybe he ought to have gone into epidemiology, he mused. The audacity of ignorance.

Meanwhile the hitherto chaotic Democratic Party contest to select someone to run against him in November is finally down to Bernie Sanders or Joe Biden (there were 24 or 25 candidates in the running at one stage, which just looked absurd, an organisation not serious about its business). Biden is 77 years old, if he wins in November he'll be 78 by the time he'll be sworn into office, older than Ronald Reagan was when he left office, by which time Reagan was a nappy-wearing senile mess.

And Biden is clearly senile as it is, to some extent, some considerable extent indeed: at an event the other evening he introduced his wife as his youngest sister! In a campaign speech a little while ago he couldn't bring to mind the most celebrated words of the Declaration of Independence. And in one of the debates he meant to ask people who wanted to contribute to his campaign to call or text a number but couldn't bring the number to mind. And, just in this cycle alone, there are about 20 other things of the like, that is to say, without going into the archives and digging up stuff from previous cycles (Joe, who was born in 1942, first ran for the presidency in the late 1980s, the cycle that saw George HW Bush elected). Many of these can be dismissed as 'Joe-isms', in fairness — he's famous for his loveable gaffs and harmless little failures and missteps — but, even with the best will in the world, not all of them can be. The guy's got serious senior citizen type issues, no doubt about it.

And that added to the fact that, as one newspaper columnist put it, Joe's 'as underwhelming as he is inoffensive' — the guy stands for absolutely nothing at all, except more of the same, the same that got Trump elected in the first place: Trump represented change, disruption, brick-through-a-plate-glass-window type change. Biden is a weak sauce version of Hillary Clinton — he's a likeable (relatable) bloke with great American teeth, that's all, avuncular (an uncle Alfie type), and he's poor at this game, which is why he's failed at it every time so far, and failed badly too, I mean he wasn't even a serious player in 2007 and '08 when he was running for the nomination, he was an 'also ran' behind Obama and Clinton, which is worrying. Man-on-man I think Trump would knock 6 colours of shit out of him; Trump has tripped-up, bowled over and knocked out far better performers than Joe fucking Biden — Chris Christie, Ted Cruz, Jed Bush and John Kasich to name just a few. The only thing going for him is that the anti-Trump feeling is such that a sack of potato-peel ought to be competitive — Trump's disapproval/approval is 53/42, something like that — but with hundreds and hundreds of millions of campaign dollars to spend Trump's people will go to work on these numbers.

In any event Trump's disapproval/approval numbers have always been poor, he got elected in 2016 with poor disapproval/approval numbers; people aren't voting for him because they approve of him, they're voting for him because they're sick of the system that Joe Biden and Hillary Clinton represent, a system which has seen the Clintons and the Bidens become billionaires and millionaires while at the same time wages stagnate for the working class people they claim to champion, opportunities diminish, and income inequality sky-rocket in terms of the top 10% versus the rest.

The alternative is Bernie Sanders, also 78! I was all for Bernie in 2016 but I'm much less so this time. I'm certainly not hostile to the guy, don't get me wrong, it's just my choice — and I believe the right choice for the Democratic Party — this cycle would have been Elizabeth Warren. She's good on policy and she's smart enough to take a win and cash her chips and walk away a winner, as opposed to Bernie who, even if he was elected, would never get anything done because he doesn't know how to build coalitions, which is what politics is about. Republicans stone-walled Obama, can you imagine what they'd do to a self-identifying 'Democratic Socialist', someone who honeymooned in the Soviet Union, for fuck sake!

But, sadly, and maybe tragically, the party has rejected what Warren has to offer, the progressives rallying around Bernie and the establishment behind Biden. (The really smart thing would have been for the moderates and the establishment to get behind Warren and make it a Warren v Sanders fight for the nomination.) It's a horrible choice — Biden or Bernie — personally I'd prefer Bernie — certainly in terms of policy — but I don't think it matters because after Super Tuesday it looks like it's going to be Biden whether we like it or not. Biden's a bad choice. I've a horrible feeling this is going to go the way Brexit in the UK did, whereby there's a clear majority against but the opposition groupings hate each other more than they hate the real enemy.

Happily Joe Biden is not reviled in the way Clinton is and was (which she and her supporters would say is and was because she's a woman but in my view that's not so at all, it's because she's a fucking Clinton, and a charmless one at that), so it might be OK. The sooner the Dems settle on someone and get behind that candidate the better because nothing trumps defeating Trump, surely. Best of all would be if Bernie sees that there's no pathway to the nomination — and sees this early, long before the end of the primary schedule — and says he's going to row in behind Biden, asking all his followers to do so too because as I say nothing ought to get in the way of booting this bastard and his crew out of office (and out of Washington). And I genuinely believe this is how Bernie sees it too.

Friday, 13 March 2020

West Cork has its first Covid-19 case, someone in Bantry. Word of mouth saying that there's another case in Schull, someone up the Colla Road as I've heard it.

Spain's gone from 1,200 cases at the beginning of the week to over 3,000 infected now — the figures published by the ECDC are the figures from the close of business yesterday, Thursday — with 84 dead.

Gott in himmel, just seen item on BBC website — posted this afternoon, Friday afternoon — saying the number of cases in Spain is now 4,200! — i.e., up 1,200 in one day! — and the number of dead now 120 — up from 84 at the close of business yesterday.

Spain's gone to 'level 2' of emergency measures, quarantining 70,000 people in the northeast and restricting the movement of people and vehicles. Schools &c already closed, or closing after this weekend at any rate. Spanish PM says it could be up to 10,000 by next week, which is up where Italy was at the start of this week.

Just spoken to Tim & Laurence on the phone and wisely (I think) they've decided to stay put, i.e., not risk going on the road and finding borders closed or the van breaking down or even the risks associated with being on a ferry which I imagine would be something of a risk at this stage. But mostly the stress of it all.

They've been told they can continue in the apartment so there's no problem in that respect, and they've no pressing business back here, and they can afford to do so, so it's clearly the wisest thing to do in the circumstances.

However Laurence wants to rent a house in the country (Tim wants to too, apparently), somewhere out in the olive groves. She doesn't feel safe in the town, she says. I'd stay put but it's not up to me. Anyway I'm happy they're OK and feel OK about staying there for a couple of months or however long it takes, which I think the sensible thing to do rather than run the risks of 3 or 4 days on the road — basically, including the ferry crossing, they'd be travelling all of next week, 4 or 5 days and nights (4 nights and 5 days, probably, door to door), and that's with everything going without a hitch.

250 deaths in Italy in the past 24 hours (just heard on the 6 o'clock news)! The numbers are starting to get horrific and the thing hasn't even started properly yet if the epidemiologists' forecasts anywhere near the mark.

No way can this be contained, it looks like, all we can hope to do is stagger the thing so the peak of it isn't totally overwhelming. They say about 70% of the population needs to be infected before we achieve 'herd immunity', which is to say, so many people have had it and survived it — developed a level of naturally occurring immunity — that the virus cannot spread in the population so easily thereafter. We've got nothing else to throw at it right now.

Ultimately physical distancing and so forth will not really protect us but it will help stagger the spread, making it more difficult for the virus to transfer from person to person.

It's going to be with us for years apparently, returning seasonally — and perhaps recurring in those who've been infected — however, in the future, they say, it will not be as virulent as it is right now, and, of course, by then we'll have some drugs (vaccines and/or treatments), hopefully.

Saturday, 14 March

90 people infected in the Republic and 119 on the island as a whole. As indicated previously, these are just the cases we know of, and for every one we know of there could be another 10 out there not showing symptoms, or showing only mild symptoms such that they're dismissed.

Authorities north and south turning this thing into a Loyalist-Nationalist issue, disgracefully, highlighting the nature of the characters concerned, and the political cultures they're steeped in. It started when we here in the Republic went to emergency measures without apprising the authorities in the north.

Arlene Foster complained about not having been consulted before-hand: Mrs Foster meet Irony, it may be that you two have not met one another previously because being uber-British she has never wanted any consultations with the authorities in the south before and had to be corralled into doing the little she does agree to do, acknowledging that the Republic has a legitimate interest in Northern Ireland.

Little point in consulting her anyway because she's four-square behind the stand-alone British position vis-a-vis not closing schools and banning mass gatherings &c as every other country in Europe has done at this stage (I'll have more to say on the UK position in a minute).

Meanwhile deputy-First Minister Michelle O'Neill has called for the closing of schools and colleges &c, following and in line with what's been done down south, thereby making it harder for Mrs Foster to do a turnaround, politically speaking. Foster has been out there parroting the Downing Street line that the advice she's been getting is that it's too early to go to emergency measures. She could have acknowledged that she's just following Boris Johnson's lead like a hillside sheepdog but, no, she's gone and said that her own scientific and medical advisers have given her the same advice as the advice BJ is getting in London, which suggests that science in Belfast and London says one thing and science in Dublin, Belgium, Paris and Edinburgh saying something else in which event it's not really science, is it.

And, worse, it appears that London is about to do a 180 and ban crowd gatherings — at this stage they're simply following their people, in fact, because Premiership and EFL soccer fixtures have been abandoned, rugby fixtures also suspended, the London marathon has been postponed to the autumn and I don't know how much more — and it seems next week they will announce that schools will close early for the Easter holidays. Downing Street has lost this battle — the attempt to stand aloof from the rest of Europe — with newspapers and other media and opinion-makers of all stripes turning away from the government (not to mention the authorities in Scotland and Wales). So now sloe-faced Arlene is going to have to do a turn-around too, and in doing so she will need to say that she's not simply responding to the shepherd's dog-whistles but that the advice she's been given over the weekend has changed. Awkward.

The British are being dishonest, in fact. Their real policy is to attempt to manage their way to achieving so-called 'herd immunity,' hoping to have the peak of infection between May and August, which'll mean *circa* 200,000 corpses at a minimum.

But of course they cannot acknowledge this, the like would be sweaty, unstable political semtex! So they're getting caught up in a tangle of their own disingenuousness.

It seems to me that at least here in Ireland the policy is still to attempt to prevent the thing from exploding if at all possible, hoping for the best but preparing for worse. It seems like the policy will fail ultimately and, if the epidemiologists' models are accurate, we'll have worse anyway. But cold-bloodedly the Brits have gone, 'OK, it's going to happen so let's manage the situation', in practical terms it amounts to the same thing, and you could argue that the Brits deserve credit for being clear-minded and pragmatic, however, point is, they don't want to appear to be so cold-blooded and calculating.

And anyway, my guess is, if it's as bad as they say it's going to be, it'll be a lot more than 200,000 corpses. If there's a 1% mortality rate (which is at the low end of the estimate-range so far as I'm aware) and you have 60% of the population infected (the pop of the UK is 60 million), that's *circa* 360,000 corpses by my reckoning (60% of 60 million is 36 million).

And, in fact, say, 10% of those infected seriously ill then the NHS will be totally overwhelmed, no matter how much management of the thing you do. The vast majority of these people will need to suffer at home, which will mean many more dead than if all of them had been hospitalized and given reasonably good treatment. Imagine being in a council flat in a tower block in London or Manchester or Glasgow and being seriously ill, pneumonia, respiratory failure, fever, and no prospect of hospitalization or any form of serious nursing. Maybe no nursing of any description, which is what'll happen for many poor people because no system could hope to cope.

But, like with the Brexit negotiations, spoiled-brat Boris wants to have his cake and eat it too: on one hand he wants to be clear-eyed and hard-nosed about it all — almost an eugenical clear-out: all the people that are going to die are old and poor and weak and sick anyhow, unproductive units, worse a fucking burden on the system, we'll be well rid of them — but at the same time he wants to preserve the patina of being a bluff and jovial One Nation Tory for future campaigns.

You may be sure the Spock-like Dominic Cummings is saying 'Let's not waste the opportunities offered by so thoroughgoing a crisis as this, prime minister, let's do some of the things we've talked about doing, there may never be another opportunity.' And BJ is enough of a student of history to know that this is so and be sorely tempted — history is made by the brave, the men of destiny, not by the managerial maintenance men, the caretakers.

Meanwhile, yesterday in the United States Trump declared a National Emergency ('two very big words'). As I've written previously, just a couple of weeks ago he was mocking the whole thing, saying it was nothing, that the whole thing will have blown through by April, that the faux concern of the fake news media was designed to damage him politically in the run-up to the presidential election, that the whole thing was a 'Democrat hoax', now he declares it a National Emergency, committing $50 billion to the fight against something that two weeks ago was just a scare-story.

Afterwards, after he'd made his announcement in the Rose Garden, one of the gathered reporters asked him about abolishing the Pandemic Unit of the NSA — Obama's Directorate for Global Bio-security and Defence — and, after saying that the question was a 'nasty question' (Trump code for hostile question asked by a woman of colour who doesn't know her place) he said he didn't know anything about any Pandemic Unit abolition. Which means he's lying or he doesn't know what's happening in his own admin-istration — and in the NSA at that! one of his core areas of responsibility. Anyway, fact is he's lying — as he's lied almost every day of his presidency — because there's video of him defending the decision to abolish the unit at the time, several videos because it was controversial but because there's been so many controversies it's regarded as one of the minor ones.

When the reporter attempted a follow-up question they cut her mic, real tin-pot authoritarian shite. This is America, Trump's America.

Several other reporters' questions yesterday found him saying 'I'm not responsible for that' or 'I don't know anything about that' and the like, textbook what not to do in leadership, let alone leadership in a crisis.

Also yesterday he was saying that there were only 40 dead in the U.S. (so far) and there were only 40 dead because of his leadership, in partic-ular his decisiveness in stopping travel from China early on and then the ban on Europeans just announced! What's he going to say next week or next month when there are 400 dead, or a couple of months from now when there may be 4,000 dead?

The U.S. had fewer than a thousand confirmed cases a week ago, today — i.e., close of business yesterday — they have 2,174. They're on precisely the same graph-line as Italy, where there are over 1,250 dead. The U.S. is about 2 weeks away from having c. 5,000 known infections and hundreds dead. And they haven't even started testing as yet — altogether, they haven't done 10,000 tests in the U.S. as yet. The CDC test kits are not reliable apparently[2] and now the U.S. is in the market trying to purchase half a million test kits, but of course no one wants to sell them any because they're needed in Europe or in India or in Japan and so on, so now, irony of ironies, they're having to go to the Chinese to get some, whereas South Korea, for instance, are doing 10,000 tests a week, something like that [actually it's 10,000 a *day* in SK!]. Hear me now quote me later, by the time they've a million tests done they'll find that the United States is the new epicentre of the outbreak.

Monday, 16 March 2020

This is the beginning of my second full week in isolation — not total isolation as the following makes clear but almost total. I saw or interacted with no one at all last week. Although of course I went into the Farmers' Market on Saturday morning whereat I went to one stall and bought half

---

[2] The World Health Organization developed a test kit for this virus — a test originally developed in Germany — and 60 countries signed up for it, however the U.S. didn't, saying it would develop its own. However this aspect of American exceptionalism turned out a disappointing failure — giving inconclusive results — and now in the middle of an epidemic they're attempting to change rides mid-race. A national humiliation is what it is, yet another instance of American decline. America First my ass. By the bye, just before Trump's Oval Office address on Wednesday night, on one of the TV channels was Sarah Palin [GOP vice-presidential candidate in 2008, and for some years afterwards an influential figure in U.S. politics, right wing politics anyhow] in some sort of C-list Celebs Got Talent type TV show — The Masked Singer on Fox — in a furry pink bear costume rapping 'Baby Got Back', looking like serious backwoods white trash, a trucker's spunk-bunny in some off-highway honkytonk, something which has to be seen to be believed. Talk about American decline! This character might have been commander-in-chief of several trillion dollars of military hardware and leader of the western world! America First in embarrassing absurdities.

a dozen things — food things from Alison. It *feels like* I interacted with no one last week is what I ought to say. I think an open air market is perfectly fine, by the bye. Going into supermarkets — enclosed spaces — I feel insecure about. I was in the Farmers' Market about 10 minutes altogether. And washed my hands thoroughly as soon as I got back to the house.

I'm not exactly sure when I started this isolation — not least because I live a fairly isolated life anyhow so it's difficult to tell — but I believe I started the first week of March, so that I may be in isolation for about 10 days now. And, like I say, it's not total isolation, it's about 97%.

I stopped going to Kalbo's [for lunch] during the first week in March, indeed I'm not even sure I was in there at all that week. However, even though I didn't go to Kalbo's that week, I did go into Fields. I went in there at least twice. I was actually buying up stuff for a siege — at that time I hadn't clocked that Fields' home delivery system was so well-established.

That last time I got caught in a couple of conversations, which irritated me a good deal, to be honest, particularly that Liverpool guy who just cannot shut the fuck up once he gets an opening. I spent about 10 minutes edging away from him and eventually had to say 'Look, mate, I'm paranoid about this coronavirus thing, gotta go…' and just walked away before he switched from whatever he was on about to doing ten minutes on the virus crisis.

He's OK, to be fair, not too different from myself in many ways, an old, opinionated bloke who just can't shut the fuck up once he starts. The time before that when I met him — which was only 3 or 4 days before! — he started on about this song he'd written and was due to begin recording a version of (with Brian Hennessy) and fuck me didn't he start reciting the lyrics of the fucking song!, a long Dylanesque type thing with several verses and 7 or 8 lines to each verse. After about 3 verses again I had to say 'Look, mate, sorry but I gotta go here I got stuff I gotta to get done…' and walked off.

I will still need to go into supermarkets from time to time but I won't do so again now until I have the masks I've ordered — I've ordered some from a dressmaker in Clon who's switched to doing facemasks and she's overwhelmed with orders apparently. And by that time, hopefully, others will be wearing them too. Anyway, even if they're not, I'm going to do so, partly because they'll offer some level of protection and partly because for me they're a sign that says fuck off and don't attempt to come near me reciting your fucking song lyrics, or anything else for that matter.

Didn't sleep too well last night, listening to the World Service for most of the night. In the end I got up at about 5am. After breakfast went out for a walk. It was a wonderful walk. I love that bit before sun-up, it's bright but the sun's not yet up above the horizon. Wonderful colours in the sky, greys and reds and purples and yellows and blues and oranges… birdsong everywhere, even when you're in among the buildings.

I was home again by the time the sun peeped up over the horizon. Hardly any traffic, 3 or 4 vehicles but none anywhere near me. May well do that again (early morning walk) as it would drive you doolally to be stuck in the house all the time.

54 new cases in the Rep. of Ireland today, now 223 in total, plus 52 in N. Ireland, so 275 on the island altogether.

Speaking at a press briefing this evening Leo Varadkar said it could be there will be 15,000 cases in the Republic by the end of next month. They expect the numbers to increase by 30% every couple of days, which is to say, double every week, more or less.

Impossible to know to what extent this represents the spread of the virus or the fact that they're now doing more testing. Despite the government's fairly good PR effort the reality (apparently) is that the testing side of things is a bit of a chaotic mess, even so they're clearly doing far more testing than they were a week ago or two weeks ago. There are probably tens of thousands already infected. And, if so, there's probably no stopping it infecting 60% or 80% of the population. We will only know after the fact.

In the UK Boris Johnson, the chief medical officer one side of him and the chief scientist the other, are doing live TV and radio press briefings every day now and in today's briefing — although they weren't fully explicit about this — it seemed clear the policy in the UK has now moved away from having managed herd immunity, which appeared to be the policy hitherto, to combatting it altogether, i.e., see if they can do a Korea on it. The idea of having a policy which accepts that you'd have 250,000 to 500,000 corpses (in addition to the half a million or so who would have died anyway in 2020) is simply too horrendous. It would be a political stain that would never wash out. That number of people may die anyway but you cannot appear like you were accepting of it from the get-go, a Marshal Pétain like defeatist/collaborationist.

Friday, 20 March

Order came today to not open the church anymore. Which suits me fine, to be honest. The hall is wholly closed for business. Services in the church also called off, until the end of the month at least (at which time the matter is to be reviewed), but the church remained open in case people wanted to go in and pray.

Couldn't sleep last night so got up before 4 AM this morning, so, obviously, been feeling exhausted all day. Tried to sleep this afternoon but managed only a few minutes, which is better than nothing but far from sufficient.

Walking around town a few times this week. Lots of shops have notices sellotaped to doors and windows, however I didn't read all of them. Some said they'd be closed until further notice, some that they'd be closed until 29th of March, but all had some communication/notice. The banks are open it seems but they want people to observe physical distancing, i.e., only one or two people in the bank at a time and whether in the bank or waiting to go in one is to preserve at least 2 meters apart from one another. Some shops (Sean Murray's, for example) have some or all of the foregoing but have changed their opening hours and are now open 10 AM to 4 PM and some (Cathal Donovan's bookshop) have asked customers not to bring children into the shop. Drinagh Hardware say only one member of a family to come in at any one time (how is this supposed to be policed?).

Gift shops and hairdressers certainly closed. And pubs. Coffee shops too however I didn't see any notice on the windows at Kalbo's; my guess is the café side is closed but maybe the takeaway side is still operating. I'm walking around at 5 and 6 o'clock in the morning so it's difficult to be fully sure.

The government hasn't said you must close up, it has just asked that you do so. However I think pubs and clubs are now closed by order.

As I say, I'm walking around at 5 and 6 in the AM, which is actually a wonderful time to walk around — when I go out at that time I usually walk for about an hour and I'm just coming back towards Abbeystrewry when the sun ups over the horizon turning the stonework at the very top of the belfry pinky-orange with the most delicate of light.

The town is quiet these days and at most the Fairfield is 40% filled with vehicles at peak times, and as I say most of the shops are closed until further notice, yet there's more early morning traffic than I'd have thought, builders still finishing jobs, perhaps, going to pick up labourers, postal workers going to work and maybe people who are on their way up to the city or Clonakilty or Bandon or wherever their place of work is. You do get good stretches of silence but the closer you get to, say, 6:30 the busier it gets. However, even at that it's only about one vehicle every 5 minutes or so. From 7 on it begins to be a little more normal like, except down by about 50%.

Sun-up is at around 7 AM at present but of course it's light for about 40 or 50 minutes before the sun's direct rays come to be seen. It's still dark when I head out and after about 5 or 10 minutes it begins to get to quarter light and then half-light.

I've been doing a few jobs around the grounds too, gardening, in the afternoons.

The following is from something published on the RTE News website this evening, giving an update on what's been happening during the day.

> There have been a further 126 cases of Covid-19 confirmed in Ireland, the Department of Health has said.

> The latest increase brings the total number of cases here to 683 since the first case was reported here earlier this month.

> Three people diagnosed with Covid-19 have died since the outbreak began here.

> 12 people diagnosed with Covid-19 have been admitted to intensive care units and, all told, 140 people hospitalised.

> Overall, 769 have been diagnosed with Covid-19 on the island.

> Dublin has the highest number of cases at 51%, followed by Cork 15% and Limerick and Wicklow have 3% of cases each.

In the UK scientific advisers to the government now acknowledge that there are likely to be restrictions in force to a greater or lesser extent for the next 12 months, something I thought obvious for some time. The present level of lockdown will flatten the peak (I trust) but the present level of lockdown is unsustainable for long. If the thing cannot be supressed and driven from our shores altogether then the authorities are going to want to have as much of it happen in the summer months consistent with not having truckloads of corpses in convey going to working-to-the-max crematoria.

What they do not want under any circumstances is to be attempting to cope with this in winter.

Therefore, for me step one is to survive this first assault and get to the summer. Then in the summer make preparations for a long winter, a long siege, one which will go on from September to next April, by which time we'll be back to approaching summer weather again but also, hopefully, by then there will be a vaccine.

Tuesday, 24 March

A little bit of good news out of Italy, potentially: the country has recorded a smaller day-to-day increase in new coronavirus cases for the second day straight, officials say, while warning it's too soon to know if the worst is behind the country with the world's second-biggest caseload. Need to have at least 5 or 6 days of figures showing a levelling off — or at least a decreased rate of increase — before they can feel they may have begun to turn the tide.

Data from the civil protection agency on Monday showed 4,789 new cases, nearly 700 fewer than the increase of 5,560 reported on Sunday.

Also the number of deaths did not rise by as many. There were just over 600 registered on Monday compared with 651 on Sunday.

But, by contrast, Spain continuing to descend into the depths of this thing; the following is from an item on the RTE News website:

> Spanish soldiers deployed to help fight the coronavirus outbreak have been finding elderly patients abandoned, and sometimes dead, at care homes.
>
> The army has been charged with helping to disinfect retirement homes in Spain, one of the countries worst hit by the pandemic.
>
> Dozens of deaths from Covid-19 have been recorded at facilities across the country.
>
> "We are going to be strict and inflexible when dealing with the way old people are treated in these residences," Defence Minister Margarita Robles said in an interview with television channel Telecinco.
>
> "The army, during certain visits, found some old people completely abandoned, sometimes even dead in their beds," she added.
>
> An investigation has been launched, the general prosecutor announced.
>
> The coronavirus death toll in Spain surged to 2,182 yesterday after 462 people died within 24 hours, according to health ministry figures.

But the big news from yesterday, however, (at least if you live in these islands) is that last night Boris Johnson addressed the nation in a formal leader-to-people address (sitting behind a desk) and announced a 3-week lockdown for the UK. Everything to shutter-up except for essential services. As in France and Spain and Italy people are to stay home other than to go food-shopping, get medicines or anything else health related (like getting yourself tested or to assist someone), and you are allowed to take one outing for exercise each day, a walk, a run, a cycle. Other than that, be house-bound unless you work in one of the essential services. 335 dead in the UK so far and, as the PM acknowledged in his address, worse figures expected in coming weeks.

Ireland will surely follow before the end of the week. Quite a lot of things are shut in Ireland already but that's just in response to the government asking people to do so — although pubs and clubs have been ordered to close. What BJ did yesterday evening was to order everything non-essential to shutter-up — an order that's backed by emergency police powers and other emergency regulatory instruments — and that is what will need to happen here now too. Several non-essential shops still open here in Skibb, for example, not that I've been out during business hours, of course, but judging by the notices in the windows — Sean Murray's, Peter O'Sullivan, Cathal O'Donovan's bookshop, Thornhill's, however, in fairness, most places have closed, about 80% of places closed, maybe more; there are places — lawyers and accountants, for example — that have their doors closed but the notice on the door says 'Business as usual' but telephone or email us.

I hope so, it needs to happen and, in my opinion, ought to be in place already.

As expected, Tokyo Olympics (2020) postponed (to 2021). Every damn thing has been postponed or cancelled altogether. Never seen such a total wipe-out, which is all across the globe; sometimes you can have a whole season of stuff disrupted, or disruption in one area, or region — in the wake of 9/11, for example, or the disruption caused by the Icelandic ash cloud eruption in 2010 — but this is everything everywhere. 2020 is in the toilet.

Wednesday, 25 March

There are now over 300,000 confirmed infections across the globe (13,000 deaths). It took 67 days to get to 100,000 confirmed infections, however it took just 11 days to go from 100,000 to 200,000, and just 4 days to go from 200,000 to 300,000.

That was the state of play on Sunday. Yesterday, Tuesday, the 400,000 mark was passed (with something like 19,000 dead). So two days to clock up another 100,000; in fact, we went well past the 400,000 mark on Tuesday, it was 420,000.

Italy reported a jump of 743 deaths yesterday — total now 6,820 — which is horrifying of course — another new record for deaths in one day — however the rate of new cases continues to show signs of levelling off: the rate of increase has been decreasing, and has been doing so for three or four successive days. If that continues (to seven days, say) we'll feel we're getting somewhere at long last. Mind you these are still big numbers — 5,249 new cases yesterday.

News out of Spain continues to be grim, they are still going down into the depths of this thing: 2,696 people have now died in the country (514 yesterday!) and close to 40,000 infected. In Madrid they're storing corpses in an ice-rink (Palacio de Hielo) because mortuaries overwhelmed.

The death toll in France jumped by 240 yesterday to reach 1,100. There were 2,444 new confirmed cases, bringing the total number of infected in the country to 22,300.

India has imposed a nationwide lockdown in an attempt to slow the spread of the virus. The restrictions will apply from midnight local time (i.e., Tuesday night) and will be enforced for 21 days.

But the big story emerging this week is the way the United States is looking like it is going to become the epicentre of the coronavirus crisis. Things look to be escalating to crazytown levels over there. New York alone now has over 25,000 confirmed virus cases and at least 210 deaths.

There are over 52,000 confirmed cases of infection in the U.S. and (so far) nearly 680 deaths attributed to Covid-19.

In Ireland 204 new cases announced yesterday in the Republic, and there's been another death, bringing the total dead to 7.

24 new cases in Northern Ireland where there's been 2 more deaths.

18,000 tests have been conducted in the Republic (as of midnight on Monday, 23 March) and 2,989 in Northern Ireland, which (the latter) is an exceptionally poor performance. The performance in the Republic is well below par at this stage too — they ought to be doing 18,000 tests a week — but NI is third world standard.

Friday, 27 March

The numbers being generated by this virus crisis are simply jaw-dropping. Here are a couple from the United States, for example.

Yesterday it was reported that in one week — the week ending 21 March — 3.3 million people registered as unemployed. That's more than five times the previous one-week record set in 1982 (695,000).

The second astonishing number is 49 over 45: in a recent Gallup poll for the first time since around the time when he was elected Trump is out of underwater on approval/disapproval ratings. This is astonishing. I understand and appreciate that presidents get a spike in approval ratings in times of crisis and/or emergencies, people rallying round the flag and all that, circle the waggons, but this guy is so clearly incompetent and so motivated solely by his own self-interest, and so responsible for the extent to which the United States is going to get pummelled by this, *is* getting pummelled by this (getting rid of the pandemic unit in the NSA, cutting the CDC budget to give tax cuts to billionaires, denying that the coronavirus was a genuine thing until the bodies began to accumulate, and first going one way — making like he was going to get behind attempting to supress this thing [back when he declared the situation a National Emergency] — and then changing tack again a couple of weeks afterwards saying America needed to get back to work, which is to say, going one way and then the other and, of course, accomplishing neither), that this completely flummoxes me.

However, moronic inferno the country may be nevertheless I cannot see this 49/45 thing holding. Once the body count goes above that of 9/11 and the war in Iraq — the war in Iraq at least as far as Americans are concerned anyhow — which it will do before May (it's already over a thousand, approaching 1,500, so it may surpass that 9/11 death toll mark before the end of *this* month!), I think Trump will be in a world of hurt politically.

The U.S. is now the epicentre of the outbreak: it now has more confirmed cases than China or Italy or anywhere else, over 85,000 as opposed to China's 81,782 and Italy's 80,589 (according to the Johns Hopkins count)! America's Number One!!! Congratulations.

The U.S. has 85,500 (and counting) confirmed cases of infection, 1,300 dead so far, and they've now conducted just over 552,000 tests.

In a WH presser yesterday Trump tried to spin it this way, saying that the growing number of cases was a tribute to the amount of testing being done in the U.S.! Nobody's done more testing than we have, he said, a tremendous amount of testing, probably more than anyone else (not true).

365 additional deaths from coronavirus in France on Thursday, taking the total to 1,696. And the country saw 231 deaths Wednesday so things starting to get seriously ugly in France.

A total of 712 people died from the coronavirus in Italy yesterday, bringing the death toll to 8,215.

And the new infections rate is up again in Italy too, rising to 80,539 from a previous 74,386, the highest number of new cases since 21 March.

A total of 4,089 people have died in Spain, with 56,188 confirmed cases across the country. The Spanish parliament has agreed to extend the country's state of emergency until at least 12 April to tackle the outbreak, which will mean the whole country on pretty much full lockdown for a month altogether.

Big jump up in the UK numbers yesterday too: over a hundred dead in one day; 578 dead now. 104,866 people tested for the virus in the UK, 93,208 negative and 11,568 positive.

But the headline news out of the UK today is that Prime Minister Boris Johnson and health secretary Matt Hancock have tested positive for the virus. Both are now in isolation. Impossible to believe that other members of the cabinet not infected also, along with staff at Number 10 and associated civil servants.

Saturday, 28 March

Nearly 900 coronavirus related deaths in Italy yesterday! 9,134 the number of dead there now.

However, only 4,401 new infections (4,492 the day before) so the rate of increase is certainly falling. Earlier in the week they were getting 5,000 new infections a day and last weekend 6,000 a day.

The death toll in Spain soared to over 4,800 yesterday after 769 deaths reported in 24 hours, a record one-day figure for fatalities in the country. Spain has the world's second-highest death toll after Italy — 4,858 deaths so far — while the number of cases jumped to 64,059 — that's 8,000 new cases in one day!

Three more people have died from Covid-19 in the Republic of Ireland. Now 22 coronavirus-related deaths in the Republic.

302 new confirmed cases of infection, so now 2,121 confirmed cases in the Republic of Ireland.

13 dead in Northern Ireland, all totalled, and 275 confirmed cases.

Combined that's 2,396 confirmed cases on the island of Ireland with 35 dead.

From midnight tonight the Republic will go to what will be full, housebound lockdown (until Easter Sunday, i.e., April 12th) — I'm writing this as I'm watching and listening to the Taoiseach announce these tightened measures:

> Leo Varadkar says from tonight, for a two-week period, everybody must stay at home in all circumstances, except in exceptional circumstances such as work [essential workers only, i.e., those engaged in providing essential services] and for the purposes of getting basic household goods or for medical or social care purposes.
>
> All public and private gatherings outside of a single household prohibited.
>
> 'Cocooning' will be introduced for those over 70 years of age and for all groups especially vulnerable to Covid-19 [i.e., full isolation — I guess hitherto this was only asked for/advised/strongly recommended whereas now it's mandated].
>
> All public transport and passenger travel to be restricted to essential service workers, and one can travel no more than 2km from one's dwelling place. [One can exercise once a day but not venture further than 2km from one's dwelling place.]

APRIL 2020

Friday, 3 April

Today, Friday, 3 April, the U.S. clocked up the most dead in one 24 hour period anywhere in the world so far as this epidemic/pandemic is concerned, over 1,300 — previous to this Spain and Italy were holders of this unenviable record, posting up to 950 dead in a 24 hour period — so the US 'Number 1' yet again. Congratulations.

There are now more than 7,000 dead in the US, and nearly 300,000 cases of Covid-19 diagnosed.

Not so long ago Trump was saying that there were 15 cases in the US but that was all, and that these 15 would be cured by mid-April and then it'll be all over. The whole coronavirus fuss was a fake news hoax designed to make him look bad, he said, designed to tether his reelection prospects. First there was Jim Comey's 'dodgy dossier' investigation, then Mueller's witch hunt probe, then the impeachment hoax, and now this, this phoney virus scare... He's a changed man these days.

Actually, strike that; no, he's not (what am I saying!), he's the same narcissistic exhibition piece as ever, only now he's generally more subdued, partly because now he appears to know that he's in serious trouble with this, and that he cannot bluster and bullshit and tweet his way out of this shit swamp, and partly because in an attempt to make the best of a bad lot he's now doing his impression of a wartime leader — he has self-identified as a wartime leader, this 'China virus' being the enemy.

The other day in the midst of a news conference to do with updating the public on the pandemic which is going to result in millions of deaths, including hundreds of thousands of Americans, he boasted about the TV ratings his coronavirus press briefings are getting! Seriously. Better than those for the finale of The Bachelor, he said.

It's unbelievable, even after 3 or 4 years listening to and seeing such gross and inappropriate self-centeredness it's still a stretch to compute what he comes out with.

Another day, again in the White House press briefing room, he broke off from whatever he was talking about to say (apropos nothing at all) "You know, by the way, I have more followers on Facebook than anyone else. Did you know that?"

First of all, not correct: he has circa 30 million followers on Facebook but Obama, for example, has 50 million, but that's neither here nor there (other than that it speaks to how careless he is with the content of the statements he makes — fact-checking be damned), what's key here is that he's briefing the nation about a situation in which thousands of Americans are dying, and because of some intruding thought about how fantastic he is, he breaks off to brag about the number of followers he has on fucking Facebook! And in doing so he lies, at least insofar as it's a totally made up assertion, straight out of his bloated ass: he might as well have said 'Donald Trump is simply fantastic' and leave Facebook out of it altogether. In addition to being jaw-droppingly incredible, it's just so offensively inappropriate.

And then in today's press briefing the following (from an item on the BBC News website) to do with the CDC's advisory that people wear facemasks...

'Mr Trump announced the CDC's guidance at the White House daily coronavirus briefing, but repeatedly emphasised that the advisory was "voluntary".

"'You don't have to do it," he said. "I'm choosing not to do it, but some people may want to do it and that's OK. It may be good. Probably will."

'Asked why, he said: "I just don't want to be doing [that], somehow sitting in the Oval Office behind that beautiful resolute desk, the great Resolute Desk."

"'I think wearing a face mask as I greet presidents, prime ministers, dictators, kings, queens, I don't know, somehow I don't see it for myself. I just don't. Maybe I'll change my mind.'"

What kings and queens and dictators is he talking about? Half the world's on lockdown. Airlines across the developed world have grounded their fleets. The Olympics has been cancelled, Wimbledon's been cancelled, all golf tournaments are cancelled, NBA, hockey, soccer, everyfuckingthing from A to Z. There are no world leaders jetting in to have meets and greets with you, you fucking assclown. '…sitting in the Oval Office behind that beautiful resolute desk, the great Resolute Desk.' The guy is such an absolute fucking moron! A gross moronic creature. Donald Trump is ego cancer, he's a cancerous tumour of ego.

Or, as Bill Maher put it (at least I think it was Bill Maher), Trump is all the bad kids in the Willie Wonka Chocolate Factory combined into one personality.

Sunday, 5 April

Lead news out of Britain is that Boris Johnson has been taken to hospital because of his coronavirus infection! He's been ill with it for 10 days now and although they keep telling us his symptoms are mild and he's still running the government, albeit isolated in his Downing Street flat (Carrie Symonds, his latest ladyfriend has left — she's pregnant — however she too has Covid-19 symptoms apparently), clearly things are a little more serious than the Downing Street spokespeople have been portraying. They say he's gone into hospital for 'tests' but there are reports this evening that he's gone in because he's struggling to breath. Probably a mix of the two. Despite what the Downing Street spokespeople have been spinning BJ really does look ill — he's posted several self-recorded smartphone videos during his confinement and in each he's looked worse than in the one before.

Nothing could underscore the extent to which this is a deadly pandemic more than if the PM were to cop it! Which is to say, this is something that is of concern not only to old people in old peoples' homes but to people of all ages, and you can die of it even when you can afford the best medical treatment London has to offer.

Matt Hancock, the Health Secretary, also diagnosed with Covid, appears to be fully recovered and is back at work. (But then again Hancock is not pear-shaped like Fatty Johnson.)

By the way, Keir Starmer elected Labour Party leader in the UK; a good choice, he's not charismatic but he looks the part and of course he's capable (i.e., he could really do the job — be PM — Corbyn never looked the part). Hopefully he'll bring Yvette Cooper, Hilary Benn, Ed Miliband & Co back to the front bench and we'll begin to have a credible looking alternative cabinet on the opposition benches again after the dispiriting clown-show of the past few years: Diane Abbott, Home Secretary, John Macdonald, Chancellor of the Exchequer, Emily Thornbury, Foreign Secretary and Jeremy Corbyn prime minister, for fuck sake, it's like a sitcom pitch!

And the Labour Party in Ireland has a new leader too, 44-year-old Alan Kelly, replacing Brendan Howlin, the greyest figure imaginable, over the past 4 years almost totally invisible. And it was even worse when he did make an appearance, made you think he'd do better remaining off-stage.

Monday, 6 April

Boris Johnson is to spend a second night in hospital in London (St Thomas'), however Downing Street still maintain there's nothing to see here so move along, folks: the PM is still getting his red boxes, they say, he's still fully briefed, and he's still fully in command of the ship of state; however, unless they're telling the truth they're going to make themselves look silly and untrustworthy. Apparently BJ has been attempting to do a Churchill — working his way through his ministerial boxes while still in bed — but he'd be better off if he quit his playacting and took his situation seriously; indeed, had he taken the situation seriously he'd have had a much better chance of not getting infected in the first place — apparently he went shaking hands with Covid patients in some hospital back in March! Fucking langer.

Tuesday, 7 April

Boris Johnson moved into Intensive Care yesterday evening. Told you; you don't go into hospital unless the situation is serious, and you sure as shit don't go to an ICU unless things are serious, really serious, life & death serious. Even so, it's still a bit of a shocker.

According to reports he's stable, he's been given supplemental oxygen but is not on a ventilator. However Downing Street have now got themselves into a situation where no one believes a word they say. What they say is just noise. Some reports saying a bed was first prepared for him last Thursday, therefore while the Downing Street press office were still telling us he had only mild symptoms and he was working fully up in the flat, steering the ship of state, clearly his doctors were saying 'Prime Minister, we think you ought to go into hospital.'

Wednesday, 8 April

Over 1,800 Covid-related deaths in the US yesterday! 731 in New York alone, which has now surpassed Italy for the number of confirmed cases — NY 138,836 to Italy's 135,586. NY now has 5,489 dead (and counting).

France passed the 10,000 dead mark yesterday.

Boris Johnson still in ICU, no change they tell us, but like I said yesterday no one puts much store by what the Downing Street press office say on this subject anymore, instead we'll wait until the prime minister comes out of the hospital — which is to say, in what type of vehicle he leaves the hospital.

In Ireland the police have been given extraordinary powers for the next 4 days (the new powers they've been given are time-limited), from now until Easter Sunday (but apparently they can be renewed again for other holiday weekends), designed to prevent people flooding out to holiday homes and holiday hotspots undermining the lockdown. Powers are so extensive that apparently it caused a split in Cabinet, not that the powers are too great especially but they're so great that if wrongly used it may result in undermining the strong sense of social solidarity rather than bolstering it.

One of the tabloid newspapers has a great headline today: 'Get Out Yer Backs And Tan.' Irish editions of British tabloids often try to do what the originals do so very well — 'Shoots You, Sir' / 'Lawn Order' / 'Elf and Safety' and so on — however so far as I know they've never hit the heights of what the Brits do in this respect — to me always seeming like lame wannabes by comparison — but this one is right up there with the best in the genre. Fair play. I'm sorry not to be able to credit the newspaper concerned, I heard of it in the 'It Says in the Papers' section of Morning Ireland this morning.

938 deaths announced in the UK today! Highest daily death total yet in the UK.

UK now has over 7,000 dead, however, based on National Statistics Office numbers — as opposed to the Department for Health figures — a report on Channel 4 News yesterday evening said that official figure could be doubled because UK still not fully counting deaths in old people's homes and in the community more widely: that 7,000 figure is mostly just *hospital* deaths.

The numbers are all over the place all over the place, apparently, every country counting up differently so that all these numbers we're seeing are the product of self-reporting, hence some of the incredible numbers you see for different countries (India, China and Russia to name but three).

Over the weekend I heard a report from Ecuador on the BBC World Service and the reporter said that there were bodies on the street in the capital. The health system has completely collapsed there, the reporter reported (a report on Newsday early in the morning), the hospitals having closed their doors because they're full to capacity, way more than capacity — every corridor and alcove filled with people on trollies and in wheelchairs &c. People turning up at the hospitals with sick relatives and leaving them there, where of course they perish in short order.

And downtown the reporter said people are putting their dead out with the rubbish on the sidewalk. The report had an interview with the city's mayor who was both pleading for assistance and also keen to communicate that the corpses on the streets were not her responsibility — the binmen, of course, do not take the bodies. A fucking horror show.

And yet if you look at the number of Covid-related deaths for Ecuador it's only 220, they claim, and only 3,995 confirmed cases.

Friday, 10 April

Aunt Mary died today, my father's youngest sister. Of that family only Lily left now. We celebrated Lily's 94th birthday in January. Mary born in the autumn of 1932, apparently, so must have been 87.

When I was a child — before she had children of her own — I was her special favourite. However after my primary school years, say, I have no memory of seeing her. Next time I remember seeing her was at Frank's funeral when she 100% and pointedly snubbed me, presumably for my having made no effort to communicate with her for so many decades: if I wanted to be such a stranger, her snub seemed to say, I could continue to be for all she cared — in saying hello I leaned in for a kiss on the cheek and she pulled away out of my phoney embrace like as if I was a drunk on a street corner and she on her way home from Sunday mass. And so strangers we remained to the end.

I saw her at John Long's funeral in January and, in her wheelchair, full of drugs for the day, she was all smiles as she shook hands with me, not knowing who I was from a bucket of sand & cement because by then she'd lost her mind and with it her ancient resentments.

Meanwhile the coronavirus-related dying continues: 25 more deaths from Covid-19 in Ireland today (the Republic of Ireland), bringing the total number of deaths from the disease here to 288.

And 480 new cases have been identified, bringing the total number of cases to 7,054.

However when results from tests sent to labs in Germany included, the total number of confirmed cases is 8,089. A large number of swab tests sent to Germany for analysis to clear the backlog of testing in Ireland.

Another 980 deaths in the UK in the past 24 hours (8,958 dead in the UK now).

Boris Johnson out of ICU but still in hospital, however, apparently he's recovering.

987 deaths in France in the past 24 hours (13,197).

And before this day is fully through the US will have overtaken Italy for most coronavirus-related deaths (Italy 18,849 and the US on 18,330, however there's still plenty day left on the western side of America). And if not today then tomorrow. Right now the US is also about to top half a million confirmed cases.

And, finally, on Wednesday I have a note about a BBC World Service report from Ecuador about the collapse of the health system there and the bodies on the street and so on. I said that the report was from the capital city but I may have been mistaken (I heard the report at some point in the middle of the night or very early in the morning when I was debating whether or not to get up, so it's possible I made error), however this evening on YouTube I see a very similar report from Chanel 4 News and this report says that the crisis is in *Guayaquil*, and, now I hear the name of that city I realise that that was the city the BBC reporter was talking about too.

I could go back and change what I wrote on Wed, however, I'd want to include this item anyway as it's a second confirmation of what's happening there, and, presumably, in several other territories around the world.

Also, just to mention this was not the same report as the BBC report because the BBC report was built around an interview with the mayor of the city whereas this Chanel 4 News report was centred on the scene at the city's main burial ground (outside of which is a long snaking queue of pick-up trucks with coffins wrapped in cling film, and cars with coffins on their roof racks also with the caskets wrapped in cling film type wrapping — presumably the authorities will not let you into the burial ground unless you have the casket cling-film-wrapped).

Wednesday, 15 April

Aunt Mary, my father's sister, died on Good Friday (aged 87). She died in a care home up in Kildare (near where Norma now lives), and arrangements had to be made to bring her down to Cork where she was supposed to be buried today in Innishannon in the same graveyard plot in which we buried her husband in January. On Friday it was said she had a brain bleed (i.e., cause of death), however today just before the funeral service word came that she'd tested positive for Covid-19, chaos ensuing, the funeral service and all related cancelled and, presumably, everyone involved — two groups of undertakers (one lot brought Mary from Kildare to Cork and another handling the business in Cork, i.e., Cork to Innishannon) — including Norma and Paula (who were with her when she passed) will now need to self-isolate. And, presumably, Norma & Paula's respective families.

More than 30,000 dead in the U.S. Trump lashing out at everyone, reporters in the WH briefing room one day and next day announcing that he's going to pull American funding for the WHO, who he says are 'China-centric', believing China's account of what happened [with respect to the origin of this virus] and failing to effectively warn the world of what was afoot until it was too late. He's seeking to blame anyone he can as long as the turd doesn't end up in his lunchbox. He appears unhinged.

Some countries in Europe beginning to lift restrictions — Spain (construction workers going back to work), for example, and Denmark (kindergartens and junior primary schools reopening). Austria too, I think.

Numbers continue to improve in Spain and Italy. France and the UK now getting the worst of it. However, the UK's official numbers are nothing like the full picture because they're only counting hospital deaths, and yet thousands are dying in care homes, which is to say, thousands who aren't being counted in the Department for Health tallies.

Italy follows the US with 21,067 deaths, Spain's on 18,579, France 15,729 and Britain 12,107 (but, as I say, this British number is not the full story, in reality another 8,000 or 10,000 could be added to that UK total).

Here in Ireland I think I notice a little more activity going on too, even though officially we're still in full lockdown. More vans and trucks going hither and yon as it seems to me, and, for example, while the Vodafone shop across the street used to have its storefront shutter half closed for at least half of each business day (a very West Cork middle ground between open and closed), today and yesterday I notice the place is now fully and openly open.

Thursday, 16 April

43 people diagnosed with Covid died in the Republic today, bringing the death total to 486.

The total number of diagnosed Covid cases now 13,271.

43 is the highest number of dead in one day in the Republic so far, so that's a headline, obviously, however the lead item today is that the reproduction rate for the virus is now believed to be less than one (the so-called 'R' number). Hitherto that's been up at somewhere between 2 and 4, which is to say, on average an infected person will infect somewhere between 2 and 4 others and each of these will in turn go on to infect between 2 and 4 others and so on, which means the virus can quickly travel through a population. However, if the R number is less than 1 the virus cannot long sustain itself in a population, it runs out of avenues into which it can travel.

Finished the Videography for Beginners course with Dom Casey this evening. The whole thing was thrown into crisis two or three weeks into it when everything shut down. Dom finished the course online by way of Zoom. It was a bit of a mess at first but, in fairness, he coped fairly well with what was a difficult situation to find yourself in. All in all Dom's gone way up in my estimation, and not just because of how he managed this course.

I got as much out of it as I was hoping to, so I'm well pleased. I wanted to learn a bit about what hardware and software I'd need to do fairly simple little videos and, in fairness, I feel I've done this.

Made a little video for the course: one about the Covid-19 notices in the shops here in town and the emptiness of the place on lockdown:

(titled) 'Dawn Walk, Skibbereen', which I'm quite pleased with (it has about 5 or 6 layers of composition on filmora9), music Max Richter's 'Vladimir's Blues' from The Blue Notebooks. On YouTube: https://www. youtube.com/watch?v=fVj5jeThOI8

Monday, 27 April

Boris Johnson back in Downing Street and back at work; since leaving hospital he's been recuperating at Chequers out in rural Buckinghamshire.

Italy and Spain certainly past the worst of it now: now they're getting figures like they haven't seen since early to mid-March; still 200 to 300 dead a day but if you've been where they've been that'll seem like good news, comparatively. Both countries now beginning to relax their lockdown restrictions a little: in Spain, children 14 and under allowed outdoors for an hour or so for the first time in 6 or 7 weeks (Spain has had the strictest of all lockdowns, literally housebound, not even allowed out to walk the dog).

All the talk everywhere is about easing back on lockdown restrictions. Junior schools opened in Norway today, for example, New Zealand almost fully back to work — 75% of the economy reopened, I believe — and the Premier League seems to think it can finish out the 2019-20 season between mid-June and the end of July, playing matches behind closed doors with lots of the games on free-to-air TV (presumably Sky and BT Sport and whoever else has paid billions for the rights will have the pick of the crop then the rest will be free-to-air).

In the Netherlands the football authorities simply declared the 2019-20 season over, everything as you were at the time of the lockdown, nobody goes up and nobody goes down. The clubs in European competition qualifying positions at the time the lockdown came into effect go forward for whatever competitions they've qualified for. Simple.

Not so simple in England, however, where TV companies have paid billions for the rights to show Premiership matches, and they've sold these rights on to other broadcasters all across the globe — premiership keenly followed in Hong Kong and Japan, all across Asia and Arabia and Africa, the premiership being a genuinely global commercial product — so unless they're going to start piking back some of these billions the games need to be staged in some way, shape or form (even at that almost certainly there will be a whole host of legal proceedings that'll continue on for years to come).

As with Dutch club football, the 2019-20 rugby season is simply declared over, certainly the Pro-14. The Gallagher Premiership in England is still talking about restarting in the summer and finishing the season but how is one to practice physical distancing in a ruck, a maul or a scrum?

By the way, New Zealand is another model to study viz well-managed response to coronavirus (Premier Ardern becoming a global political pop star, she's hardly put a foot wrong so far as I can see from here, which of course is as far away as one can get from NZ): NZ went to full alert early and has had one of the strictest of lockdowns, quarantining anyone coming into the country way back in March, and now — in a country of something like 5 million — at the present moment they have less than 1,200 infections and less than 20 deaths. Australia's figures also impressive: 6,750 infections and just 84 deaths. Going forward Australia and NZ to form their own travel bubble and anyone coming into those territories will need to be quarantined, tested &c.

The world passed the 3 million infections mark today (not that the figures put out by a great many countries are worth reporting), and also today we passed the 200,000 dead mark. Actually we passed that 200,000 mark yesterday, apparently — it's now 209,729 — so closing in on the next milestone which is quarter of a million dead.

MAY 2020

Friday, 1 May

May Day, something that, for so many reasons, has so much resonance. The calendar first of summer maybe but I don't want to move into summer yet, I want to stay in springtime, to me everything still looks and feels so spring-like.

This week extraordinarily gorgeous. It rained all day Tuesday, for about 8 hours of it anyhow — sun up these days at about 6 AM and sinking down again at about 9 PM. I think it started raining about lunchtime on Tuesday and it rained for the whole of the rest of the day, really heavy for stretches of it. I went down to check the front gates before going to bed and it had just stopped at that time. A Bangor slate coloured day you wouldn't turn a fox out into.

Monday was sunny but it was one of those days that was winding itself up for a full day's downpour. I remember marvelling at the shivering leaves on the Magnolia tree Monday afternoon; the day wasn't windy but that sort of rain-coming non-windy shiver was in the atmosphere and all the leaves on all the trees had something of it going on, anticipating the downpour to come, presumably. They were looking forward to it, not dreading it (the feeling wasn't fearful, it was excitement), because it's been dry, so dry that for weeks now I've had to spend about an hour each day bucketing water to stuff, and not just potted things, every rooted thing parched, dried-out crusted lips pleading for a drop of something. Not that I mind doing so, I may add, it's not chore-like, it's lovely work, and it's good for me to care for stuff, I get as much from the giving as the shrubs and plants do from the getting.

Then, after Tuesday's rain, Wednesday morning was Garden of Eden like as it seemed to me. I was rendered almost breathless by the incredibly delicate perfection of it all, everything sparkling with rainwater and the most innocent dawn light illuminating it all. I cannot now recall what it was that took me out into the grounds at that early hour — certainly I didn't go 'I bet the everything will look lovely this morning...' and then go out to see how it measured up to my expectation. No, that I went out at that early hour was an accident, or incidental perhaps I should say, because I remember being surprised by it, arrested by the magnificence of it, and I remember staying out there meditatively walking by the banks and beds and under fresh-leaved, still-dripping trees — every square foot of the place drenched, refreshed and exquisite looking, even the brambley bits which normally really annoy & offend me — and, at one point, thinking 'Who in their right mind would walk away from all this to go indoors to a writing desk (or to anything else for that matter)?' It was one of those timeless little stretches when the self just melts away altogether and for a little while you are the eyes of the godhead itself, or at least it feels something like this.

And then — who knows why (certainly not me anyhow) — one starts up thinking again, thinking 'Isn't this fabulous. Who in their right mind would walk away from all this to go to a writing desk?' and with that the shy godhead type bit dissolves and you're just yourself again admiring your garden, your dwelling, your handiwork, which is to say, you become self-conscious again. It's as though for a brief little while the self takes a deep dive in the 'This is Water' water, so to say, and for that little while it's just another creature swimming along in the first light of day, but then needing air it surfaces again — becoming a floater again — and so as a consequence you're alone again, yourself a bit of an invading bramble in the grounds of someone else's temple, carrying on from one day to the next for no good reason. However the afterglow of the experience remains with you for a while, happily, indeed I can feel a little of it still, two and a half days on.

Today, yesterday & Wednesday all gorgeous days weather-wise. It's a bit cold for the time of year I suppose — about 12 to 14 in the afternoons and only 2 or 3 degrees at its coldest in the night — but in fact it doesn't feel that cold, it's nice for working in that's for sure.

Did I record that the UK now has more dead than Spain? The UK on 26,770 dead and Spain 25,000 or something like that. Italy on 28,000. The USA out on its own with 65,000 dead (or will be 65,000 sometime today). France on 24,476 so looks set to overtake Spain too.

Figures out this week show that the US economy shrank by 5% in the first quarter of 2020, that's *huge* in GDP terms. And that has only about two or three weeks of coronavirus lockdown in it. Wait until the Q2 figures come out, which will be just as the US presidential election campaign proper is kicking off; people on the radio saying the shrinkage for Q2 could be as much as 20%, maybe even 30%. Two or three points of GDP shrinkage is a normal recession, a bad quarter would be if it dropped half a point. But if Q1 is minus 5% and Q2 minus 20% or 30% then Q3 and Q4 would need to be exceptional to prevent it being a record-making year, the kind of record you don't want, especially heading into an election.

Trump barking like a one-eyed dog tied to a lamppost at the end of the pier yesterday, saying he believed Q3 and Q4 were going to be great. Q3 would be transitionary, he said, but Q4 would be like nothing we've ever seen before. This is the way he talks, like a fucking ne'erdowell wife-beating shyster on a Jersey shore boardwalk, Paulie Walnuts in the White House. And next year, he says, is going to be even better.

Nobody believes what he's saying. He sounds deranged. Q3 figures are going to be bad too — there's 30 million unemployed, 30 million and counting.... And Q4 will also be godawful. This is a proper slump-type situation and the more he denies it the more unfit to govern he appears to be.

Here at home there was a review of the lockdown in Ireland today — well, the review has been going on all week, presumably — the result of which is that there will be a slight easing of the restrictions from next week, however most of the restrictions still in place for another two weeks at least.

Saturday, 9 May 2020

Today the first really warm day this year, officially its 21 degrees but it feels more. I've been out twice today, about 20 minutes each time (and moving about doing stuff when I've been out there), and I've been burned, not bad burned but reddened. I need to do stuff in the grounds — cut the church lawns in particular — but it's too hot, I'm going to need to wait until after 6pm, or do it tomorrow when it's due to be overcast. I'm not complaining, mind you, it's glorious, fabulous to look out at. The birdlife loves it, almost every bird I've seen today has been having fun as it seems to me, either gliding high up in the blue yonder (seagulls) or pigeons racing one another for fun, or magpies who seemed to be playing hide and seek in a mass of ivy, probably some kind of lovers' foreplay. And swallows, of course, who almost always seem to be having fun.

The silence continues, remarkably, a weekend such as this in regular times would be humming, shoppers stocking up for the week or weekend, overspill of pubs with their stupid amplified music and jets of semi-pissed laughter. Now as I walk around the grounds — as I've just been doing this last half hour (but I've come indoors again because it's still far too hot, even though it's 5 o'clock in the afternoon) — it is so still and quiet, birds and insect life is all I'm hearing, I feel like the last monk in some forgotten monastery. I'm intensely conscious of what a remarkable time this is and what a privilege it is to be here in these grounds, this walled parkland on the very edge of the civilized world. The like will never be experienced again, not in my lifetime anyhow, and maybe not until this whole place is a forgotten flooded ruin someday.

Monday, 11 May

Forgot to mention Tim & Laurence arrived home from Spain over the weekend: they got the ferry in France Friday evening and docked at Rosslare noon Saturday.

They arrived home at about 8pm Saturday evening. At least it was about 8pm, I'm not wholly sure — I was absorbed a movie when the phone call came — in the background Laurence was cooking up some supper.

They started out on the road Tuesday morning. Tuesday evening they were just south of Burgos (sleeping in the van); Laurence had 4 days of food and supplies of all sorts prepared and scheduled for the journey.

Wednesday night they were somewhere near Bordeaux. And Thursday they made it to Cherbourg.

They spent a week and more preparing for the dash, collecting permits and papers of every description, including getting in contact with Christopher O'Sullivan, the bird-watching TD who they know through Dan, who got in contact with Simon Coveney [Foreign Affairs minister] who provided them with a letter saying that these two people — a British national and a Belgian — were resident in the Republic of Ireland and asking all concerned to assist in getting them back home, or he directed someone in his office to write up such a letter; they also had a letter from the Guardia Civil which they got via the priest in Trabuco, plus they had permits for France and everything else they could possibly need.

As it turned out they didn't need so much at all. As long as you weren't going in and out of towns and cities the motorways were open. In all of France and Spain they were spoken to twice by authorities, both encounters perfectly civil and friendly. Indeed Tim said that between Rosslare and Skibbereen they were stopped & checked by Irish police more often than they were in all of France and Spain.

They took the 'Captain's Cabin' on the ferry over; not actually the captain's quarters, obviously, but that's what it's marketed as, the most expensive cabin on the ferry, which actually only cost €100 more than a regular cabin. The Captain's Cabin gave them more space than they had in that whole house in the olive grove in Trabuco, Tim said; sounds like they were getting seriously sick of confinement down there.

I was against them doing this run. I felt that — in their own interest — they should continue to shelter in place until the end of May at least, but Tim's daughters, Lisa and the one in Castleknock, were saying 'No, this is the best time to do the run; do it before everyone starts going out and about again.'

When I said to Tim that people have been jailed here in Ireland for offending in terms of the lockdown regulations, making non-essential journeys and so on (which they have), Tim said "Quite right", consciously or otherwise missing the point. I didn't push at it but in truth it can hardly be said to be an essential journey, can it? Remember that here in Ireland we're still on full lockdown and will be until Monday, 18 May, at least.

On the other hand it does look like they got the timing spot on because things really starting to loosen up all across Europe now; this week and next will see huge increases in movement. I heard someone on the radio today saying she'd come into London's Kings Cross railway station this morning and it was busy, almost like a normal Monday morning.

Look, I'm glad they're home, and home safe. I presume and hope they're safe & well — they're going to quarantine for the next 14 days now, as they're obliged to do.

Tuesday, 12 May 2020

Trump in all sorts of trouble: he's now ordered everyone in the White House to wear facemasks however he himself continues not to. Meanwhile, aside from Katie Miller — Stephen Miller's wife, Mike Pence's press secretary — and one of his valets testing positive for the virus, four of his Coronavirus Taskforce are now self-isolating, including VP Mike Pence, head of the taskforce, also Dr Anthony Fauci, head of the Nat Inst of Allergy and Infectious Diseases, the head of the CDC and the head of the FDA. Trump got the hump with some of the questions coming at him yesterday at an event in the Rose Garden designed to trumpet America's great success with testing — if he cannot keep his own workplace safe how can he possibly say that regular citizens should return to work? He got the hump and walked out of his own presser. Reporters clearly have zero respect for him and are now answering him back. He's losing control.

His new election slogan is 'Transitioning to Greatness', which clearly he thinks a winner — obviously he's thought this one up himself and no one around him has the strength of character to say 'Mr President, in terms of effective sloganizing, that's absolutely shite in a bucket'. In 2016 he ran with 'Make America Great Again' — a straight lift from Reagan's 1980 campaign — and this year he was going to go with 'Keep America Great' (they've the caps and t-shirts printed already) but of course with 80,000 dead (soon to be 100,000 and more) and 35 million unemployed and the whole economy sinking into the swamp mud they're not going to run with that now. Hence the new formulation, 'Transitioning to Greatness', have you ever heard of anything so absurd?

Trump keeps saying that while the first two quarters of 2020 are disappointing because of this 'China virus,' the next two quarters will see America transitioning out of this mess, and next year will be better than anything we've ever seen. When he talks like this he sounds less like a president and more like a salesman trying to flog you an apartment in a development in Florida, one which isn't built yet but everyone is saying is going to be the best ever, better than anything ever seen before. Transitioning to Greatness! As Stephen Colbert says, it sounds like the kind of thing a cult leader comes out with just before he starts mixing cyanide into the Kool-Aid.

Saturday, 16 May

Bundesliga restarted in Germany this weekend, games taking place in empty stadia and following strict health and safety protocols. All of Europe watching closely because if the Germans make it work — and very likely they will — then other leagues will feel more confident about starting up too — they'll claim they're following exactly the same protocols.

Town clearly busier this weekend, lots of out-of-town vehicles and the Fairfield more than half full for most of most days. And in addition to the NeighbourFood set-up about half a dozen market people turned up in the Fairfield this morning, people selling poultry and fruit and veg — people selling stuff out of the back of their vehicles, the kinds of folks who would never have anything to do with NeighbourFood or any such set up. I didn't go out so I'm not too sure who was there exactly but O'Leary's Poultry people certainly were, for example, although of course I went out to NeighbourFood but that was at about 1:30 PM and all those other stallholders had packed up and gone home by then.

Saturday, 23 May

Farmers' Market back in the Fairfield this week. I've not been out — although I will be going out in a little while to pick up my NeighbourFood stuff — but, judging from what I can see from my viewing places, it looks like the market's back in full, or very near it. Certainly 75% of what it would be on any given Saturday in the latter end of May or early June, which is to say, the place is just about full. And, so far as I can see, not one person wearing a mask — although, in fairness, it's open air, and I don't think I'd be wearing one if I was out there either — but, more importantly, no one observing physical distancing either it seems to me. People milling around stalls as per normal it looks like.

That said, yesterday morning — or possibly Thursday morning — on RTE radio they had an item saying that as of now — this week — there is believed to be but c. 1,800 infectious people in the Republic, which, if true, means one doesn't need to be too concerned about being out in the Farmers' Market in Skibbereen, I suppose.

JUNE 2020

Monday, 1 June

The weather's been amazing, really fine and sunny, record-breakingly fine & sunny.

The Americas the epicentre of the coronavirus thing now, the United States, Brazil and Peru to name but three of the worst.

And on top of everything else the US now has race riots going on in 20 or 30 cities as a result of the death of a man in Minnesota last week, as clear a case of police homicide as you can get. Very similar to the Eric Garner situation from a few years back: a big black guy pinned to the tarmac and even after he's subdued and cuffed the cop has his knee on the guy's neck (altogether for nearly 9 minutes), even though (like Garner) the bloke is saying "I can't breathe, I can't breathe…"

The incident was phone-camera-captured by a number of people. There were 4 cops involved altogether, 3 standing by while the murderer did his murderous business.

Also last week a white woman in Central Park had her dog unleashed in an area where dogs are supposed to be kept on-leash and when a black bloke complained she called 911 and claimed that "an African American man was intimidating" her and "threatening" her so she sought NYPD help and protection. Several times she used trigger-terms such as "large African American man threatening me" with her posh white woman's voice, clearly hoping that cops like the cops that killed Eric Garner showed up.

But the man in the park was in no way threatening, we know this because he was filming the incident and the fact that he was filming the incident is what enraged her. The bloke was a bird-watcher, and that part of the park (The Rambles) is reserved for birders primarily.

The thing went viral and it turned out the woman was an Obama supporter! At least she'd made campaign contributions. Just goes to show being an Obama-supporting liberal doesn't mean you can't be an everyday racist, and quite a vicious and manipulative one at that. The woman was clearly attempting to take advantage of the bad relationship between cops and black folks. The birdwatcher could easily be another dead black bloke who'd been 'resisting arrest' or whatever explanatory story the cops fabricated, a potential rapist maybe (it happens every day).

But universal phone cameras — good quality cameras too — make all the difference. In the following days as the bloke's video went viral on social media the woman ended up getting sacked from her finance job, the firm not wanting to be associated with her ugliness (it's a devastating video: she really does look like someone abusing the law, abusing it from several points of view; she was enraged that a black bloke challenged her posh white privilege, and, for having the temerity to do so, she wanted to see him banged up in a detention centre, or just simply have his day fucked up for a few hours, and if he happened to get shot in the course of that well then that would be on him, wouldn't it, for being a jumped-up Negro and resisting lawful arrest).

And a week or so before that a black guy in Georgia was shot at point blank range for the crime of jogging while black. The rednecks that shot him said they were 'investigating' a spate of recent burglaries in the area, the suspects for which were black. But this guy jogging was a church-going college student (and the shooters looked like they'd be better occupied investigating soap and water).

Anyhow, between one thing and another the whole situation has exploded, people comparing it to the outbreak of violence across America in the wake of the acquittal of the cops who beat up on Rodney King back in the 1990s and the violence across America in the wake of MLK's murder. And it's not just black communities protesting, there's as many white people on the streets as black, partly because this is not the 1960s or the 1990s, a really good number of white people wholly agree that the way cops treat black people in the US is unacceptable (which it is) and partly because this is now morphed into an anti-Trump thing too.

So first we had fully-armed right wing militia types demonstrating against the health-and-safety-coronavirus-lockdown in Michigan and elsewhere and now this anti-Trump anger. Trump very quick to get behind the cops in any situation, even in situations where the cop is clearly in the wrong: impossible to get any sort of condemnatory expression out of Trump about the murder of George Floyd, for instance, his line is 'There's going to be an investigation, let's see what the facts are first', but of course in hundreds of other instances he will have no interest in waiting to see what the facts are first, he'll poo-tweet about it while he's pooping his morning poo, jumping on something with both feet; and everybody in the country gets the messaging in Trump's out-of-character reticence: a cop killing a black guy is no crime at all. Trump has threatened to put troops on the street to quell the disorder; the National Guard is already out on the streets in several states but Trump is talking about units centrally commanded by him, not the National Guard called out by state and local governments, Trump now talking about being the 'Law & Order President' and 'When the looting starts the shooting starts' — a tweet of his which knowingly or not deliberately echoes a Southern racist police chief from back in the 1960s — and the need to 'dominate' the streets, for which read/hear 'Show em who's boss'/'Get your boot on their throat and keep it there'.

Just what's needed in the middle of a pandemic which has a death toll of over 100,000 and counting. Try social distancing in the middle of a riot! But Trump is loving it: it has taken the rocketing coronavirus death toll off the front pages and out of the headlines and instead he can focus on being the law & order candidate, someone offering to dominate the revolting negros.

The US is coming apart at the seams. With 30 or 40 million unemployed and hundreds of thousands dead in a pandemic and a breakdown of law and order I cannot see how Trump wins an election. This election in November will be a referendum on Trump's presidency, it cannot possibly be anything else, and I cannot see how he wins such a referendum.

However, it seems to me he's in an increasingly ride or die situation. If he loses the election and leaves office he's going to face the full onslaught of a legal reckoning, he may even see the inside of a detention centre. Trump could not do lockup time. Impossible. With troops on the streets and the need for more and more emergency measures he may be able to see his way to an alternative future. He's crazy enough and desperate enough and stupid enough to attempt almost anything.

Friday, 5 June

Today Leo Varadkar announced that the Republic would move to 'Phase 2' of unlockdown from Monday, 8 June.

From 8 June people will be able to travel up to 20 km from their dwelling place.

Groups of up to 6 can meet up, even indoors.

Sporting and cultural activities can resume for groups of up to 15, although in such instances appropriate physical distancing protocols will need to continue to be observed.

Libraries, museums and other heritage places to reopen.

All retail can reopen from Monday, but the Taoiseach said those shops reopening from Monday will be required to operate staggered hours, opening no earlier than 10.30 AM and allocating dedicated times for elderly, vulnerable and at-risk groups.

The hospitality sector will be reopening in the next phase of unlockdown (Phase 3) which will be from 29 June.

Saturday, 13 June

We've now had two weekends of riot-like disturbances in the UK, last week it was Black Lives Matter and associated this weekend it's lots of right wing groups who've come into London to protect British monuments — last weekend Churchill's statue in Parliament Square was daubed with red paint and graffiti saying 'Racist' — however, the protectors of the heritage of England — which included lots of football club groups, white skinheads, and groups with names such as the Loyalist Defence League — were necking cans of larger at 9 AM and involved in running cat and mouse encounters with the cops by noon and pissing and puking on the monuments they came to protect later that same afternoon, so much so tomorrow morning's (Brexit-advocating) *Mail on Sunday* has the front-page headline: **What HAS become of the Tolerant Britain we love?** with a picture of a football hooligan type clocking a black person in the face with a right hook — the photo is taken from behind the black person so cannot see if it's a man or a woman but s/he has a mass of dreadlocks or braids and all that hair is sent flying at the impact of the punch in a wonderfully photographic fashion. And underneath it all The Mail has a red strip-line which says 'Unrivalled Analysis of a Nation in Turmoil'.

I don't know if I actually did write this in these diaries last year or the year before but I remember predicting that there'd be trouble on the streets in the wake of Brexit. And I *do* think all this turmoil is Brexit-related ultimately. These disturbances are culture war disturbances but so too is Brexit a battle in that same culture war. On one level the stuff last week and this has been about the death of George Floyd in Minnesota — and the Occupied Territories treatment of black people generally in the US and in lots of other places too — and, as a counter punch, right wing groups mobilizing to defend British monuments — last week in Bristol protesters pulled down a bronze statue of 17th century merchant and slaver Edward Colston and dragged it through the streets and threw it into the harbour — but as Edmund Burke argued, when you tear up parts of a constitution that has been layered into being over generations don't be surprised if you find you've uprooted much more than you sought to uproot.

None can predict the occasion of the disturbances — the second lot of the Brixton riots kicked off with the shooting of Cherry Gross, for instance, and the riots in Broadwater Farm in Tottenham kicked off when another woman died in another police raid — it might be a long hot summer, or an economic downturn in conjunction with a long hot summer, or any of several other flashpoint incidents but as it has happened it's racial justice issues in the midst of a viral pandemic, but in fact all of it — Brexit, Edward Colston's statue, the Churchill monument — it's all about who we are: what is it to be British?

And I further predict a lot more of such disturbances this summer and in summers to come. Just wait til the full impact of Brexit manifests. Johnson, Gove, Cummings, Rees-Mogg & Co may have advanced their careers with Brexit but they've no notion what they've unleashed, and I don't think they care. I suppose they figure that by then they'll have got what they set out to get and they'll have cashed their chips and be off somewhere sipping chilled white wine and reading books about the history of Rome.

But the irony of The Mail and Mail on Sunday who, when Supreme Court justices were handing down judgements that frustrated the government viz Brexit — which is to say, rulings that the government had acted unlawfully — were printing pictures of the judges and giving out telling details about them and branding them 'Enemies of the People,' wondering what happened to the tolerant Britain we love is simply mustard pungent.

Monday, 15 June 2020

FF, FG and the Greens have agreed a programme for government at long last (128 days after the GE in February). The *leadership* of the three parties have agreed a programme for government anyhow, they must now get their respective parties to vote for it, which is no forgone conclusion, especially viz the Greens who are in the middle of a leadership contest: Catherine Martin challenging present leader Eamon Ryan who is seen as far too accommodating, which, in fairness, is true, he is far too nice for this game — this is senior hurling as Seams Brennan used to say.

Micheál Martin and Leo Varadkar will job-share the office of Taoiseach: Micheál Martin will serve as Taoiseach until December 2022 (until 15 December 2022 — just after the centenary of the foundation of the Irish Free State) then Varadkar will return as Taoiseach until the next GE, which, all going to plan, will be in the early part of 2025. Varadkar will be Tánaiste and hold a ministerial role too. It's the first time a coalition government will include a plan to share the office of Taoiseach.

No word yet on other ministers who technically will be appointed by Micheál Martin, but deciding who will be in Cabinet will be in consultation with Leo Varadkar and Eamon Ryan. My guess is that, in addition to serving as Tánaiste, Leo will be minister for Foreign Affairs as he clearly enjoys all that hob-nobbing with foreign leaders and he's good at it, and he already has a lot of good relationships across Europe and more widely so he'll be well respected, and with Brexit issues still not wrapped & stamped it's an important position and, of course, being Taoiseach, he'll be fully briefed already, plus it's good for his career after politics which I'm sure he has half an eye on already — an EU commission position maybe, or a UN job, WHO something of that nature. And, if that's what he wants — to be in the ministry for Foreign Affairs — it's his for the asking.

And presumably Micheál Martin will serve as Tánaiste when Leo V is Taoiseach, although there may well be a new leader of FF by then, who knows, lots of people in FF keen to get rid of Micheál Martin. They're unlikely to move against him now that he's about to become Taoiseach but he may well make a move himself before the next election, giving the new leader time to settle in. He'll certainly go after the next election, even if he has a good campaign and picks up an additional 20 seats, say (which would put them on 58/59 — they were down to just 20 seats when he took over as party leader after the 2011 meltdown).

FF are to have 6 senior ministries. Presumably FG will have likewise. And then maybe a couple for the Greens along with a few junior ministries — jobs for most of the Greens presumably as there's only 12 of them.

Wednesday, 17 June

Spoke to John Ardis today — we met in the grounds as I was doing a job on one of the lawns and he was on his way into the church to do something — and he told me that services will resume (Abbeystrewry church only for now) on Sunday, 5 July, so just over two weeks from now.

So my splendid isolation is over. I wasn't surprised to hear of it, everything is due to be open by then, including pubs and restaurants &c.

The premiership restarting this evening (English Prem), Villa v Sheffield and later on Arsenal v Man City. These are two matches outstanding from the last round before everything was suspended in March. After these two games 9 rounds of games to go.

All of these will be played behind closed doors. Football already restarted in Germany and even in Spain.

Saturday, 27 June

All the formalities of a new government coming into office today: Micheál Martin Taoiseach, Leo Varadkar Tánaiste and minister for Enterprise, Trade and Employment, Simon Coveney remains at Foreign Affairs and also doubles as Defence minister, Paschal Donohoe remains at Finance and FF's Michael McGrath becomes minister for Public Finance and Reform, and Green Party leader Eamon Ryan heads a super ministry for Action on Climate Change, Transport and Communications.

Catherine Martin, deputy leader for the Greens becomes minister for Media, Tourism, Arts, Culture and Sport.

Stephen Donnelly (once of the Social Democrats but now FF) becomes the new Health minister and Simon Harris the minister for Higher Education, Innovation, and Science.

Helen McEntee, who was Europe minister and always at Leo V's side at EU events, is now Justice minister, and Heather Humphreys goes from Arts and Culture to the Department for Social Protection.

Barry Cowen becomes minister for Agriculture and Darragh O'Brien, another FF guy, will be in charge of Housing and Local Government.

Trump in serious trouble so much so even he shows signs of recognising it, there's even talk of him withdrawing from the contest rather than face the humiliation that's surely coming his way — nearly 130,000 dead from a virus he said was no worse than a common cold and would be gone with the return of warm weather in April, and now there's a resurgence of it because of his haste in undoing the lockdown and persistently undermining it when in place, projections now suggest the death toll will be approaching 200,000 by the time of the election in November — plus he's just totally lost his way and his once madly enthusiastic supporters are beginning to drift away: he held an indoor rally in Tulsa, Oklahoma, last week where they [the campaign to re-elect the president] were expecting tens of thousands — so much so they built overflow areas — and just over 6,000 showed up. He's about 10 points behind in the opinion polls and he's losing badly in all the battleground states and worse yet for Republicans he's bringing other Republican candidates down with him so that the Dems look like they may increase their hold on the House and take back the Senate too. He's got absolutely nothing to run on and no agenda for a second term, he's just attempting to redo the set list from the successful 2016 tour — it's just a Fat Elvis in Vegas show at this stage.

47,341 new cases in the US yesterday! And nearly as many in Brazil: 46,907. Brazil had over a thousand dead yesterday. 56,109 the cumulative death total in Brazil at the close of business yesterday. Brazil now has 1,280,054 cases of infection; at the rate they're going they'll catch up with and surpass the US, which has 2,552,956 cases with 127,640 dead. Both countries led by virus deniers, so, obviously, no coincidence that these countries top these shameful charts. It's no exaggeration to say that Trump and Bolsonaro are directly responsible for the deaths of thousands, and maybe tens of thousands.

Sunday, 28 June

Department of Health reports one further death of a person diagnosed with Covid today along with three new cases of infection.

Now 1,735 Covid-related deaths in the Republic of Ireland, and a total of 25,439 confirmed cases.

In Northern Ireland, another person has died as a result of the virus, taking the official health department death toll there to 550. And one new case of infection, taking the cumulative total to 5,751.

Therefore, altogether, 31,190 confirmed cases on the island of Ireland and 2,285 Covid-related deaths.

	Population	Infections	Deaths	Tests/1m pop
1. USA	330,806,424	2,548,996	125,804	98,475
2. Brazil	212,405,664	1,344,143	57,622	14,196
3. Russia	145,928,315	634,437	9,073	132,487
4. India	1,378,604,014	548,318	16,475	6,086
5. UK	67,859,075	311,151	43,550	135,453
6. Peru	32,932,217	279,419	9,317	49,901
7. Chile	19,105,644	271,982	5,509	56,481
8. Spain	46,752,999	248,770	28,343	110,425
9. Italy	60,470,472	240,310	34,738	87,900
10. Iran	83,921,387	222,669	10,508	19,517
11. Mexico	128,844,230	216,852	26,648	4,314
12. Pakistan	220,673,722	206,512	4,167	5,715
13. Turkey	84,244,944	197,239	5,097	38,896
14. Germany	83,757,235	193,761	8,961	64,603
15. S. Arabia	34,776,977	182,493	1,551	45,712
16. Argentina	45,244,432	173,355	3,232	14,082
17. France	65,259,187	162,936	29,778	21,213
18. S. Africa	59,316,193	138,134	2,503	46,729
19. Bangladesh	164,802,127	137,787	1,738	6,823

JULY 2020

Sunday, 5 July

Lockdowns being reintroduced all over the place because of re-ups in infections and hospital admissions and other critical indicators: the city and surrounds of Leicester in the UK, for example (944 new cases of Covid in Leicester in the past 2 weeks — 10% of all new cases in the UK), various areas in Germany, Melbourne, Beijing, Florida, Texas, Arizona and areas in Catalonia and Galicia. This is the future, local lockdowns rather than national shutdowns.

This thing far from over. Yesterday the pubs in England opened again — at least the ones that claimed they could manage one-metre physical distancing and all the other protocols that places have to comply with in order to return to trading — and this morning's papers full of pictures of crowded pubs and bars with zero physical distancing going on!

And in the US this week Donald Trump held another couple of super-spreader events, one at Mount Rushmore, where 7,000 non-mask-wearing Trumpists attended his mad event, and another at the White House where he held a huge 4th of July party in spite of the fact that almost the whole of the rest of the country had cancelled all Independence Day events.

Friday, 24 July

Trump announced yesterday that they were cancelling the Republican Party's nominating convention this year, the in-person get-together version of it anyhow (Dems decided to have a virtual convention months ago). Originally the Republicans were going to have their convention in North Carolina but because of the coronavirus situation the local authorities imposed too many health & safety restrictions and Trump got the hump and said 'OK, fuck you, we'll take the business elsewhere,' perhaps expecting the North Carolinians to come running after him pleading with him not to take his business down the interstate. But instead the NCs said, *Yeah, OK, you do that, pal, good luck; I'm sure there are lots of states that'll be happy to host your super-spreading shit-show.*

Trump took the event down to his adopted home-state, Florida. This was before this second virus spike. Now Florida is on an Italy type track and not only do the Floridians want to impose as many restrictions and obligations as the NCs did, in fact, now they don't want the event there at all good, bad or indifferent.

No doubt Trump and his people tried to move it to some other town or city but at this stage no one wants this assclown rodeo as it would be utterly irresponsible to bring 20,000 Trumpist nutters (most of whom refuse to wear PPE) into your district — an army of people who regard mask-wearing and other pandemic protocols as offensive to their constitutional liberty (these people, many of whom claim to be Christians, object to being obliged to look out for the well-being of their fellow citizens). Even if a state or city wanted to do so because they were die-hard Trump supporters, it is not unlikely that at this stage it would be adjudged so irresponsible they might leave themselves open to lawsuits by people who became infected.

Anyhow, yesterday Trump sought to make a virtue of a necessity, saying that on consideration he's come to the conclusion that his main concern in calling off the four-night convention is his deep-rooted and abiding concern for the welfare of others.

"It's a different world, and it will be for a little while," he said, adding that he "just felt it was wrong" to put potentially tens of thousands of attendees at risk.

"We didn't want to take any chances," he told reporters. "We have to be careful and we have to set an example."

Yeah, right! He held a rally in Tulsa, Oklahoma, last month which brought infected people into that area — he had 6,000 people in an arena almost none of whom were wearing any form of respiratory protection, and the crowd-size was an enormous disappointment to the campaign because it was a 20,000-seat arena, moreover they'd built overflow areas to host thousands more — and he attempted to hold another such rally up in Maine after that which they cancelled for fear of having another PR disaster on their hands — they say they cancelled it because of an incoming storm, which is total BS, and anyway the storm they were concerned about never came in — and, as I say, he's been trying to get his maggoty convention into several places but like a mangey, unwanted dog that's frothing at the mouth and leaking sewage out its ass it's been chased from town to town and now won't be let in anywhere.

However Trump says he will still be making a convention speech in some form.

In his Trump voice and persona, last night Stephen Colbert picked up on that last line about making a convention speech 'in some form' and delivered the following:

> I'll still be doing a convention speech but in a different form; perhaps I will take the form of a ravenous wolf-headed creature, or maybe a giant blood-thirsty bird who shrieks through a razor-sharp beak, or maybe an obscenely bloated spider-shaped creature with a hideous human face who devours light and spins it's web to tangle every flicker of human hope in my cocoon of madness and despair.

Thursday, 30 July

I'm in a not-so-good mood at the minute. Not especially sure why this is — what specifically is upsetting me.

Partly it's the weather and the passing of the summer into fall — knowing that that is but an anteroom to the darkness and death of winter, and, with this pandemic, this coming cycle round the far side of the sun will be especially trying.

The weather's been awful, June was disappointing but July's been worse. It rained all day yesterday, and I mean really fucking rained, non-stop, west of Ireland rain, which from before breakfast until after bedtime was really quite heavy. Before 10 AM it was softish kind of rain, however it was still wet enough to require an umbrella, as I know for sure as I had one or two things to get which I did early in the morning because the day was forecast to deteriorate. Indeed, yesterday morning, despite the protection offered by an umbrella, out and about doing the few things I had to do, I got wet enough that I had to change out of the clothes I was wearing when I got back home.

Yesterday evening I pulled the curtains to at about 8:30pm, doing so felt like it was a wet evening in October.

Today is supposed to brighten up but it hasn't done so as yet. Right now it looks like we may see the sun at some point this afternoon, an hour or two of mottled sunshine, but equally we might get a soaking in a couple of downpours.

The coming weekend — the August bank holiday weekend — is set to be broken, not wet (as I understand it) but mixed and cool for the time of year.

I know they say if you don't inflate you won't deflate, and, as these diaries testify, I certainly did inflate earlier this year, April, May and early June especially, which were extra special this year because of the silence and splendid solitude courtesy of the pandemic lockdown, not just here in Abbeystrewry but the town and territory all over, which now seems quite dream-like, unreal. I enjoyed those weeks, as I'm sure I've recorded, but in retrospect those weeks seems even more magical than they probably were in quotidian reality.

All this week I've been running about squirrelling things for the winter to come, which I suppose has made me more winter-conscious than I ought to be, but also doing the like means a constant run on my dwindling cash reserves which certainly does put me into my grumpy pants because at this rate, unless I figure out some way of generating some additional income (and fast) I'm going to be back down to zero fairly soon — back to borrowing from the CU to finance the deficits in my poorly resourced financial system. This pandemic has been expensive.

I seem to keep saying I'll get this stuff now and then come — whenever (depending on the scenario) — I'll need to spend less and so I'll be in a position to save something. In the present instance 'whenever' is September; but if the past 5 or 6 months are anything to go by then it'll be something else in September and October and then shortly after that it'll be the Christmas season.

That time when the grass grows all day long and the cattle get fat and big and strong and all I have to do is sit back under a spreading chestnut tree and watch it happen never comes.

Friday, 31 July

In a series of tweets yesterday — right after a set of devastating economic figures came out — Donald Trump floated the question of postponing the election in November because mail-in voting, he said — which people are going to have to do because of this pandemic — will mean 'the most FRADULENT & INACCURATE Election in history.'

In *history*? The guy clearly doesn't know too much about Russia, eastern Europe, Africa, Asia, or even the Americas for that matter — including the US — ever heard of Mayor Daley or Jim Crow?

It's clearly a dead cat effort to change the lead in the news cycle, and even though people know this is what it is, it still worked such that 9 times out of 10 Trump's provocative tweets have led news cycles everywhere for the past 24 hours.

However, it seems clear to me — and to others too of course — that in addition to changing the topic of conversation such tweets also are part of a long-running attempt to undermine the legitimacy of the forthcoming presidential election, either because if he loses he'll seek to say that the elections were clearly blighted by fraud such that they cannot be trusted and he'll need to continue in office for a little while until the mess is sorted, or else he packs his trunks and withdraws to Florida but he's able to say if it was an honest election he would have won. A Deep State coup d'etat, he'll say, thereby sinking a crowbar under the foundations of the new administration so that if they do come after him — which they're quite likely to do — he'll be able to credibly threaten widespread disorder because there's no doubt he has enough nutters following him to credibly make that threat, and the nutters following him likely to be armed & dangerous.

Trump does not have the power to change the date of the election, Congress has that power and Congress will not want to have anything to do with any such proposal, certainly not the House but not the Senate either. There are many Republicans in both House and Senate who look forward to this election, even though the GOP is going to get a kicking, because it'll mean getting rid of this unfunny domineering assclown; the party might not survive him as it is but they certainly won't survive another extended period of him; many in the party already focused on making plans for 2024. However there are many ways in which Trump and his loyalists may be able to achieve measures of what they want between now and the middle of January next year. Until then he's the commander-in-chief and he has his people in the Dept of Justice, in the Treasury and in the State Dept. Lots and lots of levers to try.

It is so shocking to hear POTUS suggest postponing an election — and as I say undermining its legitimacy — for his own selfish ends — to protect his own gangster enterprise and his gangster associates — while claiming to be concerned for the legitimacy and authenticity of the poll, especially bearing in mind that not only were Federal elections held during both World Wars but also during the Great Depression and even during the Civil War — not to mention all the other sociobiological epidemics and pandemics the US has been heir to down the years.

AUGUST 2020

Sunday, 2 August

Unbelievably busy in town yesterday, as busy and bustling an August bank holiday weekend as ever I've seen. Apparently there were complaints about the congestion and crowding at the market last weekend so this week it was well-policed — over-policed in my view — both actual police and market-appointed stewards in hi-viz bibs. Plus they had these absurd one-way systems which meant one could only move one way round the market, everybody going in a unidirectional flow, which to my mind made a nonsense of what being in an open market is all about, which is to say, the back and forth that's involved in humming and hawing about whether you really need that olivewood bowl or antique naval officer's hat or cascading houseplant or whatever whim or absurdity it might be.

In addition these stewards sought to ensure that only 500 or so people in the market at any one time — or whatever the guidelines for outdoor gatherings are at the minute — so that, as with really busy shopping malls and supermarkets, there was a one-out/one-in policy. The queue to go into the market yesterday went from the back of the Church Restaurant all the way up to Aldi! Which was absurd because so far as I could see there was little physical distancing in that queue so, if public health and welfare was genuinely the concern, the cure was worse than the ailment. As with airport security, all such crap is not for the sake of the thing they say it's for at all, it's just for show, everyone participating in a fucking charade.

And then all stall-holders were PPE'd to an absurd extent, even the small farmer types selling potatoes and cabbages out of the boot of their mountainy vehicles! It looked absurd and comical to me.

Luckily my only go-to was the NeighbourFood stall, which is right out on the edge of things, and the time-slot for my pick-up 1:00 to 1:30 by which time the main rush was over and the stewards appeared to have gone off to lunch or wherever, so I didn't need to queue to get in which I would have been reluctant to do. In any case, as I say, on the edge of things the NeighbourFood stall appeared to be outside the area they were most concerned to corral and police; I went directly to the NF stall, ducked in under the ropes, collected my stuff and was back inside my house in less than 5 or 6 minutes.

Uptown things were just as crowded, traffic almost at a standstill everywhere — 'traffic almost at a standstill' not a figure of speech, it's a literal description of the situation, the town's whole traffic system appeared to be in all-out gridlock, at least it was as I made my way up to Kalbo's on North Street at about 11am, and, on the return trip, little appeared to have moved — and all the pavements thronged such that if one wanted to practice any measure of physical distancing one needed to walk on the roadways, which with vehicles at a standstill, was perfectly safe to do.

I confess I found it exciting to see the town so out-of-the-ordinary full — I'd certainly have got off on it when I was younger, and back when I had a bookshop too, of course — but now a grumpy old man (an Ed Riordan of the western seaboard) I find it less enchanting; however, as I say I confess that although I found it a little frustrating at a few points yesterday I also found it a little bit exciting too, but only from a novelty pov, such a powerful contrast to the intense isolation experienced most of this year.

People holidaying at home this year, and more folks coming here from the UK too it looks like. I can well imagine if you were living in London or Birmingham or some such Ireland with its low coronavirus numbers when compared to those of any region of England must look attractive, a safe place to venture into when compared not only to England and the UK but anywhere else in Europe.

Devon, Cornwall and the whole of the West Country and the beaches of Wales also overwhelmed apparently, not that I would say we're 'overwhelmed' here exactly but certainly things appear to be full to capacity, maybe even stretching the seams a little. I've seen articles on the BBC website about how West Country people are complaining about being pushed off the pavements in their own towns and elderly and other vulnerables afraid to go to their local supermarkets — for fear of city folk bringing the virus into the local area.

England (and indeed the whole of the UK) enjoying a heatwave right now — 28 and 29 up in Scotland but 34 and 35 in southeast England. However, it turns out it's not just England and the UK, it's the whole of Europe: 40 degrees in Barcelona yesterday apparently, and states of emergency have been declared in several parts of France because of fears of forest fires. Everywhere in northwest Europe basking in it except this island where, as I say, although it is sunny today, and was so yesterday, it's nothing spectacular, and the week leading up to this weekend was well-broken, raining all day Wednesday, and heavy rain at that — Kenmare town centre flooded Wednesday and Thursday.

Got a text from Betty Chapple yesterday evening informing me that yoga and the Country Market starting up in the Parish Hall again from this week onwards.

And I suppose Pat Hughes will be starting up again also — St Patrick's Day stuff still up in those playschool rooms, which, now, in this harvest time of year, looks Marie Celeste-like. She has to do so: it's her business and as such presumably her main source of income, if not her only source.

She's my age at least, maybe more, and so is Judith (Judith's in her 60s, I believe), and I know I wouldn't fancy being circa 60 years old (overweight) and facing into a kindergarten schoolroom each morning in the midst of a pandemic which is particularly bad for over-50s, especially people north of 50 and overweight.

And the regulations attending the like — because of coronavirus — must be mind-melting, in addition to all the other stuff to do with dealing with children, I mean.

I plan to steer well clear of it all.

We're almost at the end of summer — the summer holidays, I mean, as opposed to the actual season — it's been the most remarkable spring and summer. But, as I say, what with yoga and the Country Market — and, presumably, the Ilen River Playschool returning again in September —

from here on things will begin to drift back in ones and twos. Of course it'll never be back as it was — cannot see Bridge and Bingo returning anytime soon, for example, and I cannot see the Turkey Suppers happening this year — unless they do it as a take-away service only — or the November Bazaar. Ah well, it was good while it lasted, wonderful — blissful in fact — a time to treasure.

Friday, 7 August

I'm sure I'll have noted this before in a diary entry but after a while one becomes numb to these virus numbers. Yesterday, for instance, it was reported that there were 69 new cases of the infection reported in RoI in the 24 hours up to the close of business yesterday evening. In early July we were down to single figures in terms of new cases each day, we even had a handful of days with no new cases, then it went up into double digits, which we noted, then it was 20 or 30 a day which again we noticed (furrowed brows now), and then it went from there to an average of 40 or 50 a day which by comparison we hardly noticed at all (i.e., that upslide from 20/30 to 40/50). Now we're reporting very nearly 70 new cases in a 24-hour period!

The enormity of that 69 figure didn't really strike me until this morning at the breakfast table when I was reading a report on the fact that the R-number is now believed to be circa 1.8 in Ireland, and in the course of that report again I came upon this 69 (new cases in one day) number; moreover, the report I was reading said the number of new cases today is expected to be equally high.

Big news today in terms of coronavirus in Ireland is that from midnight tonight there is going to be a reintroduction of lockdown restrictions for the counties of Kildare, Offaly and Laois because more than half the new cases we're getting at the minute are coming from workplaces in these areas, a couple of meat processing plants in particular which have now ceased operations, obviously — most of these cases today and yesterday resulting from the fact that all the workers in these plants have been tested, but what's most worrying is that most of the people testing positive for the virus were completely asymptomatic, which means these workers have been circulating in the community totally unaware they were infected and infectious. Residents will not be permitted to travel outside of their counties except in limited circumstances.

The Department of Health has been notified of 4 additional deaths today and 98 more cases of Covid-19.

So now a total of 1,772 Covid-19 related deaths in the Republic of Ireland and 26,470 confirmed cases.

Saturday, 8 August

One further Covid death and 174 additional cases of infection reported to the Department of Health today.

This is the first time new case numbers above 100 since Friday, May 22, when 115 people were confirmed to have tested positive for the virus.

It is understood there have now been more than 150 cases at the Kildare Chilling factory. O'Brien Fine Foods has had 86 confirmed cases.

And there have been 53 cases linked to a pet food factory in Naas and another 11 cases linked to the Carroll's meats factory in Tullamore, Co Offaly.

Altogether 32,535 confirmed cases on the island of Ireland and, so far, 2,502 Covid-related deaths.

Tuesday, 11 August

So clearly moving into the autumn time of year now. This week really fine, however, and the weekend just gone too — 19 to 24 or 25 degrees each day and 9 or 10 to 14 at night — although this fine, dry, sunny spell is due to break up later this week. Indeed, these 7 or 8 days — or however long it turns out to be — are good enough to rank alongside that spell we had in the latter half of May.

Southeast of England and most of Europe having another heatwave right now — 33, 34, 35 degrees and the like; I do not envy them, what we're having here right now is what I feel is really pleasant. It's not so hot that one is reluctant to go out in the middle of the day — somehow 22 and 23 degrees at this time of the year doesn't seem as hot as the same temps might be in high summer. Indeed in the mornings — up until 11am, say — and in the evenings too (after 6pm) there's an autumnal pick in the air, not so cold that you *must* have a coat or jacket but sufficient to make you wonder — as soon as you step outside — if you ought to turn around and get a coat or jacket before continuing to wherever it is you're headed.

Mornings have harvest-time-of-year mists quite often too or, if not, full fogbanks which take a couple of early morning hours to burn off, or else there'll be that condensation on the inside of windows indicating the overnight temp inside is significantly higher than outside which points unmistakably to autumnal night-time chilliness.

But most of all it's the colour of the light, especially in the mornings, there's a harvest-coloured orange tinge to the morning sun right now which is unlike anything you get in June or July when one can also get orange-coloured morning sun, especially in the very early hours. The sunlight seems weaker now, more fragile, and more angled, casting long and lengthening shadows. Which is not surprising, of course, because the sun *is* withdrawing from the northern hemisphere, so to say, so the sunlight really *is* more angled and really *is* weaker — because it has further to travel to light up the dewy lawns of Abbeystrewry and elsewhere. After all we're very nearly two months away from the zenith of summer's midpoint.

Thursday, 13 August

Fine weather we've been enjoying has finally broken as it was forecast to do and now, following 5 or 6 days of glorious unbroken late-in-the-summer-season sunshine, we are facing 5 days of rain. At least that's what the forecast says, rain until Monday, if not full days of continuous rain then clouded over with thundery downpours and the possibility/probability of localized flooding.

Indeed, there's flooding already: I heard on the radio news this morning that the N71 was impassable in two places due to flooding, one place between Leap and Ross and the other between Ross and Clon.

Heavy rain falling now (and all night last night as the preceding para indicates), in addition to which this morning is as dark as dark can be during daylight hours. At the breakfast table this morning looking out the back window I could just about make out the ivy-covered wall which is no more than 5 feet from the window, that's how fucking dark it was — this was at circa 8am, by which time, if the sun was showing, we'd be nearly two hours into daylight. No exaggeration, it looked like it was 4pm on a wet Wednesday in December.

In the UK they've now completed their review of Covid-related deaths and they've come up with circa 5,000 deaths which, they say, were deaths of people who had tested positive for the virus, got sick, recovered, and then some weeks or months later died because of some other unrelated condition (this is what they're *saying*, I stress, in reality they're kneading the numbers because the numbers for the UK are among the worst in Europe and they're ashamed of them). Yesterday, 12 August, the official UK death toll was 46,706, now it is said to be 41,329, which is to say, 5,377 fewer Covid-related deaths in the UK. (Previously, they did a similar thing with the way cases of infection were counted, taking 30,000 off that total; now they're trying the same trick with the death toll.)

Truth is Boris Johnson and his government were reluctant to move toward a shutdown because they feared the economic cost of so doing and they thought they could make hay if they did not do so while everyone else in Europe battened the hatches and cowered under their beds and dining tables in hopes of the pandemic passing by — initially their attitude to this virus was much as Trump's and Bolsonaro's, which is to say, *So a few thousand poor and weak people die, their lives are not worth billions, indeed they're not worth anything at all, throw them on the trash heap where they belong and let us continue making money*, and that delay, that critical couple of weeks, has resulted in tens of thousands more deaths than would have occurred had they moved towards lockdown as quickly as other European governments for which there is no excuse because at the time we had the examples of Italy and Spain to go by. That plus the fact that the much-vaunted NHS, which they continually trumpet as the best health service in the world, is quite clearly not, nor anything of the kind. Going by the figures for this pandemic it seems to me that the German health service is at least 2 or 3 times better at looking after you when you get sick, and, critically, detecting and preventing sickness in the first instance. The UK government is repainting the shithouse in hopes of brightening the gaff for the photographer.

Going forward, if someone dies more than 28 days after testing positive for this virus it will not be counted as a Covid-related death — despite the fact that one often hears of people dying after four and five weeks on a ventilator, and often people don't need to be ventilated until at least a couple of weeks after they've tested positive.

Thursday, 20 August

136 additional cases of infection and another death reported today.

Now a total of 1,776 coronavirus-related deaths in the Republic of Ireland and 27,676 confirmed cases.

> The HSE published data today to do with examining the prevalence of the virus in Ireland. Using data from the survey it "estimates that 59,500 people in Ireland in the age group 12 to 69 years had been infected with SARS-CoV-2 up to mid-July".

This is three times more than that detected through the surveillance of notified cases.

The study, the first of its type in Ireland, measured antibodies to the SARS-CoV-2 virus, which are an indication of past infection with Covid-19.

It was conducted with a random sample of 1,733 people aged 12 to 69 in Dublin and Sligo in June and July.

It reported a prevalence of infection of 0.6% in Sligo and 3.1% in Dublin The HPSC said it was then able to estimate that the national prevalence rate was 1.7%.

Friday, 21 August

Yesterday my cousin, Margaret, asked me to compose a few words for Lily's funeral.

I was first alerted to the fact that what was surely terminal decline had set in last weekend, another phone call from Margaret. I've also had a couple of messages from Liam.

Lily passed away yesterday afternoon, not a Covid-related death — in fact, no instances of Covid in the Bons Secours home, apparently.

I'm not going to be able to go to the funeral: I simply don't think the risk worth it and anyhow with these renewed restrictions I'm not sure many will be able to do so. One person representing each family I suppose. Angela is going to go, and Liam of course, and Tim and Margaret, and I suppose the Farnalough boys will do so. Not sure Norma will be able to make it as she lives in one of the 3 counties on lockdown.

Margaret has asked me to write a few words to be read out at the funeral. No easy thing because I can hardly claim to have known Lily, not in any meaningful sense anyhow. Some tricky waters to pilot through there too.

Elizabeth (Lily) O'Donovan
1926-2020

Of the children born in Ahilnane in the 1920s and 30s, Lily — Elizabeth — is the last to pass away, these being the children of Patrick O'Donovan of Ahilnane and Mary Kingston of Drinagh East, colloquially Sonny and Minnie.

Sonny and Minnie were married in Carrigfadda church in 1919. Their first-born, Kathleen and Denis, were born when the treaty that ended the War of Independence was agreed and enacted. Then came the twins, William and Ellen, born in 1924, Lily in 1926 and, finally, Mary in 1932.

Sonny and Minnie died in the 1970s.

Ellen — Nelly — died in infancy. William, Denis and Kathleen were laid to rest in the closing decades of the last century. We buried Mary earlier this year, in April. And now, in this harvest time of year, we lay to rest the last of these Free State children.

Though she had not seen the light of dawn there for half a century and more, my cousin Margaret tells me that up to and including the last of her days Lily dreamed of Ahilnane, vividly, and sometimes felt herself out of place in not being 'at home' — home for her being looking south over Fort Robert and Carrigmore into the fertile river valley below; home was the Mash and the Meadow beyond it, the field by Crowleys and the field where the geese were kept, the Break, the Grove, the haggard and hayshed, Minnie's potted geraniums by the window, Thou Shalt Not on the wall and apple-tree blossoms in May.

Margaret says she thinks this terribly sad, but I don't think so. I think it wonderful to be so rooted, to feel that there's somewhere that's forever home, a place where you rightly belong, a place that no passage of time, nor any subsequent experience, can erase or compete with.

In this world there are people from somewhere and there are people from nowhere. Lily — Elizabeth — O'Donovan, daughter of Patrick and Mary O'Donovan of Ahilnane, was from here, this place, this parish, where she was christened and schooled and confirmed in her faith.

And now she's laid to rest here, with her father and mother, a brother and sister and aunts and uncles. May she rest in peace.

SEPTEMBER 2020

Tuesday, 1 September

Being September it's the most obvious thing to say but it's *so* autumnal already! Despite the fact that there was a heatwave in much of Europe in August, here in Ireland the month was broken and, particularly the latter half of it, distinctly chilly, especially early mornings, and evenings too after about 6pm, such that one wouldn't venture forth in those transition hours without a coat and scarf and maybe a cap too. And now it's quite cold (I don't feel it too much to say 'cold') — condensation on all the windows every morning which speaks to the fact that the temp overnight is well down into single figures while the temp indoors much higher.

I've not put on the central heating as yet, aside from a couple of mornings when I've given it once-off blasts for an hour or so because there's still quite a bit of summer heat in the house, especially upstairs; heat (and cold) tends to linger in these old stone-walled houses. I've not put CH on to a *regularized cycle* as yet is what I'm saying. However, I probably will do so this week because as I say it's distinctly chilly nowadays for three quarters of the 24 hours: presently, at its lowest it's between 2 and 8 degrees at night and between, say, 12 and 20 during the best of the day.

However this (not regularizing the CH as yet) also to do with have/ have not security: because I have a full tank of heating oil which is paid for already I feel secure, knowing I can flick a switch and have as much heat as I want for as long as I want — within reason, obviously — whereas if I was struggling financially, just barely able to pay for food and rent and scrambling to draw together emergency measures to provide heat on a hand-to-mouth basis (so to say), I'd feel much colder in these conditions. I have clear memories of having a *not* full-to-the-brim oil tank and, despite that fact, feeling I had to put on the CH mornings and evenings *in August*, which indeed I may even have written about in these diaries once or twice because, even when you're lucky enough to have a full tank of heating oil, putting on the heating in August is a disaster in the sense that if you do so you will not make it through to the end of the cold seasons — which in Ireland is autumn, winter and spring: Irish springs being bracing almost always, and quite cold not infrequently, including frosts even as late as April; indeed snowfalls in February and March wouldn't be remarkable, wouldn't be common but they wouldn't be noteworthy either; April often bright and brightening but cold, as indeed it was this year, so much so that the DSP extended the winter fuel payment until the end of April — usually it ceases at the end of March; in my opinion they ought to pay it in April and September every year anyway because these are cold months, months in which you absolutely need to have heating systems on; and, as I say, if you're poor and insecure somehow you seem to feel cold (and hunger) more keenly.

In addition to which we've had two proper storms already this year. One of them really quite severe such that one had to secure wheelie bins and outdoor furniture and look about for other hazards, i.e., in August one had to put one's winter goggles on — the equivalent of searching about for one's shorts, sunglasses and sunscreen lotion in March or April when there's an unexpectedly warm and sunny spell. And, also in August, there's been flooding in several towns as a result: Kenmare, Skibbereen (only minor here, resulting from a new storm drain not working as it ought to for some reason), the N71 closed at several points either side of Rosscarbery, and part of a road quite washed away in Rosscarbery my cousin Margaret tells me, probably that shoreline road that forks over to where her place is.

So the world (this part of the world anyhow) feels quite wintered already. 'Wintered' may perhaps be going too far for there are still rambling roses blooming and lots of butterflies everywhere, and swifts and swallows, although at the end of last week and over the weekend the swallows have begun gathering in troop formations on electrical and telecom wires such that one of these days we'll look up and they'll be there no more, which 100% is the end of summer, just as the joyful sight of their arrival heralds summer's onset. 'Winter-washed' might be more like it. Or winter-weathered/winter-withered.

Ilen River Playschool started up again this week. So now 4 things back in the parish hall: the Special Needs people in the back room, yoga Tuesdays and Thursdays, the playschool, and, as reported previously, the Country Market on Friday mornings.

My guess is Bridge and Bingo will not be coming back, not this year anyhow (nor next year either, probably). Irish dancing, I don't know, probably will as they're young and it'd be easy enough to have them in OK-sized groups. On the other hand dancing is physically exerting, which might be fine in a hall like the parish hall but not so much in other spaces and I suppose it would have to be a one-rule-for-all type regulation.

I must acknowledge it's been a blessedly gentle re-entry series, so much so that even with these 4 things back you'd hardly notice it, things still wonderfully quite around here. Obviously the playschool kids make a flock-of-randy-geese type racket when they're out on the lawns, however, firstly, that's only when it's dry, which, goodness knows, isn't every day, secondly, even on fine days, it's only an hour or two at most, and thirdly, it's actually quite a nice sound, I think, after all there's only about 20 of them altogether. I can easily imagine it having worked out otherwise whereby one went from the intense silence and stillness in which I've been immersed these 5 or 6 months past to the unpleasant shock of noise and traffic and footfall and all sorts of kerfuffle. But, happily, not a bit of it, it's been as gentle a fade-in as one could reasonably wish for.

I cut the lawns at the end of last week because I was conscious of the fact that the playschool would be back this week and if the kids came out and flattened the grass when it was too long it'd be a hell of a job getting it right again. Also that day (Friday) was the only day last week when it was dry enough to do a cut. Anyway, as I was doing it Pat Hughes came in to set up. (She's already been in a couple of other days, I've noticed, but I hadn't seen her, just seen her vehicle parked in front of the hall.)

We had quite a good chat; she's frightened at the prospect of the year ahead (the virus). She's about my age (maybe even a few years older) and like me she's overweight. And Judith (her assistant) is certainly in her 60s (which I know because she told me so), however, physically Judith's in fairly good shape.

Pat says she'd prefer to pay some young one to run the business for a year or two (until a vaccine is developed) but, she says, the enterprise doesn't pay enough to allow for that.

My guess is that if she really wanted to do this it could be organised — she would simply take less out of the business for herself — but, no doubt, she fears that the young one would take over the show, maybe going independent and stealing half her client base and hop-step-and-jump she'd have handed over her business to someone else.

Pat needs the income clearly, so much so she's willing to put her health in the balance for it.

I have sympathy for her. It's a proper crisis. On the upside for her is the fact that 85% of people suffer no or very minor symptoms even when they do get infected. And, secondly, even if things get quite bad this winter, here in Skibbereen you're going to be in as safe a place as you can be consistent with having a money-making enterprise — no doubt one would be safer in some isolated village or headland or island but in such places it's harder to coin the price of a trolley of groceries. So — what I'm saying is — there's a reasonably good chance she and Judith will come through OK. I'm not sure what the odds of contracting this virus are but I'm fairly sure that here in Skibbereen they're better than in Cork or Carrigaline, say, and, similarly, anywhere in Cork they're better than in the Greater Dublin area. Even in a city my guess is there's a reasonable chance of never being exposed to the virus at all, at least not for long enough to become infected. After all, there are nearly 7 million people on this island and in 9 months only just over 36,000 confirmed infections; even if you double or triple that to account for people who are totally asymptomatic and therefore do not show up in the numbers at all, it's still only a tiny fraction of the population; even at 100,000 it's less than 2%. If things get really bad they'll get bad up the country a few weeks before they do so down here, which'll give them time to think about what they want to do. And if things don't get too bad, as I say, they've a reasonably good chance of making it through OK.

That said, I would not do what they're doing. Too much risk for my blood. But this is how it is when you get hooked on an income, whatever it might be. (Judith might not be overweight but her aged parents live with her so that *she* might not be too much at risk but they must be because of her.)

Pat says she's going to do as much outdoors as she can manage. And of course she's got the hall which is a reasonably good-sized space. However, it's a kindergarten and when a kid cries s/he will need to be picked up, and some (if not all) of those kids need help going to the loo and so on. By its very nature it's a hands-on let-me-wipe-your-nose/arse/mouth/ hands type job, there's no getting around or away from that.

They've been advised not to wear masks because masks might be off-putting for infants but, she says, she's going to wear a visor and face-mask anyway. She's just not going to be comfortable otherwise, she says.

Parents — nor any adult aside from Pat and Judith — not allowed into the hall during playschool hours going forward, and all sorts of protocols in place for coming in and going out. A thorny thicket of regulations.

I'm steering well clear of it all, you may be sure. I open up the grounds in the morning — just the gates, I don't go anywhere near the hall or the church anymore — and I close them up again as soon as I can afterwards — and I do another cycle around the grounds again in the evenings, checking everything's secure — but that's about all. And like I say I'm still doing the lawns.

Sunday, 13 September

Political furore in the UK (and in Ireland and the EU) this week because the UK government has put a bill before parliament, the Internal Markets Bill, parts of which are designed to negate/overwrite key elements of the recently agreed UK-EU Withdrawal Agreement, concluded at the end of last year following three years of torturous wrangling, negotiations and political upheaval (when at times Britain looked like it was at war with itself, Union Jack waving Brexiteers vs EU flag-waving Remainers, and the latter weren't just Guardian-reader types like me, it was also fairly hardcore Conservatives — Philip Hammond, Dominic Grieve, Nicholas

Soames, Oliver Letwin, Justine Greening, Ed Vaizey…, former ministers or key office-holders, nationalists in Scotland and Northern Ireland but also some Northern Ireland unionists too, old school unionists, non-DUP unionists). As Keir Starmer says, this is simply to reopen hardly healed wounds.

Oh, and by the bye, the British government concedes that if passed as is this bill — by which I mean the provisions referred to above — will be in contravention of international law, in particular the Brexit Withdrawal Agreement, an international treaty. Indeed, the provisions referred to specifically state that in cases where the provisions of the bill are in conflict with any treaty obligations, or with any other domestic legislation, then this bill predominates. Moreover the bill's provisions abrogate to ministers the power to apply or disapply all sorts of rules and regulations to do with trade and tariffs and customs regulations such that the situation will be that the law applying will be whatever ministers say it is at the time, the very essence of lawlessness.

The subject is mightily complicated, far too in-the-weeds to explain — for me to do so anyhow — but it is profoundly important. I now think it likely that the UK and the EU end up with quite sour relations, which'll have all sorts of knock-on consequences.

The Brits accuse the EU of 'bad faith' with respect to the recently agreed Withdrawal Agreement but this is classic projection. Clearly, as it appears to me, Johnson never intended honouring what he signed up for at the end of last year. His objective was to sign up to something he could go to the country with, force a general election, win the election, and then turn around and tell the EU to go swivel. Which is exactly what's happened and what's happening.

Even at the end of last year, and at the beginning of this year during the election campaign, BJ was telling the DUP and his own supporters that there would be no regulatory border down the Irish Sea, no checks, no threat to the unity of the United Kingdom, despite the fact that this is certainly what he signed up for in the Withdrawal Agreement, in particular in the so-called 'Irish Protocol' section of that agreement, the protocol to do with preserving an open border on the island of Ireland, which, because of Brexit, isn't just a British-Irish border it's also an EU-UK (EU/non-EU) border now. When this was pointed out to him — that he was saying one thing to his supporters and associated allies and another opposite thing to the EU in the negotiated agreement — he blustered and blathered his way through and past such challenges. He had to be lying to someone; everybody (including me) suspected that he was lying to his own people, but we were wrong, turns out he was lying to Ireland and to the EU.

On Friday, *The Financial Times* put up a YouTube video by David Allen Green, one of their writers, someone with legal expertise clearly. The video is titled 'Opinion: Can the government breach the Brexit Withdrawal Agreement?' It is a really well made video, as it seems to me, clearly explaining the facts of the matter, pointing to all the key bits in all the key documents in a way I found informative: https://youtu.be/ XJOGLcvh-9o

Appreciating the work, I left a brief positive comment attached to the video.

This got a reply from David Allen Green which said (simply) 'Thank you.'

So far, so pleasant.

However, after that the crazies start to circle and gather. The following (which is threaded onto my exchange of pleasantries with DAG) tells you something of the present atmosphere, and the way things have been for the past few years, like a British version of Trumpian virus. (In reproducing the following I'm preserving semi-literate punctuation, spellings &c as the like seems characterful.)

> **Roy Wiseman**: Here's the problem with all of this video. It tried to pretend that the UK are in the wrong, and the EU can do no wrong. The EU carefully and deliberately worded the WA as a means to trap and put economic pressure on the UK. If any person believes that the WA had anything to do with "peace in NI", please tip your surgeon, that lobotomy worked.
>
> EVERY act that the EU has done has been to try and split up the UK and to trap the UK into the ECJ etc.
>
> This is a terrible video because it grovellingly operates as a "ball sac licking device" for the EU.

The EU has already breached the WA, AND have stated their intent to try and use the WA to blockade NI from the rest of the UK (which would be, frankly, criminal and unacceptable). The Internal Market Bill seeks to counter the EU's clear breach of international law.

Now, if you are the kind of person that grovels to and licks the balls of the EU and pretends that the EU is a wonderland of unicorns and custard, then you will scream about this (manufactured faux outrage).

If you are an unbiased person that wants the facts however, then the deceit and lies of the EU are clearly exposed for all to see, and this video just seems to be people that grovel to the EU on everything.

When the EU are so corrupt that their promised report on corruption was just ditched and hidden without a word, when the EU are so corrupt that we'd be here all day going through their corruption and when the EU tell you who they are, why not believe them?

Not a single thing that the EU has done in this negotiation has been in good faith. The EU operate exclusively on dishonesty and deceit.

So much for wise men and wisdom.

And here look at how Wiseman online-Alpha-males the next guy, Mikey Mike, into subservience.

Mikey Mike: Roy Wiseman Of course the EU worded the WA in their favour and to support their interests. Wouldn't you if you were them ? It's Johnson's government that cocked up by accepting it as is and they are now trying to backtrack out of it. It's embarrassing

Roy Wiseman: @Mikey Mike Sure I would. Just to be clear: are you ok with the EU lying a [*sic*] deceiving to hurt you and your family (if you are British)? Is that harm to you and your family all good because you just grovel to whatever faeces the EU shovel down your throat?

Mikey Mike: Roy Wiseman You are right of course. We at least have the higher moral ground where we can trust fully everything Johnson government says and does. We know for a fact that that [*sic*] there'll be no U turns down the line in any policy's [*sic*] that they come up with.

Roy Wiseman: @Mikey Mike I have no problem with U-turns in policies and neither do you. If any other country but the UK does a U-turn in policy you support that and think that is wonderful "it shows statesmanship for Varadkur [*sic*] to U-turn on this important issue!" you would say (though that twat is gone). Possibly you would criticise Trump as well. But let's be clear, EVERYTHING that you think here is 100% ideologically driven. You see the EU as "the land of unicorns and custard" and you hate your own country because ... low IQ ? Inability to work out that EU is determined to do you and your family as much harm as possible ? A combination of the two ? Which of these is it?

Gringo Bandito: Roy Wiseman what's with all the ball licking? Freudian slip?

MEGA: It doesn't mention the Miller case which is key.

Roy Wiseman: @MEGA Gina Miller is maybe the biggest unsung hero of Brexit. Without her, May's deal would have gone through and the UK would be a vassal state of the EU right now.

And so it goes on. And these are just the sub-comments to my altogether uncontroversial 'Thank you' exchange with David Allen Green. I've looked at the replies to a few other comments and I see that Roy Wiseman has cut & pasted the exact same 'Here's the problem with all of this video' rant under several people's comments. Like some kind of troll under a bridge coming out from under the arches every time someone crosses the bridge to show us his ringed-up swollen ball-sac or whatever it is he wants people to see. In addition to having his ball-sac ringed-up he's also on about having shit shoved down his throat, I notice. Wonder what he gets up to when he's not online trolling non-Brexiteers? Trolling non-Brexiteers along with policing stragglers who are not sufficiently Brexity for his liking as he does above with Mikey Mike and MEGA.

All this stuff to do with Brexit is a British version of the Culture Wars virus that has infected and completely debilitated the body politic in the US, something far more serious than the coronavirus pandemic as it seems to me because it even gets in the way of responding to the virus in a sensible way — wearing masks/not wearing masks is a political statement in the US these days. Similarly the Brexit referendum in 2016 wasn't really about Europe, I believe, or at least it wasn't wholly about the European Union, it was about stuff which I've written about in these diary pages before: for many people it was a rejection of the EU but it was also a rejection of the general direction of travel, a rejection of the fact that essentially there's no difference between Cameron and Blair, nor the Milibands and Yvette Coopers and the up-and-comings surrounding Cameron, Osborne, and Clegg, not as far as the people on the Feckham, Peckham and Clapham omnibuses are concerned anyhow. Different rosettes but same plastic Oxbridge repulsives whichever way you vote. And indeed a rejection of the whole meritocracy model of organisation in general, if I'm not mistaken, which by this stage (in Britain anyhow) is, generally speaking, a lie, and a bigger lie with each generation. In reality to prosper in this world you got to be born to the right parents and have the right postcode and go the right schools and universities and have the right kinds of social contacts to secure the right internship pathways and so on, otherwise 99 times out of a hundred you're just fuck-hutch fodder, people to sell soap and biscuits and new cars to. If you have talent as well that'll help but if it's a choice between having natural born talent on one hand and having all the advantages listed above, you'd be better off with the geo-social advantages. CEOs paying themselves 4 and 6 and 8 and 10 million dollars a year because they believe they're worth it, while workers on the ground take home 400 dollars/euros a week, 600 or 700 if they have a particularly good gig, and 800 to 1,000 if they perform some level of platoon corporal type function. Politics, media, business, managing capital and IP, technology, the legal industry… it's all one system, a system designed to squeeze the last drop of value out of everything for them that already have far too much. Nick Clegg goes from being deputy PM to being head of 'ethics' for Facebook. Osborne becomes editor of The Evening Standard and *at the same time* trousering £650,000 a year as an advisor to the BlackRock investment fund. David Miliband goes into the international charity racket on a million dollar remuneration package. 2016 was a rejection of all that, all that direction of travel. And, unfortunately, both in the US with Trump and here with Brexit, this frustration and outlash has taken on a nationalist, right-wing tilt.

In one of the Sunday newspapers this morning Tony Blair and Sir John Major have penned a joint article condemning this Internal Markets Bill move as damaging to the reputation of the UK in terms of being a law-abiding nation and the Brexiteers are already batting the concerns of these former prime ministers away as the squawking of the 'Remoaner

Establishment' reawakened. These people need to return to their coffins in the political crypt, Brexiteers say.

By the bye, Theresa May and Gordon Brown have also spoken out against this threatened act of bad faith by the British, which is to say, altogether 4 former prime ministers. (Having led us into this mess, David Cameron is still in hiding somewhere in the Oxfordshire countryside, writing his phoney memoirs or whatever the glib tosser is at — anyways he's keeping schtum.) Even former Tory leader Michael Howard has spoken out in opposition to this, and he's a genuine Brexiteer. Howard was pro-Brexit before Boris Johnson found it politically expedient to sign up for the Make Britain Great Again campaign.

No doubt Boris Johnson is attempting to get out of what he pretended to agree to this time last year. After all he's a notorious liar, just ask his ex-wife, or the mothers of any of the children he's fathered around town, or the women who've aborted his seminal legacies, or any of several of his former employers — he was sacked from his first job at The Times for making up quotes and then lying about it, he was sacked by Michael Howard when Howard was leader of the Tory party for lying about one of the affairs he was conducting, he told The Spectator he would not seek a seat in parliament when he interviewed for the editor's desk, also a lie, and so on and on, his whole career is a lattice of brazen lies, but, as it seems to me, following a terrible spring and summer in which he's been in serious trouble about his attitude to the pandemic — nearly 50,000 Britons dead for goodness sakes, one of the worst records in Europe, and the mess with A-level results and two or three other high-profile missteps (refusing to sack Dominic Cummings for not abiding by public health regulations imposed on everyone else, for example) — he's also attempting to rally his Brexity base with this move. And nothing rallies his base so well as upsetting Guardian types and bed-wetting Tories, and the authorities in Dublin and Brussels. As I say, I see this as something from the Trumpist playbook.

Thursday, 17 September

An additional 240 confirmed cases of infection reported today, while one further person diagnosed with the virus has died.

Death toll now stands at 1,789, and the overall number of cases now 32,023.

And a further 149 confirmed cases in Northern Ireland.

Therefore, altogether, 40,803 confirmed cases of infection on the island of Ireland and, to date, 2,362 Covid-related deaths.

10 million people in the UK living under some level of restriction as of today. Two million in the northeast is the latest tranche from midnight tonight, including a 10pm curfew for pubs and restaurants &c. Sounds like its equal to level 3 of the 5-level system we have here in Ireland.

Indeed Dublin — and maybe the Greater Dublin area too — is about to be moved onto level 3 according to reports (presently all 26 counties on level 2).

Israel has announced that it's about to go into a second full-on lockdown, another 3 weeks of it. Buckle up, ladies and gentlemen, we're heading into a wintery swell and the forecast's unhappy looking, not to say bleak and foreboding.

Friday, 18 September

Beautiful day today, azure sky, cotton-ball clouds, pleasant breeze, and warm. It's 9 o'clock in the morning right now and it's 14 degrees. Later in the day it'll rise to about 20. It's been 20 or 21 or 22 (or even 23) degrees every day this week. A so-called Indian Summer, which, by the bye, refers to Native Americans rather than something out of British Empire India which hitherto I had always imagined/presumed for some reason, according to Wikipedia anyhow:

> 'a period of unseasonably warm, dry weather that sometimes occurs in autumn in temperate regions in the northern hemisphere during September, [October and] November [...] research shows that the

earliest known reference to [an 'Indian Summer'] in its current sense occurs in an essay written in the United States in the late 1770s (probably 1778) by J. Hector St. John de Crevecoeur [the original published in French]. Although the exact origins of the term are uncertain, it was perhaps so-called because it was first noted in regions inhabited by American Indians, or because the Indians first characterized it for Europeans, or [maybe it's] based on the warm and hazy conditions in autumn when American Indians hunted. In literature and history, the term is sometimes used metaphorically [...] an era of inconsistency, infertility, and depleted capabilities, a period of seemingly robust strength that is only an imitation of an earlier season of actual strength. William Dean Howell's 1886 novel, *Indian Summer*, uses the term to mean a time when one may recover some of the happiness of youth. The main character, jilted as a young man, leads a solitary life until he rediscovers romance in early middle age.'

But — not unusually for me — I digress.

It has not been sunny all week. It has been along the east side of this island, apparently, and in England, especially down in the already much too favoured southeast, where they've had temps up to 30 degrees, at least according to the newspapers — predictable 'Phew! Wota Scorcher' headlines along with pic of busty starlet or celeb in a bikini looking prick-teasingly tarty or faux-coy, and of course for all their sniffiness broadsheets have their own versions of the like. Here, however, it's been clammy and muggy for the most part, lots of fog which doesn't clear until nearly lunchtime and then maybe three or four hours of patchy sunshine before everything goes into sun-setting mode. And a couple of days it's not been sunny at all, not even patchy sunshine, just overcast and warm.

But, like I say, today is a beauty.

Great season for butterflies which are everywhere at the minute. If I went from here to where the wheelie bins are and back again — which is a dog-leg trip of about 40 yards — I'd be quite likely to see half a dozen of em. They're on almost everything one looks at — windows, gable ends, shrubs and grass-level, they're dancing in the air in front of you, above you, and all around you. I do not know whether there are so many because of the weather or because of the extent to which the grassy part of the Old Schoolyard — and the Master's Garden above it — has been let go so wild looking in recent years — Matt doesn't do a tap back in this area anymore. Or a combo of both.

Anyhow, the main thing I wanted to say here right now is that I've just been out to the wheelie bins and on my way back I looked up at the wonderful blue sky and (about 30 feet above the belfry) saw the ash-coloured bellies of what must have been 30 or 40 swallows!

I saw some on Monday, but since then haven't seen any at all, so — not unreasonably, I think — I concluded they'd finally gone this week. But, no, they're still here, some of them anyhow.

However, while this warm weather is due to continue into the weekend, it's due to turn colder (and wetter) next week apparently, so I'm sure this weekend is the last hurrah for our lovely friends from the warm south.

All the coronavirus news is bad. Dublin has been moved up to level 3 in the Irish 5-level system of classification. And as I've mentioned in bits and pieces during recent weeks so too is most of northern England. Parts of the English midlands also. News coming out of France grim: Nice, Lyon and Marseille all on lockdown (or at least fairly serious levels of restriction), the latter in particular trouble, almost at capacity in terms of ICU facilities; in France they had over 10,000 new cases of infection in one 24-hour period earlier this week, which is crisisville to be sure.

In the Czech Republic there were 3,130 new infections recorded on Thursday alone, almost as many as for the whole month of March — and officials are warning of the risk of an exponential increase.

Like I say, the news is bad all over Europe. Modelling projections suggest that here in Ireland we might have 1,000 new cases a day by mid-October, which, if the like came to pass, is worse than anything we experienced earlier this year — and as yet we're a long long way from the depths of winter! If we did have 1,000 new cases a day — or anything like it — in October, what the fuck would it be like in December, January and February?

300,000 new cases reported across Europe last week according to the WHO, which exceeds anything in March of this year. By the bye, according to WHO figures, 228,000 deaths in Europe since the pandemic began, which is worse than the US where the number of dead is just about to cross the 200,000 threshold. And, in fairness, I think it is *all of Europe* — or the EU at the very least — that ought be compared to the US, not just individual countries — Germany or France or the UK — comparisons that make the situation in the US look particularly bad. The Trump administration has been attempting to make this perfectly reasonable point all summer and, as I say, I think it a fair point to make.

Numbers rising so fast in the UK the government is reported to be considering a short, sharp 'circuit-breaking lockdown' for a couple of weeks so as not to have to resort to something worse later on.

Just saying, buckle up and hang on to your skirts and hats.

Monday, 21 September

Today in the UK the chief scientist and the chief medical officer held a press conference in which they spoke of the possibility of having up to 50,000 new cases a day by mid-October — which would mean up to 200 dead each day 4 or 5 weeks after that — if people failed to follow the regulations and recommendations now in force, the so-called 'rule of 6' and all the rest of it which, clearly, people are not, which is why the government is considering a 2- or 3-week circuit-breaking shutdown to coincide with the schools' mid-term break in October because if things go on as they are presently modelled to go the situation will be out of control before the end of the year. The fear is that as things stand the UK is just a few weeks away from what's happening in France and Spain — which are in really bad places with respect to the second wave of this thing — and they want to avoid following the same (or similar) paths if at all possible.

Saturday, 26 September

Another 6,042 new cases reported in the UK today (6,874 yesterday and 6,634 the day before that). I suppose they can consider themselves fortunate that — for the moment anyhow — the number of new cases appears to have stabilized somewhere between 6,000 and 7,000 a day, although we'll see how that goes next week and the week after, which is to say, I very much doubt it will stay in that range.

34 deaths reported in the UK today.

Interesting to compare and contrast Italy and Spain. Both had it really bad in spring but now, while Spain appears to be caught up in a second wave which looks like it will be just as bad as the first (and probably worse before we get to Christmas), Italy not so much for some reason.

Spain has reported over 150,000 new cases in the past 14 days and it has been reporting between 100 and 300 deaths per day for the past two weeks whereas the equivalent figures for Italy are 21,439 new cases in the past 14 days and between 10 and 30 deaths per day. Altogether, so far, Italy has had just over 300,000 confirmed cases and 35,000 deaths and to date Spain has had over 700,000 cases and 31,232 deaths — in fact I've seen reports that the authorities in Spain have been doing some fancy footwork in accounting terms to minimize the full extent of how really dreadful things are there; but of course in Spain things so toxic politically you cannot always credit the reports that come out of that country about what one side or the other are supposed to be up to; nevertheless I mention it because as I say I've seen such reports and on the face of it that death count for Spain appears to me to be quite low when compared with other countries that have had so many cases of infection.

The Civil War has utterly toxified politics in Spain, which, after all, is still within living memory, just about — disgracefully they're still squabbling about Franco's remains for goodness sakes!

Speaking of political toxicity, I was watching PMQs a week or so ago and BJ was bemoaning the fact that Keir Starmer is always carping from the sidelines, essentially suggesting that Starmer was responsible for much of the chaotic response to this pandemic because he [Starmer] is an impediment to national unity, as opposed to the government he [Johnson] leads with his stonking great Brexit majority in parliament, and he [Johnson] went on to attempt to do a Churchillian rallying of the nation to get behind the government for this great fight — this United Kingdom, this Awesome Foursome, this happy family and so on — but it sounded not only flat and unconvincing to my ears it actually sounded absurd, unpleasantly so.

Now this repulsive fuck who lied us into breaking off from the European Union, and did so for no higher cause than the furtherance of his own cursed ambition, wants unity — and of course he only wants unity because national unity at this time is what will save him from the fate he so richly deserves! And it is most certainly *not* a *united* kingdom, and he has done as much as anyone to render it disunited. He is actively and purposely and knowingly sowing the seeds of disunity in Northern Ireland, setting one side of that unhappy territory against the other, careless of the cost or consequence, and I'm convinced that this Brexit thing is the final steel spike in the chest of the union between England and Scotland. However, you just watch, the guy is such a coward he'll run away before the final split happens so he doesn't go down in history as the prime minister who broke the 300-year-old union. But he won't run away from the judgement of history so easily because that more than any other thing is what he'll be known for. Indeed, if I'm not mistaken, it's the only thing he'll be known for.

Above I refer to the cost and consequence of Brexit in general and the faithless and cavalier actions of Boris Johnson's government in particular with respect to Northern Ireland; let me record this here and now: I now believe we'll see a border poll in Northern Ireland before too long and a majority will vote to leave the union. What goes round comes round. Of course the UK government has the power to say when and whether this poll takes place, and like they did with the Scotland referendum in 2014, they'll seek to stage it at a time that's best suited to a unionist response, however, the UK government may not be in control of events like it was in 2014. It'll be difficult to continue refusing the Scots another referendum, I believe, what with Brexit and the SNP winning overwhelming majorities in the Westminster elections and in the Holyrood elections — Brexit changes everything — and if there is a second referendum in Scotland I believe this time the vote will be for independence (and, after a short period, a return to the European Union). At present opinion polls suggest this is how the vote would go, and the direction of travel is one-way only — BJ's porcine face and posh English antics play really badly north of the border and, at the same time Nicola Sturgeon is having a good coronavirus crisis, so far anyhow, certainly by comparison with BJ. And if that happens and then there's a border poll in Northern Ireland then I think it very likely NI will also vote to leave Boris Johnson's 'Awesome Foursome'. After that he'll be left with a somewhat less awesome twosome.

The thing is whether SF can hold their horses. SF pushing for a border poll *now* which is foolish in my view. As I say, it'd be smarter to play the medium-term play here. So much so it wouldn't surprise me if the Brits gave them what they're seeking, which is to say, granting it *before* they're pushed into granting another ref in Scotland, thereby disrupting the sequence outlined above. However, like I say, London may not be able to control events quite as much as it thinks it may be able to (or as much as it has been able to do in times past).

But, just to be clear, however it actually plays out, I feel we'll see both Scotland and Northern Ireland uncouple from the United Kingdom in the not too distant future. It might be 5 years, it might be 10 or 15 — it might even be 20 or 25 years from now (it may require a whole generation to move through the pipes) — but like I say it's coming. And, as indicated, I believe it'll happen in my lifetime (assuming I live to the end of the 2030s, that is).

Wednesday, 30 September 2020

Last night's US presidential debate was, as Dana Bash on CNN put it, 'a shit show'. She actually said this live on air which caused me to clutch my pearls because, famously, Americans are far more conservative about the language they use on television broadcasts than we here on these islands so, even though I swear like a drunken trooper myself, it was a little bit shocking to me, someone being so forthright, unexpected. But it was nothing other than the truth of the matter.

Actually Jake Tapper was the first to speak in that after-the-debate panel discussion on CNN; CNN went straight from the venue in Cleveland to Jake Tapper in studio and, after a moment's silence —

looking deadpan into the camera — Tapper says "That was a hot mess inside a dumpster fire inside of a train wreck", which I feel sure is going to be clipped and become part of the newsreel footage about the last days of the Trump era, something that'll be played and replayed for generations to come.

And in so saying Tapper summed up what most Americans were thinking at that moment, I suspect — most of those watching CNN at least — the hardies who hung on until the end of that stomp-and-shout fest masquerading as a presidential 'debate'. Only political junkies would have stayed with it until the bitter end, regular folks — which is to say, people with jobs to do, kids to get up on a school morning, mortgage repayments to meet and all the rest of it — having tuned out and switched over to other channels long before the horrifying final section in which Trump again made it clear that he may or may not accept the result of the election; it'll depend on how the land lies in November, he says, smirking that sick smirk of his.

Or, as Mike Madrid of the Lincoln Project said in their post-debate podcast discussion, it wasn't 'a debate', it was 'a spectacle', politics as ratings-chasing spectacle. It was 90 minutes of undiluted Twitter Trump. It was the political equivalent of an episode of the Jerry Springer Show. The contemptuous trashing of the — admittedly rather quaint-seeming — democratic ritual of the Candidates' Debate, the whole concept of candidates for top office coming before the citizenry and conducting a debate of ideas and philosophies and programmes for government for the benefit of the citizens, putting before them the issues at stake and the solutions proposed, something that goes back to the very bedrock of western political traditions.

Or as George Stephanopoulos put it the following morning on Good Morning America, "How about 'A disgrace'?" he suggested as fellow GMA presenters stumbled about in the wreckage of their political lexicon searching for words and phrases to begin to characterize what we'd witnessed the night before.

This was the first of 3 presidential debates in this election cycle, however I feel that after what happened last night there's some chance that that event in Cleveland will be the first and last presidential debate we see in this 2020 cycle.

Trump simply wouldn't shut up! He sounded like he was on drugs, one too many pep-me-up pills, Adderall or some such. (Before the debate he was calling for Joe Biden to be drug-tested and Trump is famous/infamous for projecting onto others his own faults and failings, just like he's been accusing Hunter Biden, Joe Biden's son, of being the kept boy of Russian oligarchs, for instance, or like he accuses everyone else of trafficking 'Fake News' which, more than anything else, has been Donald Trump's stock-in-trade for 40 or 50 years.) Hectoring, bullying, verbal and rhetorical incontinence... He tried to do to Joe Biden what he did to Hilary Clinton 4 years ago, however all his bullyboy stuff has grown (exponentially) more grotesque on 4 years of POTUS steroids such that, while he thought he was doing to JB what he did to HC in 2016, it was actually about 8 times worse, such that it was, as the commentariat say, a grotesque spectacle, a shit show, a total disgrace — and this from commentators from both right and left.

Twice (and unmistakably) Trump was given opportunities to denounce White Supremacists — who clearly see Trump as some kind of John the Baptist type figure — and pointedly Trump declined to do so. He said he would do so but then didn't, saying that left wing activists and protestors were the real problem — which, by the bye, he classifies as 'terrorists' despite the fact that his own FBI says it is right wing militia groups and white supremacist groups that are the 'Number 1' terrorist threat inside the US at the minute, not activists and protestors protesting racist killer cops. But the debate moderator — Chris Wallace of Fox News — was unwilling to allow the president to wriggle away from the question so easily, repeatedly bringing him back to the question at hand: 'Will you disavow the support of Nazis and other White Supremacist hate groups?' — groups which are very keen on Trump, Making America Great Again, America First, and 'Taking back our country' (i.e., taking it back from black and brown people, and from the queers and quiche-eating tree-huggers and feminist radicals), all in for the man from Trump Tower they are. Cornered on national television Trump said, 'OK, ok, who is it you want me to condemn or disavow or whatever it is you want of me?' (I'm paraphrasing here but this was the gist of it.)

As one commentator put it in one of the discussions I watched afterwards, it's like asking someone to condemn violence against women and, being cornered, the bloke says "OK, ok, ok... So, what we talking about here? A slap in the mouth once in a while? Locking them up in a windowless room, rape, gangbanging, verbal abuse...? I mean what *kind* of violence against women do you want me to disavow?" And of course it goes without saying that one ought to condemn *all* forms of violence against women, and do so without hesitation, equivocation or distinction, you fucking monster! Much less needing to be *cornered and harried into doing so!*; and even then being willing only to condemn/disavow specifically named entities — for fear of tarring all such activities with the same broad-brush, lazy characterizations — because, as he's said previously, "There's good people on both sides", isn't there!

So, like I say, cornered, eventually Trump says "OK. Who? Who is it you want me to disassociate from? Give me some names." Biden chipped in with the Proud Boys group as an example of the kind of group Wallace was referring to. And Trump says, "Yeah, ok, whatever, Proud Boys stand down and stand by, but, like I say, Antifa is the real issue here..." and with that the shit show rolled on. However, that's what the president said: "Proud Boys stand down [but] stand by" and, although the president's supporters have since been spinning "Well, he didn't really mean 'Stand by' in the way you're suggesting... — you're injecting malign meaning into the president's innocent words", there's no doubt about what the Proud Boys themselves heard because within the hour they had memes up on social media saying 'Proud Boys Standing By' and so on.

We've been through all this before with Trump, back around the time of the Unite the Right rally in Charlottesville in 2017, for example, when, eventually, after about a week, the media drew a condemnation of White Supremacist ideology out of Trump — which, when it did come, came in the form of a statement clearly written for the president by staffers which he read off the teleprompter like a troublesome schoolboy made to read his composition assignment out in front of the class, which meant it was drenched in insincerity and contempt — but by that time he'd made enough cryptic and double-meaning remarks, and he'd stonewalled the liberal media's demands for a show of decency for so long that all supremacist groups in the US fully understood that this president was firmly on their side in reality but, for political expediency and for the optics of it, he had to make this BS show of contrition/disavowal.

And we had it before that as well when (then candidate) Trump pretended not to know David Duke (former Grand Wizard of the KKK) who had endorsed Trump's candidacy for the GOP nomination.

And before that again with all that business about Obama's birth cert, and before that, back in the 1990s, with the Central Park 5 and so on.

Also, for instance, in the debate last night Trump vowed to put an end to racial sensitivity training programmes, saying that in his view such programmes taught Americans to hate their country, which is to say (in effect), that if you're against the grotesque brutality of slavery and the injustice of the apartheid Jim Crow regimes, and the multifarious toxic legacies thereof, then you hate America!), which is wholly a David Duke/Richard Spencer/Tea Party position.

And indeed Trump has been perfectly clear about how the (treasonous) Confederate flag and Confederate monuments are part of the proud heritage of the United States. It's who we are, he says.

So there's no mistaking where Trump is under this heading.

But combine all that with the fact that in the debate again (for the 12th time this year) he refused to commit to accepting the outcome of the election and a peaceful transfer of power should he lose the election — all that stuff which, you know, we kind of take for granted in the western world — similarly, pointedly refusing to do so. (He seems to enjoy refusing to do so; threatening the very nervous system of the body politic.) He says he's willing to commit to accepting the result of a 'free and fair election', but it's clear that what he means by 'a free and fair election' is an electoral process that discounts votes that are likely to be anti-Trump and, by contrast, privileges votes more likely to be pro-Trump.

All together, the whole thing was simply an assault on the electoral process itself, on democracy (democratic ideals), on decency, on civic virtue, basically everything that makes our flawed and fragile system acceptable — reasonable if far from flawless.

The guy's a real bad dude. He's so awful (and crazy) he makes Dick Cheney and the like seem acceptable right now. And he makes old school conservatives like Mitt Romney and HW Bush seem positively *desirable*. It was and is alarming.

A final word on all this for now.

In many ways I think Trump did Biden a favour last night. First of all, Trump was so crazy he frightened quite a few on his own side, I'm sure. But also Trump's insane aggressiveness and rhetorical incontinence last night covered over the fact that Biden looked a bit shaky (to my eye anyhow). He did OK, there were no gaffs — I'd score him 6/10, maybe 6.5 — but he looked like a 78-year-old bloke. The fact that Trump wouldn't shut up covered over the fact that sometimes Biden struggled to find the words or the concept he sought, and to my mind he didn't have a convincing grasp of his own policy programme (that's because he doesn't really have a policy programme worth remembering, his USP is that he's not Trump, nevertheless you've gotta present the like, and do so convincingly). At one point Biden was asked about taxation and he started talking about spending pledges. All politicians do this kind of thing, of course — ignore the question asked and talk about what they've come to talk about — but, the point is, you must be able to carry it off, which Biden failed to do, he was a bit doddery doing so and Wallace pulled him on it, and for half a second you could see Old Joe checking to be sure he didn't have a senior moment with 80 million people watching; but, in fairness to him, he soldiered on and got through it without making a show of himself in a way he need be ashamed of.

Biden did one thing really well, however, which is that 6 or 7 times he looked directly down the barrel of the camera and addressed the American people at home on their sofas, reassuring them that he was tuned into their concerns, assuring them that as long as they turned up to vote this Trump madness would come to an end, and he did so convincingly, I thought, therefore I believe he did enough to convince everyone that he's not mentally deteriorated like the Trump campaign has been spinning all year, rather he's 'all there' and keen to go do what needs to be done, and capable of doing it. And he provided the sound-bite clippers with some good clips: "You're the worst president America's ever had", "Ah quit your yapping", "He's not capable of it, he's a clown", "America is poorer, sicker, more divided and more unhappy after 4 years of this administration" and so on.

And he smiled for goodness sakes! — and did so in a non-phoney way — something Trump did not do all evening (smirking aside); the contrast between the bullying wounded bitterness of Trump and his putrefying, stinking self-obsession on one side, and Biden's pleasant looking decency and American-people-focused presentation on the other, was as night and day to my way of seeing. In this sense the evening was a triumph for Biden, and, more than any wonky policy presentation, this is the whole game with these debates.

I feel Biden would be a fool to do anymore debates. He's got nothing to gain from doing so, and he has much to lose. Trump was attempting to rattle and break Biden, and he was doing so because Biden is clearly breakable. Why would you expose your guy to any more of it? Last night he did enough to show that he does not suffer significant cognitive issues like the Trump people have been saying all year, and that he's not afeared to go toe-to-toe for 90 minutes with a nasty bruiser like Trump. I don't see why he needs to do any more.

I wouldn't give a fuck what they'd say. I'd walk off now and leave the American people with that 'crackhead' impression of Trump. Why give him an opportunity to rectify that?

OCTOBER 2020

Friday, 2 October

Late last night/early this morning it emerged that Donald and Melania Trump have tested positive for Covid.

No one knows what this means for the campaign — certainly not me anyhow (I'm writing this first thing after breakfast, having listened to the BBC and RTE breakfast news radio broadcasts) — but, for example, the next presidential debate is due to be on the 15th of this month, will this go ahead now? Who would send a 78-year-old into combat with someone who mocks mask-wearing, which Trump did the other night in the debate and which he's done scores of times at rallies, even insisting that journos remove their masks when asking questions in the WH press briefing room — he cannot make out what they're saying when they're masked, he claims. The real reason he's anti-mask-wearing is that it suggests the pandemic is still fully with us and continues to be a clear and present danger at a time when the Trump campaign strategy is to make like the whole coronavirus nightmare is in the rearview already and the US is on recovery road. This especially evident during the RNC convention in August when every speaker — when they mentioned the pandemic at all — referred to it in the *past tense*, clearly campaign strategy and conference policy. Even in the debate the other night Trump did so, especially in the economic section where he had a slew of figures designed to portray a V-shaped recovery, America coming back stronger than ever. Jam tomorrow, boys and girls, and lashings of it.

Anyway, as I wrote Wednesday, Joe Biden has nothing to gain from engaging with Trump on the debate-stage anymore, and this — plus the unhinged shit show the other night in Cleveland — is the perfect opportunity to shelve plans for the remaining debates, although I'd still go ahead with the VP debate next week because I think Harris could do a job on that creep Pence, but it doesn't matter too much either way because no one pays attention to the VP debate. No need to make any statement(s), just wait and see how things play out. It may be that everyone around the president and his wife test positive too.

Last night's dramatic developments began with Hope Hicks feeling unwell on the flight back from Cleveland on Tuesday night. Hope Hicks is the WH Comms Director, that's her official position but her real job is more like being the president's body person. She's on hand for Trump in the way Gary Walsh is on hand for Selina Meyer in VEEP, or at least that was her role for the first couple of years in Trump's White House. She then went off and worked for one of Rupert Murdoch's media companies as a communications director — leaving the WH after getting tangled up in the Mueller probe because she was involved in the blizzard of lies to do with that June 2016 meeting in Trump Tower where Don Jr and Paul Manafort and the Kushner princeling were hoping to get 'dirt' from the Russians on Hilary Clinton. Then she returned again to serve as Trump's 4th or 5th (or is it 6th?) Communications Director, however she's a former model who's only work experience is working for the Trump Organisation which mostly involved bringing Donald sodas and Adderall or Viagra pills or whatever it is he calls for, and dressing like a wannabe on *The Apprentice* so everyone looks mannequin cool when walking through lobbies and whatnot, and her main qualification (if you can term it as such), her USP, is the fact that she's a friend of Ivanka and mutt-loyal.

Anyhow Hicks gets sick and gets tested for Covid and yesterday evening the test result came back positive. As I say no one (not even his wife) is closer to The Donald (*especially* not Melania who's as cold as Newfoundland with him — the contrast between Joe & Jill Biden after the debate on Tuesday night and Donald & Melania was stark, something which, in the course of the past couple of days, has received a lot of comic attention: Joe & Jill Biden clearly a genuinely loving couple and

Donald & Melania a rich Yank and his agency-lady from Slovakia or Slovenia or wherever she's from who's playing the role of First Lady of the United States for the cameras, and not a very convincing performance at that: being Mrs Trump III is clearly a business deal for Melania — you gotta put a silver dollar in the silver-dollar-slot to get a mannequin smile from her). So Donald and everyone else who'd been in contact with Hope Hicks had to self-isolate, which, presumably, was everyone in the POTUS apartment on the Airforce One flight back from Cleveland, all the principals anyhow, which would include Trump's repulsive offspring, Don Jr, Eric, Ivanka &c. (At the debate there were several cut-to shots of the families in the audience on Tuesday night and another striking contrast was the fact that all the Biden people were masked-up as per agreement and the Trump contingent not, defiantly not — apparently the people at the Cleveland Clinic asked them to mask-up as per the event agreements but on the night the Trump party refused to do so.)

So, in self-isolation yesterday evening, Trump calls in to Sean Hannity's show on Fox [Hannity is one of Trump's most fervent supporters on television] and in that call Trump tells the Hope Hicks story and says that he himself and his wife have been tested as a result of Hope's positive and at that time they were awaiting the test-results.

Then, later on, at 1 o'clock in the morning (East Coast Time), Trump tweets out that both he and Melania had tested positive and were now quarantining in the White House and that they would get through this 'TOGETHER!' (Trump's caps and exclamation mark.)

But, presumably, even if there are no more positives among the senior people at the White House, all of them would need to follow best practice protocols and self-isolate anyway until they'd had 2 or 3 lab negs over the course of 8 or 10 days.

All the president's campaign events have been cancelled and presumably most of his presidential events too, except for what can be done by telephone from the Residence. Certainly everything for the weekend must be binned and, probably, everything for next week too.

The other main result of this development is that this irreversibly secures the fact that the coronavirus crisis is and will be the central issue in the election. It is and would have been anyway but as I say the Trump campaign has been attempting to move the focus off the topic of the pandemic, which, obviously, with over 200,000 deaths and over 7 million infections — and all the numbers going in the wrong direction suggesting that we're still in the early stages of this pandemic — doesn't play well for them, attempting to move the focus onto law and order, the recovering economy, their mad-Catholic Supreme Court pick, that bullshit peace deal in the Middle East they concocted last week or the week before or whenever it was (UAE and Bahrain recognising the state of Israel and the three states congregating together in their shared determination to bear-hug one another for the cameras and destroy the theocracy in Iran, all bullshit for the election, of course, as I say an attempt to change the topic of conversation which, as such, was a flop; they didn't even achieve a change of topic for one news cycle because, of course, with over 200,000 American corpses on American soil in an election year it's *impossible* to get away from the unmoveable and insurmountable central issue).

And if the central issues of the election are Donald Trump's persona — a referendum on Donald Trump — and the coronavirus crisis then there's only going to be one outcome, I believe, which is a clear victory for Joe Biden and the Democrats. Including taking back the Senate and, probably, increasing their majority in the House of Representatives.

However, a lot can happen between now and November. Trump is 74 years old and he's overweight — clinically obese. This infection could be serious for him — it was serious for Boris Johnson who is 20 years younger and quite a bit fitter. It'd be a loss to see Trump die or be sedated and put on a ventilator before he's rejected at the polls, humiliatingly rejected, hopefully.

Saturday, 3 October

Trump airlifted to hospital yesterday evening (yesterday evening our time; afternoon in Washington) out of 'an abundance of caution' and for some tests, they say, but this is when credibility counts: no one trusts the press briefings coming out of this administration. They torched the last of the little benefit of the doubt they had long ago. Yesterday morning they told us the president was fine and working normally, albeit directing operations from the Residence, next thing Marine One is coming down onto the South Lawn and there is so much chaos in the West Wing someone unintentionally lets it slip that the president is about to be helicoptered to the Walter Reed Medical Centre.

The president walked to the helicopter — wearing a mask and giving the far-away corralled press pool a thumbs-up sign — but even when one has full flu one can, if one really must, get up and walk out and attend to something.

Before going to Walter Reed the president put out a video-message on Twitter in which, all suited-up and coiffed, he said 'Hi y'all, I'm fine; I'm just going into the hospital for some tests. Melania is fine too. Thanks for all your love and support, much appreciated.' (Not an exact quote but this was the gist of it.)

But despite his best attempt at smiling and trying to sound upbeat he looked really sick and old. He looked like a man who had a bad dose of flu. He looked like Boris Johnson did when BJ was putting out those videos from Downing Street before being taken into hospital.

'Is the fat fuck taking hydroxychloroquine now?' someone ought to ask. Earlier in the year Trump said he was taking hydroxychloroquine, saying that doing so protected him from getting infected. Looks like it doesn't really protect you, does it?

Have they attempted shining UV light inside him? (up his bloated ass, I suggest), see if it works, as the president himself suggested in one of his coronavirus briefings earlier this year. Someone ought to look into that, he suggested to the squirming-with-embarrassment medics and scientists with him in the press briefing room that day. Afterwards — when his suggested lines of medical and scientific inquiry met with gales of derision and scorn — he claimed to have been only joking at the time. "I was being sarcastic", he said in the debate on Tuesday night when Joe Biden attempted to make a hit on him on account of it. Get that, joking in a coronavirus briefing in the middle of a global pandemic. Wow, good comms. Whichever way you play it it doesn't speak well of the guy: either you're an absurd moron and you seriously think that we ought to investigate 'disinfecting' the lungs of people with Covid-19, or you're playacting in the middle of a serious situation in which event you're not fit to lead the nation in a time of crisis.

Anyhow, my guess is he's quite sick. And it's serious, I think, that he got so sick so quickly. However, that said, given that he's the president they're not going to take any chances and, sensibly, they'd rather have the embarrassment of having him walk to a helicopter to go to Walter Reed yesterday afternoon/evening than have to wheel him out on a gurney with an oxygen mask over his face tomorrow afternoon or sometime next week.

As I say we really don't know what's going on behind the scenes.

Right now, so far as we know, Donald and Melania have tested positive, so too has Hope Hicks (as I reported yesterday), but today we learned that Kellyanne Conway is also down with the bug, along with Ronna McDaniel (RNC chair), Bill Stepien, the campaign manager, but also Senators Mike Lee and Thom Tillis and so too is John Jenkins, president of Notre Dame.

It's believed several of these got infected at that White House event last weekend where Trump formally nominated Loony Coney Barrett — a law professor at Notre Dame — as a Supreme Court Associate Justice, an event at which there were hundreds of guests, not to mention staffers and associated, everyone defiantly maskless and ostentatiously air-kissing one another in open defiance of bullshit liberal concerns about this Fake News virus. (And, believe it or not, Trump did a campaign fundraiser in Bedminster, New Jersey, *after* Hope Hicks reported sick with suspected Covid symptoms, so sick she self-isolated, so that everyone at that fundraiser is now also at risk if not actually infected. In fact, I believe Trump went to that Bedminster fundraiser *after he learned that Hope Hicks had tested positive for the virus*, which is really reckless, even for this wretched administration.) So that, clearly, the infection has been circulating in the White House for a week at least; and not just the WH in general but specifically in that congested warren of offices that is the West Wing.

Sunday, 4 October

At the top of yesterday's entry I said that no one believes the briefings coming out of the Trump White House. Now there are all sorts of stories doing the rounds about what happened when and who knew what when, many of these fuelled by conflicting WH briefing statements.

Turns out Trump and his people were *not* Covid-tested before coming into the venue in Cleveland on Tuesday evening for the debate as per agreement — i.e., Cleveland Clinic/Commission for Presidential Debates tested — which the Biden people were. Team Trump turned up late, too late for testing, and as I reported yesterday, or was it the day before (I cannot remember now), the Trump people refused to wear masks at the venue, despite having agreed to do so. They blustered their way through saying they'd all been tested in the White House so they were all clear. However it turns out this was *not* true (imagine that, Trump and his people speaking untruths! difficult to believe, isn't it) — not all of them were tested that day, it now seems clear, and, as yet, journalists have not established who precisely was and was not tested that day; as things stand right now it may even prove to be that *none* of Team Trump were tested that day. Indeed, the White House is yet to confirm when exactly Trump had his last negative test before testing positive Wednesday.

And, worse still, there's speculation that Trump may already have been infectious at the time of the debate and, more than that, had reasonable grounds for suspecting he might be. Which, if so, is beyond reckless — ordinary recklessness, I mean — this would be over into the domain criminal recklessness in my view.

Look, we just don't know enough at this point, and like I say what's coming from the authorities in this administration is not helping matters (quite the contrary), but there is, it seems, enough evidence to say that the virus has been prolific in the White House for at least a week now. That event they had to formally announce the nomination of Amy Coney Barrett to the Supreme Court last weekend was a super-spreader event. And as one commentator has said, if the president and his people are putting on super-spreader events at the White House how can he possibly go before the citizenry and credibly claim that he's the guy to shepherd the country through this pandemic, which is not only a health crisis and an associated economic crisis, but with every day that passes a crisis of authority too.

Lots of attendees at that ACB event now testing positive, including two (Republican) members of the (22 member) Senate Judiciary Committee which is hoping to get those Coney Barrett hearings done this side of the election, also Chris Christie, former New Jersey governor, for instance, who was at the event and remained on at the White House afterwards prepping the president for the debate in Cleveland, who is now not only test-positive but in hospital (and with his level of obesity — which must be morbid obesity — I wouldn't fancy his chances of pulling through if things start to go south for him; as the Rick Wilson book title has it *Everything Trump Touches Dies*).

Monday, 5 October

More news clambering for inclusion than can possibly be coped with at the minute: if I recorded all of what's happening right now I'd spend all day every day here at this laptop diarizing.

This is the bit of this morning's news I'm going to focus on: yesterday evening Trump took a car journey up and down the street outside the Walter Reed hospital where he's being treated for Covid! Since Friday some few hundred of the Trump Nutter Army have gathered outside the hospital keeping 24-hour vigil for the Dear Leader. Trump decided to pleasure them by organising a drive-by for them — let my people see me/let them see the sun/a splash of bottle-bronzed sunshine in their drab little lives — so they shut down a 2-mile section of the 4-lane roadway (both directions) and organised a presidential cavalcade to cruise up and down the highway outside the hospital where his white trash supporters had gathered with their flags and 'We Love You' signs and shantytown facilities, Trump in the belly of a presidential SUV, masked, waving out at his fervent followers whom he terms 'patriots' (no, they're not 'patriots', you monstrous moron, they're just *Trump loyalists*; just because you wave an American flag doesn't make you 'a patriot', besides the pictures I saw showed a couple of Confederate flags fluttering out there too, which are not patriotic signifiers seeing as it's a traitor's flag).

But think about that: think about being sick with a deadly virus that has already resulted in the death of 210,000 Americans, or whatever the figure is presently, and what you're focused on is a Sunday evening photo-op. There were others in the vehicle with the president for that drive-by (which, as I say, coming in the midst of an election campaign, is unmistakably a campaign photo-op and nothing other, political theatre) — masked, admittedly, but masks only mitigate, they do not offer secure protection, nor anywhere near it — so, on the taxpayers' dime, you're putting others at very real risk for the sake of a campaign photo-op. And not just the people in the vehicle with him but everyone involved — presumably every door handle, every piece of glass, every brass rail, every elevator had to be deep-cleaned afterwards. Every corridor the president walked through was infected with the infection his ignorant and malignant fecklessness and recklessness and carelessness has resulted in.

All of this is bad enough but I suspect this may be the worst of it: I think Trump's need for public adulation is such that it is itself now a deadly disease. He literally couldn't go 24 hours without putting himself centre-stage again, regardless of the potential cost to himself and to others around him. He's the leading man — the ratings-getter, as he says himself — the star of the show, so he must be not only in every episode but in every storyline, and even in every scene. And seeing as he's not only the star of the show but also the executive producer, that's what'll happen. The malignancy of his narcissism is clearly untreatable and uncontainable — '...he cannot buckle his distempered cause within the belt of rule.'

Even if whatever it is is a critical disaster and it trashes whatever shreds of integrity the show is left with, it doesn't matter — I'm the leading man and I must be in every episode and every storyline must revolve around me. I haven't looked at any of the coverage of this stunt as yet this morning (I'm writing this directly after breakfast, having listened to the morning news on the radio) but I'm sure this drive-by will be regarded as a PR disaster (even from the pov of his own campaign); but that won't be a bother to him, all that matters is that he is the centre of attention. He must show himself to the people who love him and the people who love him must muster and show their love for him. It won't matter to him that the sub-text messaging of his drive-by photo-op is that one doesn't need to take this virus all that seriously — even when you're sick in hospital, as long as you have the very best of care as he is privileged to have (at the taxpayers' expense despite the fact that he doesn't pay his fair share of taxes), you can still do a little campaigning.

(Over the weekend they also put out still photos of Trump at work at a desk in the presidential suite in Walter Reed, reading briefing documents and putting his signature to stuff, the president's at work despite his sickness the pictures attempt to say. Really phoney looking photos in my view but that matters not, it's the messaging of them I'm concerned with for now.)

Trump is absolutely sick. And his sickness infects everyone around him. It is sickening to watch the White House physician, Dr Tony Conley, mislead and spin (and 24 hours later return to clean-up) like a campaign operative. First he twisted himself like Simone Biles to avoid saying the president had been oxygenated (in fact, we now know Trump had to be oxygenated on at least two occasions since last Thursday evening), because to say that — that the president needed supplemental oxygen — is to suggest that the Dear Leader was weakened. Conley now accepts that he misled the public with respect to whether or not the president needed oxygen but, he says, he didn't want to 'not be in tune with the upbeat tenor of the whole team'; but what team is it you're referring to here, Dr Conley, the campaign team? When did you commence serving as a campaign operative? Does the taxpayer pay your salary or the campaign to re-elect the president?

There's also issues to do with when precisely the president first tested positive: apparently he tested positive in one of the White House's rapid tests *before* the more comprehensive lab-based test, the result of which was communicated to the public on Thursday night, however the WH physician doesn't want to get into any of that, presumably because a genuine time-stamped account of events would not please his political overlords, and clearly at this stage Conley's commitment is to the politics of the situation rather than to the science or to any sense of legitimate public interest/service.

And there are questions to do with treatment: Trump was given an anti-viral cocktail soon after (officially) testing positive; apparently normally this would not be done until a later stage in the progress of things. Similarly he got sick and needed oxygen very quickly after officially testing positive, again normally there would be a time-lag between when one is tested and being so sick, all of which suggests that by the end of last week the president was at least a week into his illness, the treatments prescribed are consistent with this, so the question returns (as it always does with these things) who knew what and when did they know it?

In yesterday's medical briefing — whereat Conley is looking increasingly ragged because he has so many lies and misleading bits and pieces to keep in mind now, and of course he's now serving several masters, never a good look, and additionally he's facing an increasingly sceptical press corps — Conley suggested that the president might return to the White House as early as today. However at the same time we now also know that the president has been prescribed dexamethasone — a steroid usually prescribed for "severe and critical" Covid-19 cases (dexamethasone supresses the immune system, apparently, because what happens with Covid is that the immune system overreacts to the perceived viral attack and it's this overreaction more than the virus itself that does for many patients). But, like I say, the campaign comes first and foremost and Conley appears to be a servant of the campaign as much as he's a public servant, and if the campaign needs the commander-in-chief back in his command centre then that's what'll happen.

However, it must be acknowledged that the president — who put out a couple of videos over the weekend — does look well, certainly far better looking than he did in that video he recorded in the White House before getting onto Marine One to go over to Walter Reed at the end of last week. Still doesn't look 100% but certainly he doesn't look nearly so sick. And his normal self-confidence is clearly reasserting itself too. In one of the videos he put out yesterday he says he now understands Covid like he never did before; he's been schooled in Covid, he says, not book-learning schooled but true schooling, which is to say, lived experience ("I get it now" he says at one point in one of the videos), and, based on this learning he says he'll be teaching us all about Covid very soon.

However, surely this is an implicit acknowledgment that he hasn't fully understood what Covid is about until now, which means we're 9 or 10 months into a serious crisis — a crisis which has resulted in the deaths of hundreds of thousands of Americans, and an amount of economic disruption not seen since the last great war — and all the while the chief executive lacked a comprehensive understanding of what he was attempting to grapple with?

Frankly, it shows, Mr President.

This implicit acknowledgment is probably the one clear truth to emerge from this whole weekend of polluting Trumpian smog.

Tuesday, 6 October

Trump came out of hospital in a made-for-television special which ran on all networks at prime time yesterday evening. The messianic insanity the Trumpists are pedalling is that The Amazing Mr Trump, our national champion, has done battle with this plague and, hero-like, has triumphantly prevailed and is now returned to us (immune possibly). And, similarly, America will prevail.

The campaign made a little film about the triumphant return of the conquering hero, including film score musical bedding — soundtrack from The Avengers apparently — slo-mo, soft-focus and movie-like long shots of Marine One flying past historical monuments in Washington with the evening sun setting in the background and so on, which *il presidente* himself tweeted out later in the evening once they'd finished speed-editing it for publication. There's even cringe-worthy footage of them reshooting parts of the hero's re-entry into the White House and of Trump himself, show-runner-in-chief, issuing instructions to the camera-person crouched down behind a portico pillar on the Truman Balcony, sotto voce instructing her about the kinds of shots he wanted when he did his salute to the helicopter Marines before they took off again.

One last thing about this made-for-television Trump campaign event: Trump on the Truman Balcony — clearly out of breath having walked up the exterior staircase — attempting to puff out his chest before he does his salute to the helicopter Marine party that brought him back to the White House from the Walter Reed Medical Centre is, I feel sure, going to be an image on book covers and such like, it'll be one of the defining photos of the whole Trump presidency. He cannot see it himself, nor can anyone around him evidently, but he looks like nothing so much as a strongman president in some shithole republic. 'Benito Trumpolini', as someone tweeted yesterday evening; instead of the like making him look strong and heroic the whole thing makes him look little and weak. That's not the kind of thing a strong man does, it's the kind of thing a weak man does when he's attempting to project strength. (What is it with wannabe strongmen and balconies?)

And, just to be clear, I feel sure many of the people that'll end up voting for him next month *can* see what we're seeing when we look at these images — how un-American it looks, unless you're talking about Latin or South America of course — how like a little strong-arm *il presidente* he looks with all that saluting helicopters and puffing out his chest and attempting to look like a victorious wartime leader, it's just they don't care. They hate the liberals and the east and west coast elites so much they'd rather live in Benito Trumpolini's America than they would in Hilary Clinton's or Barack Obama's or Joe Biden's or Kamala Harris'.

That said, equally I'm sure a lot of them *don't* see it, just as I'm sure a lot of them look at those photos of Trump and his catwalk wife in their gaudy apartment in Trump Tower and what they see is upper-class class; but, like I say, a lot of them do see that he's a tin-pot buffoon but, the point is, he's *their* tin-pot buffoon and he's put 3 hardcore right-wingers on the Supreme Court and he's pro-gun and pro-fossil fuels and he's hostile to Negros and Mexicans and to the Chinese, and towards the libtards in the mainstream media, and that's the kind of all-you-can-eat buffet they want to feast at from Monday to Sunday and all through next week as well.

Wednesday, 7 October

Several of the top brass in the defence forces (including Mark Milley, chairman of the Joint Chiefs) are self-isolating having been in close contact with someone Covid-positive. I'm not sure what the full count is but at least 18 or 20 people around the president have tested positive, the latest this morning being that wicked creep Stephen Miller. Kayleigh Mendacity, the president's press secretary, also testing positive.

And that's not counting all those self-isolating because they've been in close contact with someone who has tested positive.

In fact, we're not getting a true picture of how many Covid-positives there are or have been because the order has gone out not to reveal the fact that you've tested positive if you test positive. Nor has the WH done any contact tracing for all the people involved in that Amy Coney Barrett roll-out event, for the same reason — they don't want the bad press (fuck public health, or even national security, the campaign's PR interests are all that matters in this White House).

Twitter wags have dubbed it the Blight House.

One last thing (for now anyway): the following is one of the blizzard of tweets the president has put out since returning to the WH — not one of which has expressed sympathy for any of the people at the WH that have tested positive for this infection (some of whom are quite sick apparently, at least as sick as he has been, however they have not had anything like the level of medical support and supervision he has been privileged to enjoy at the taxpayers' expense), including workers, cooks, valets and cleaners and such, much less for the millions all across America that have been infected and/or bereaved — which read for an insight into where the fool's mind is at (speaking about himself and his campaign in the third person like he's the king of pre-revolutionary France) — this is a series tweets that follow his saying that he'll be back on the campaign trail soon; don't pay any attention to the Fake News polls saying he's behind in this election campaign, he says, his people are all revved up and ready to go...

"You see it in enthusiasm for the President outside Walter Reed Hospital. You see it in Registrations, from Florida to Pennsylvania & West Virginia,

where Republicans are outstripping Democrats by 2 to 1. If the President bounces back onto the campaign trail, he will be an....

"*....invincible hero, who not only survived every dirty trick the Democrats threw at him, but the Chinese virus as well. He will show America we no longer have to be afraid.*"

To my mind anyhow in these — and in everything else he's at at the minute — he comes over as deluded to the point of being quite nutty. And he was nuts to begin with! Now he's in quarantine in a blighted, deserted, cavernous (not to say cadaverous) WH tweeting about 'the President', an invincible hero who has single-handedly defeated the invisible enemy — the virus which laid siege to his vitals.

I cannot see this whole situation ending well. (Another one of his tweets is a retweet of a meme in which someone is shouting into Bill Barr's face, and in the speech-bubble we see the person is screeching "ARREST SOMEBODY!!!") I can see this going the mad [Targaryen] king Aerys II storyline route, or at least a Trumpian version of same, which is to say, a cack-handed debacle, the kind of thing you might expect from someone who went bankrupt running casinos in Atlantic City.

Saturday, 10 October

902 new cases of coronavirus recorded in Northern Ireland during the past 24 hours.

902 is 178 fewer than the record daily total recorded yesterday, but based on population size it is equivalent to more than 2,300 cases in one 24-hour window in the Republic.

There have been three Covid-related deaths reported in the Republic today, and 1,012 new cases of infection.

This brings the cumulative number of cases in the Republic to 41,714 while the cumulative death toll now stands at 1,824.

Latest figures show there are 194 patients being treated in hospitals. This represents the highest number since 2 June, when there were also

194 people in hospital. The number of patients being treated for Covid in intensive care units remains stable at 31.

Therefore — altogether — 60,807 confirmed cases of infection on the island of Ireland and, to date, 2,411 Covid-related deaths.

Tuesday, 13 October

One thing I want to mention is how lovely the weather is, and has been; and it's due to be all this week again. It's been fine and dry two weeks at least, maybe more. Obviously it's not fine as in take your jacket off or anything of the kind but it's fine and sunny today, for instance, and it was so yesterday too — c. 4 or 5 at night and 13 to 16 best daytime temps — and, in fairness, it's been at least partially sunny almost every day going back into September, and even when there's been a bit of rain — and we have had a few showery days — there's been good, sunny patches too. It's really lovely. The only thing is it's seriously autumnal, everywhere you go there are accumulations of dried leaves and everywhere dried leaves twisting and tumbling to the ground and hopeful seeds helicoptering thither and yon, so much so one can hardly see the green grass of the lawns for fallen leaves. And now, although it's not wholly dark until about 7pm one tends to draw the curtains to at around 6, 6:30 at the latest. I was up at about 6:30 this morning and it was quite dark. It begins to brighten from about 7 AM but you wouldn't open the curtains at 7 AM , you'd leave it to 7:30 at least and maybe until 7:45.

Of course the clocks go back an hour a couple of weeks from now so while that'll mean it'll be bright at 7am, on the other side of the day we'll be drawing the curtains to at about 5pm, which is awfully early. It's that as much as anything that really makes winter so dark — the loss of all evenings and a good measure of the afternoons also.

Still, grateful for this late brightness. Early summer and late spring fabulous this year and now autumn too: it's been a really lovely autumn season this year, here in Cork and Kerry anyhow. Some serious rainfall in parts of the UK and in Europe in recent weeks, which even impacted the east and northeast of Ireland, so it's not something we take for granted.

Mood darkening noticeably everywhere with the realisation that this pandemic is going to be more than we'll be able to cope with in all likelihood. Czechia (the Czech Republic) about to go into another full lockdown, and I believe we'll see a few other countries follow suit because the thing is much worse than we feared much earlier.

People were pretty relaxed about things up until Donald Trump got infected and hospitalized. That had an impact not just in the US but across the globe, certainly all across the western world. Not that we care a fig for him personally, of course, but, as with Boris Johnson getting hospitalized with it earlier in the year, it focused minds.

And of course Trump getting infected coincided with some shocking jump-ups in infection rates, from well under 10,000 a day in the UK to over 10,000 a day — the UK never had more than 10,000 new cases in a day during the first wave. And here in Ireland we're suddenly getting a thousand a day in Northern Ireland — NI never had anything like 1,000 a day in the first wave — and now we're getting nearly the same down here.

France had over 26,000 new cases reported one day last week!

And as I say we're still in *October*! The most challenging months are still ahead of us. Even without being any kind of infectious disease expert one can see how things could get very bad very quickly even this side of Christmas.

And January is always unbearably bleak anyway. February will be bad too, depending on the weather conditions, but at least once in February one is clearly beginning to move towards increasing light and warmth again, which will offer hope of brighter days at least.

Friday, 16 October

1,205 new cases reported in the Republic yesterday, and 1,095 the day before, and with similar numbers coming out of Northern Ireland — i.e., circa 1,000 new cases a day (where there's half the population compared with the Republic so, therefore, the spread of the epidemic is twice as bad up there) — things beginning to look seriously ropey. Nearly 20,000 new cases on the island in the first 14 days of this month!

A few weeks ago — back in September — it was said that if we continued on as we were going at that time epidemiological models suggested we'd have c. 1,200 to 1,400 cases a day by early November. This morning on the radio one of the people interviewed said that on our present trajectory models suggest that we're headed for 1,800 to 2,500 by the end of this present month, and that by the end of the first week in November we'd be closer to the upper end of that range!

Goodness, if we're up at around 2,500 cases a day in the first week of November what the fuck is it going to be like by mid-December, or mid-January?

If it's anything like that no way systems will be able to cope. If 5% of people require hospitalization that's 100-150 people a day at some point in November, and 25-50 of these requiring critical care and/or ICU facilities. Each day! And then another 30 or 40 the day following. And more the day after that again. And so on.

Of course, they won't allow this to happen, because they simply cannot afford to have it happen, so they'll do everything possible to prevent 200 people a day turning up at hospital doors, and they'll do as much as they can to cut that 25-50 a day number too — reserving critical care and ICU facilities only for those most likely to benefit from such facilities, for example, which is to say, identifying those most likely to die anyway and simply warehousing them some place and letting them die (albeit with some rudimentary palliative care) — however, even if they cut these numbers in half by these and other means the systems (North and South) will still be overwhelmed.

And that's only November!

When one digs into the numbers as I heard this bloke doing on the radio this morning the whole situation is truly alarming. This is as alarming now as we feared it might be in springtime. However, because springtime did not turn out as dreadful as we feared it might do — in part because we took it so seriously — now people are clearly not taking it so seriously.

Things at least as bad as in April but we — the public at large — are not taking it nearly so seriously in my estimation. Yes, everyone is wearing facemasks and there are signs about washing your hands and physical distancing and being vigilant everywhere one goes, and Perspex screens around every cashier and so on, however it feels a little like this is just guff one has to be seen to do so as not to be called out for not adhering to the regulations.

At least here in Skibbereen only about half as many people wore masks in March and April but there was a tremendous sense of social solidarity back then, I felt, now everyone is masked but there's much less of the we're-all-in-this-together spirit, much less of a sense of emergency.

The country's been moved up to Level 3 restrictions but I don't think I've noticed anything different in people's behaviour or in the amount of vehicles parked in the Fairfield, for instance, nor in the mood in the town.

I feel perfectly sure that if you interviewed 10 people at random about what it means to be on Level 3 as opposed to Level 2 it would be an embarrassing mess of ignorance (and, to be honest, the results wouldn't be altered much if I was one of the 10 interviewed, for I am, I admit, a bit hazy on the details — all I know for sure is that church services have been suspended on Level 3, and cafés and restaurants can do outdoor service and take-aways but that's all, all indoor gatherings are suspended aside from schools and workplaces where workers cannot work from home, and one oughtn't to visit other people's houses, and if you do don't go indoors).

In fact, I think it's been a bit of a failure having 5 levels because Level 1 means fuck all to people and Level 2 doesn't mean too much more. And as I say most people (including myself) are a bit hazy about the differences between Levels 2 and 3, with the upshot that none of it has been taken seriously so far, which is why little of it is working in the way hoped for.

Too many bits and pieces; the first two levels are pretty much a waste of time, as it seems to me, just fucking noise. I think the Brits may have it right — in terms of comms strategy anyhow — in having just 3 tiers. That said, things not working out too well in the UK either, but a large part of the reason things not working in the UK has to do with the divisiveness of the government that brought us the profound divisiveness of Brexit which is now calling for national unity to fight this virus (the response from a huge proportion of the country is 'Fuck you, you lying, bloviating, Tory ass-rag').

And because of the piecemeal nature of the 5 Levels I'm not convinced that if they moved this county to Level 4, for instance, that it would make too much difference either.

Apparently NPHET has again called on the government to consider doing a circuit-breaker shutdown before it's too late (only this time they've done so in a sealed letter and they've made no press announcement about the contents of their communication, nevertheless — assuming it's true — the story's leaked), and I think there's some chance the government will do something noticeable in response to NPHET's recommendation this time because this Level 2, Level 3 and Level 4 shite isn't working, and, as I say, if things go on as they're going right now we'll be into unmanageability very soon anyway, at which time things will shut down by default, because everything will grind to a halt if we have hundreds and thousands ill and dying, however there'll be no benefit to it because by then the virus' spread will be completely out of control.

Northern Ireland is essentially doing a circuit-breaker shutdown from now until the end of the month — moving to the equivalent of our Level 3 or maybe 4 but, in addition, shutting down schools and colleges for two weeks — and, partly because, as I say, it's needed and partly because as NPHET says we're in The Last Chance Saloon right now, and partly because the Dublin government is into all-Ireland initiatives, and partly because if they don't show themselves to be doing everything in their power to prevent this predicted public health pile-up they'll get the blame for it when and if it happens (and ignoring the repeated recommendation of your public health emergency team is a stick they'll be beaten with), I wouldn't be surprised if there was a surprise announcement this weekend and just about everything that can be shut down is shut down for two weeks at least (reports say NPHET wants the whole country to be moved to Level 5 for 6 weeks — and remember Level 5 is not a full shutdown, it's the last step before a total shutdown).

Then on the other side of that Level 4 and Level 5 restrictions might have some meaning for people.

Society needs a jolt of something to wake up, I feel.

At the minute there are only 3 or 4 people a day dying. If that was 30 or 40 a day it would be a different story. It will be 30 or 40 a day a few weeks from now, of course, but, like I say, by then it'll be too late to be awakened.

Also, as is intended, I believe, Trump's bounce-back contributes something to people not taking it as seriously as they did earlier in the year when Boris Johnson was hospitalized, for example. Few people are going to get the level of treatment Trump got at Walter Reed but at some level people don't really factor this in, even when they are conscious of it and even say it in conversation. And in fairness it *is* true to say that even for people way down the socioeconomic pyramid treatments are much better than they were 5 or 6 months ago and, as a consequence, fewer people are dying compared with what we saw in spring and early summer. This is because of better treatments, as I say, and a greater level of preparedness in systems, but it's also because more young people getting infected now compared to earlier in the year (about 70% of cases of infections nowadays are people under 35) and such people suffer from it less, generally speaking — many of them being asymptomatic or very nearly asymptomatic — and also, frankly, I suppose quite a lot of the lowest hanging fruit have already been harvested.

But, presumably, the death-line just moves a level higher and this second wave will take out plenty more low-hangers — after all care homes are still full of residents, presumably, and while they may have enhanced safeguarding procedures this time round as compared with the first half of the year, nevertheless, it takes just one person to slip up — one cleaner, one cook, one delivery driver, one visiting maintenance person, one nursing assistant, one nurse, one visitor… — and if the virus gets into a facility it will still find many frail and vulnerable people.

Sunday, 18 October

Cabinet meets on Monday to formally decide on what it will do in response to NPHET's repeated calls for a Level 5 circuit-breaking shutdown. In my view it can hardly ignore them, yet clearly the government is reluctant to shut things down again, presumably fearing it may never get things going again because no matter what things are only going to disimprove for some time to come. If one had to shut things down for 4 or 5 weeks in the very dead of winter it wouldn't be too bad — start opening up again in February as we move towards the renewal of spring-like conditions — but if we do so now things might well be shut for 3 or 4 months, which would be catastrophic for the economy and for state finances because between one thing and another the like could cost the country €100 billion, which, what with darkening Brexit clouds massing, might be more than we can manage because, at the end of the day it's not the government who will decide what we can manage it'll be the people in the capital markets who are loaning us these billions, and in doing so writing the T&Cs for the loans.

Micheál Martin was at the EU summit at the back end of last week where, aside from the coronavirus issue, Brexit was the main topic, and now back in Dublin the leaders of the coalition parties along with the finance ministers (Donoghue and McGrath) are in crisis talks about what to agree to do before Cabinet on Monday, which suggests to me they're more likely to do something, something substantial I mean.

These meetings — and reportedly there were crisis meeting going on for most of yesterday (the heads of the coalition parties, the heads of the parties along with the finance ministers, the heads of the coalition parties along with finance ministers and health minister meeting people from NPHET, Cabinet subcommittee meetings and so on) and more scheduled for today; everything will be decided at these meetings, which is to say, nothing will be decided at Cabinet on Monday, the leading members of the Cabinet will bring a plan of action to Cabinet and Cabinet will approve it — are on a par with the crisis meetings that took place at the time of the financial meltdown a decade ago, same sort of vibe about them, as it seems to me: clusters of reporters on the wintry sidewalks outside government buildings, Cabinet ministers and top officials coming and going in utmost seriousness, reporters and camera crews keeping watch not only on front doors but also side doors and back doors. Something of importance afoot, the sausage of history being made.

Interesting to note that everyone I've spoken to (I've actually only spoken to two people this weekend so it's not much of a vox populi — Tim Macey and Darragh, the guy manning the NeighbourFood stall) think the government will move to Level 5 lockdown, and, more importantly, that they ought to do so. (And, of course, as these diary entries make clear, I'm of this opinion too, so that makes 3 out of 3.) The feeling is that people are simply not taking this thing seriously enough, things are deteriorating rapidly and, perhaps in collective anticipation of another shutdown, everyone is as busy as ever they've been this year, attempting to get whatever few things they want to get done finished before the shutdown to come. Well, the result of such selfishness is that the shutdown (which might or might not have happened) is made virtually inevitable, it's just a matter of when.

It's not certain the government will shut things down, of course — immediately, I mean — they're clearly reluctant to do so, because, for example, Level 5 still keeps schools open, however teachers' unions saying that if the situation does require a Level 5 shutdown they don't think their members ought to be made to work in conditions that require almost everything else to be shut down. And, of course, if school teachers are reluctant to work then the schools will need to close and if the schools close then many folks will need to stay home to do child-minding which will mean many in essential services not being able to work.

Also a full shutdown will mean putting 70% of the workforce on government-subsidised paycheques which, with the way things are going, the public finances can ill-afford. The government presented its budget only 4 days ago, going into a Level 5 shutdown would make nonsense of that whole presentation before it's even a week old, which would be damaging to the administration's credibility because it would begin to appear like it was being buffeted by events, blown hither and yon by events over which it has little or no control. In truth governments of small states such as the Republic of Ireland have little or no control of events when winds blow and seas rise like this, but it's about the *appearance* of being in control — to some extent anyhow — or, on the other hand, appearing to have totally lost control such that the wheelhouse appears abandoned and the captain is cowering and whimpering in his cabin, or drunk like Brian Cowen 10 years ago, or on deck but clearly mad and talking to god/gods or other unseen entities.

In fairness, these are a fairly competent group of officers in my view — Martin, Varadkar, Ryan, Donoghue, McGrath, Coveney and Donnelly — there's no fear of them appearing to be lost at sea, not at this stage anyhow; these are the times one goes into politics to be there for, my guess is that they'll do OK, steering this little vessel through this long wild night just fine.

Also we're not altogether alone, are we, we're one of a squadron of 27 vessels, and Europe has sailed through nights much worse than this is likely to be. Everyone simply needs to keep their nerve, stay at their posts, and stay in contact with the flotilla. And, in fairness, our vessel's not in too bad a shape at all. I have confidence in it and, as I say, in the officers crewing it.

Tuesday, 20 October

Micheál Martin has announced that the country will move to Level 5 restrictions for six weeks from Wednesday night (midnight).

Strong of them to take hold of the situation in this way. We are the first state in Europe to go full-bore and for this reason it's gotten quite a bit of coverage internationally. I doubt we'll be the only state to do so because the situation is very close to being out of control altogether in some places. Better to go to it before you completely surrender hope of any kind of control of the situation because then a full scale lockdown wouldn't even work as intended anyway.

Also, once one state jumps to it others will be more likely to follow. Even if they don't what we've decided to do is the right thing to do. Even if we don't manage to get the numbers down to the levels they're hoping to get them down to — R at 0.5 and 50 to 100 new cases a day — (even if we only achieve 0.5 and 100 to 200 cases a day in early December, say), it will still be worthwhile.

Also it's simply reassuring to be seen to take strong action. Action kills fear. And, as I've written before, people simply weren't taking the restrictions seriously; yes, everyone is observing all the outward forms of compliance, for the most part, but the mood of the country isn't serious enough to meet the moment. In this type of scenario one needs to comply not just with the letter of the law but with the spirit of it too.

This lockdown is the short sharp wake-up that's needed. This is serious, we simply wouldn't be able to cope if the virus was allowed to let rip.

Even though the Level 5 restrictions do not come into force until tomorrow midnight, already there is a noticeable change of mood it seems to me. The Fairfield is emptier this morning, about two thirds full — whereas this day last week it would have been 80% filled — and I expect it to be somewhere between half and two thirds empty before the end of the week.

Also, in fairness, there's a storm blowing today (all last night and all of today too), so maybe that has something to do with folks staying home today.

The really lovely mild and goldeny October spell we've been blessed with has been put to flight with this week's weather conditions which are clearly of a more wintery character. Quite a lot of leaves still on all the trees and shrubs up until this week (even though everywhere you go — especially here in the church grounds — there are banks of fallen leaves, 6 and 8 inch drifts of them, sandbars of them), this year's been particularly good for autumn colours.

Now — today — with this storm suddenly everything looks stripped naked, old and scrawny, shivering and ashamed of their nakedness.

Thursday, 22 October

Today's the first day of our second coronavirus lockdown, and, if the number of vehicles in the Fairfield is any measure, you'd have to say it's a success: at 9:15 this morning the Fairfield looked like a Sunday morning in off-season, about a 3rd full, if that.

Uncle Kevin terminally ill, it seems. A stroke, apparently, but now there are follow-on issues, kidney failure in particular. He's been in the Bons in Cork but now he's been flown to one of the Dublin hospitals. Not much hope according to Liam.

Kevin and Angela in Castledonovan are the last of that [Queensfort] family — Angela, mum, Kevin and Alfie were the 4 youngest and now Alfie and mum gone leaving just Kevin and Angela.

And with Lily all the Ahilnanes gone, of course.

Speaking of Liam, he was in town yesterday. I saw him on Main Street at about 10 or 10:30 AM; I was coming back from Kalbo's with a bunch of food supplies. He'd dropped a couple of memorial cards up to my house (putting them through the letter slot) — memorial stuff to do with Lily and Mary and John Long — in addition to which I think he said he had some sort of appointment up at the hospital.

Liam looks like a right wild man of the mountains at the minute. I've been moaning about going grey myself recently but Liam's gone much greyer. His hair is shoulder-length and he must have washed it earlier that morning because it was all puffed up like some Old English Sheepdog shampooed and blow-dried by overly enthusiastic children. You'd no longer say he was blonde, you'd now say he was grey-haired, and as I say it was all puffed up and there's lots of it and the morning sunlight caught it as I was speaking to him and set it all alight such that it was a remarkable looking sight. And of course he's bearded (a totally unkempt beard that's spread like wild fire to his ears and cheekbones and eyebrows such that it appeared to cover about three quarters of his face area, if not more), although the beard didn't seem to me to be as greyed as the head hair. Anyway it was a lot of hair to be looking at — collectively it would have filled a plastic shopping bag or a small bucket, it seemed like.

Aside from what he had to say about Kevin, and little bits & pieces about the settlement of Lily's affairs, he told me that he's just emerging out of quite a severe bout of depression, a couple of months of it at its most intense, he said, however he said he now sees that he was sliding into it for a fair few months as well. During its most intense period all he could do was do the few jobs he had to do (look after the few animals he has, do the school bus run he does, and do whatever few milkings he does) but then all he wanted to do after that was sleep but when he went to bed he couldn't get off to sleep, or at least no kind of restful sleep.

Once he got a bit of energy back again the first thing he did, he said, was 'gather up every bit of rope in the place and make a fire of em', i.e., he was seriously suicidal and frightened of the extent to which he was.

It was bad enough to cause him to seek help. He had some sort of assessment at Bantry Hospital. Which makes me wonder whether his appointment at the hospital in Skibbereen yesterday morning was with Harbour Counselling people?

I didn't quiz him about it because I got the impression that he'd shared as much as he was willing to share with me. And I'm glad he told me as much as he did.

He didn't seem too bad to me, a little slow-witted to be sure, perhaps, and once you knew what the matter was you could see evidence of it in several ways, but — I'm suggesting — if one can talk about the like, put a name to it, and if one is on the pathway where help is sought and is being got, then you're not too badly off.

I asked him what did he think was the turning point for coming out of the depths of it and he said talking to Mary [O'Brien] about how he was feeling one day — presumably from there it was she who organised whatever consultation(s) he had at Bantry Hospital.

At one point I mentioned that I go down a fair bit at the depths of each year most years and he said he gets a bit of that too but that this — what he's just been through — wasn't that; what he's just been through was the full I-see-a-darkness monty, not seasonally affected depression.

I believe him. Also he did have that aura of someone who's just come through a near-death experience: that thing where all of what's going on around you, and the kinds of things people concern themselves with — sport, politics, achievement-seeking — seem so distant, distant and trifling: I tried to josh to him about his beloved Liverpool but my provocations elicited no response at all.

Saturday, 24 October

U.S. coronavirus cases have hit a record daily high as states grapple with a renewed wave of infections. Citing data from local state health authorities, the Covid Tracking Project reported 83,010 new cases on Friday.

Meanwhile, here at home, the Department of Health has reported a further 859 cases of infection today, bringing the total number of confirmed cases to 56,108.

Four more deaths have occurred such that now there's been a total of 1,882 Covid-related deaths in the Republic of Ireland.

315 patients in hospitals, 37 of whom are in ICUs.

And in Northern Ireland, there have been six further Covid deaths in the last 24 hours along with 923 new cases of the virus.

Altogether, so far, there have been 33,209 confirmed cases in Northern Ireland.

The death toll recorded by the NI health department now stands at 645 (however according to NISRA, Northern Ireland's statistics agency, this is just the Department for Health's 28-day figure for deaths, the real number of Covid-related deaths in Northern Ireland closer to 1,000).

There are currently 309 patients with Covid-19 being treated in hospitals in the North, 34 in intensive care.

NOVEMBER 2020

Sunday, 1 November

Yesterday Boris Johnson announced a return to national lockdown (also yesterday the UK went past the 1 million mark in terms of lab-confirmed coronavirus infections) — something more restrictive than the UK's Tier 3 restrictions. He did so in what appeared to be a hastily arranged and rather poorly managed Downing Street presser because most if not all news outlets already had the back-to-lockdown story, and had it in convincing detail, so, presumably, Downing Street sought to stay up with the news if not ahead of it. And of course if there are one million lab-confirmed cases there's likely to be as many more asymptomatic or ever so slightly symptomatic cases out there, infected people who feel no need to get tested, or simply have not bothered to do so: the UK Office of National Statistics estimates over half a million people in the UK infected with the virus in the week ending 23 Oct, therefore, altogether, there could be 2 or 3 million that are or have been infected, detected and undetected (since the beginning of the pandemic).

So the UK becomes the 9th member of the One Million Club, joining the United States, India, Brazil, Russia, France, Spain, Argentina and Colombia.

By the bye, this weekend France reporting over 40,000 new cases of infection per 24 hour period, and Spain over 30,000, which I mention because that is the kind of territory the UK is headed for — presently the UK reporting about 25,000 new cases a day. Maybe with this lockdown they won't get up to those levels but I wouldn't be so sure, the whole thing has been so poorly managed; furthermore my impression is that this government is going off the rails particularly in relation to managing this pandemic. Johnson is going to go to the Commons tomorrow and present his plans to parliament — and parliament does not like it when it is presented with proposals news of which is 2-days-old already because parliament is sovereign in the British system (not prime ministers or monarchs or the people or anyone else) and it can get strikingly petulant when its sovereignty is disrespected; leaders of much greater substance have been brought low by a sullen and resentful parliament — even already there's quite a bit of rumbling and disgruntled grumbling on the Tory backbenches.

Johnson will not lose the vote in the Commons this week, of course, because, having called for this circuit-breaking lockdown, the Labour Party is bound to support it — even though they will say it ought to have happened weeks earlier, and if it doesn't work as envisioned that will be because it ought to have been done earlier &c &c — but it's a bad look for the government to be reliant on the opposition to get its business through the House. And the fact that the opposition will almost certainly vote with the government means even more MPs will feel free to register a protest, either by voting against what the government is proposing or by abstaining, therefore they will feel able to protest without fear of really putting the government in peril.

Wednesday, 4 November 2020

It's 4:30 AM as I write this: I went to bed at around 11pm last night — even though I was tempted to stay up and watch the coverage of the US elections but in the end I felt it would be better to get a few hours' sleep and get up and watch the coverage from around 5AM which would be midnight on the east coast of the US — however I had the BBC World Service on and I was getting updates every time I woke up which was every 30 or 40 minutes it felt like.

Eventually I had to get up because the news coming out of the US was so alarming. While we knew Trump would win a majority of the votes cast on Election Day itself, that would be counterbalanced by the early voting returns — record-breaking this year, something like 100 million votes cast before election day, which would be 2-to-1 for Biden — however, it looks like Trump has been more successful at getting souls to the polls than anyone appears to have credited. He campaigned like a man possessed in the last two weeks, it ought to be acknowledged, doing 4 and 5 rallies a day. He even did a rally in Florida the day before yesterday which *started* at midnight, having done 4 or 5 events already that day.

It looks like Biden is not going to win North Carolina or Florida or Texas. It's too early to call Georgia, Ohio or Pennsylvania. But what is really surprising is that it's closer than the polls were suggesting in Michigan and Wisconsin, however — right now at any rate — it seems like Biden will prevail in these states.

Arizona is looking good for Biden too, which if he holds onto what HC won in 2016 and he retakes Wisconsin and Michigan and he captures Arizona, then he'll be over the 270 mark.

But, right now, all the indicators are that it's not going to be a blowout win for Biden. Forget about anything like 320 or 330 in the EC, right now it looks like Biden will do well to get up above 300. Which is the worst result for America because this will mean some fierce fighting in days and weeks to come, fighting in the courts and maybe fighting in the streets: lots of retail outlets and other places in likely hotspots have ply-boarded their plate-glass windows already like as if the most godalmighty hurricane is about to blow through; as someone I saw interviewed yesterday said "This place doesn't look like America right now."

It seems incredible to be saying this but it seems the opinion polls have misled us again, and it looks like the media have got it wrong again, or at least the media I watch, which isn't all liberal/left-of-centre, by the bye — despite the fact that they were being super cautious, nevertheless their underlying bias in terms of expectation and disposition was clearly anti-Trump — and it looks like the Democratic Party got it wrong again, got it wrong in picking a 78-year-old for goodness sakes! Joe really has looked like a man who is nearly 80 years old in my view, despite the fact that he made it a campaign thing to jog onto almost every stage he appeared on during the campaign, and up every staircase — he did so so much it looked like a gimmick so the more he did it the more it pointed to his frailty and age in my opinion — and got it wrong in again going with someone as establishment as HC in 2016 — Joe has been living on the fat of the land in Washington DC since the late 1980s, in many ways he's even more establishment than HC for godsakes, and you'd think it'd be hard to do that but the Dems have managed it. And they've got it wrong in going with someone so determinedly conservative — Joe is an old school, church-going conservative, a throw-back to the America of 50 years ago.

Look, Joe is still going to win this thing, I believe, but it's a poor showing by the Dems, especially the establishment Dems.

On the returns we have so far it looks like Trump has increased his share of the vote with blacks (up from 8 or 9% to 10 or 11%) and with Latinos! Wtf!!

Biden might still win Ohio and Pennsylvania and maybe even Georgia, in which case, along with Arizona, Wisconsin and Michigan and all of what HC won in 2016, it will look like quite a convincing win when all the votes are counted, but right now it doesn't look or feel convincing at all.

OMG — it's just before 6 AM Irish time, so about 1 AM on the east coast of the US — Biden has just come out and effectively declared victory. I heard it as a reassuring speech — one which said keep calm and keep the faith — but TV talking heads seeing it as a victory declaration effectively. And his doing so has riled Trump, Trump immediately claiming 'They're trying to steal the election' and the White House announcing that the president will be making a statement imminently, in which, presumably, he will also claim to have won the election and that there's a lot of cheating going on by the Democrats who are trying to steal the election in the middle of the night. This is the nightmare scenario — a close election with both sides claiming victory.

I can see the logic of Biden doing this — smart to do so before Trump has got his trousers on (no doubt Trump is utterly exhausted from his admittedly impressive performance over the past couple of weeks, the last 5 or 6 days in particular) — but if it does comes down to one or two states then Biden seeking to claim victory so early is sure to cause significant backlash, almost guaranteeing that Trump will seek to characterize non-Trump votes in those last one or two states as somehow "illegal", or at least non-valid one way or another, which is to say, Biden has thrown the first punch in what is sure to be a street fight now if Biden doesn't win Georgia and Ohio, one of them at least.

What is emerging here is the nightmare scenario, punch and counter-punch leading to more and harder punches and maybe worse than that. If Biden wins by a couple of states or more it'll just be name-calling and (probably) a few wild unsupported allegations but if it all comes down to one state it'll be serious trouble, which is to say, fighting in the courts and on the airways and online and in the high streets and public squares maybe.

7 AM now and Trump is expected to make his statement any minute — all the TV networks fixed on the empty POTUS podium in the White House — which no doubt will be wild and ugly and norm-busting in all the ways we've come to expect from this wretched character, this stubby-fingered vulgarian, but for now note that the Trump campaign is hosting its watch-party at the White House — apparently there are about 300 people there (we don't know for sure because the press corps are excluded, the pictures we're seeing are pictures provided by the White House's media team) — and now he's going to make what will undoubtedly be a declaration of victory speech in the East Room, which is totally inappropriate — i.e., party business in government buildings, which are supposed to be for governing, not re-election campaign events. But, given that they staged some of the party convention events at the White House in August — including the nominee's acceptance speech — what can you expect?

It tells you something about the night to say that aside from the presidential race, the Senate races and House races not going well either. Dems expected to pick up at least 10 seats in the House but now they'll be lucky to pick up one or two. The Senate will be especially tight, with maybe the Republicans holding on to it.

The president has just come out and claimed victory, as expected. He also claimed that the Dems are attempting a massive campaign of fraud with all these postal ballots, again as expected. And finally, as expected, he said that as things stand he has won and vote-counting must now stop and he will go to the courts to put a stop to this attempted Dem coup.

As things stand he most certainly has *not* won, nor anywhere near it. However it does look like he has won Ohio so now it's all down to Pennsylvania and Georgia; assuming Biden takes Arizona, Wisconsin and Michigan, then Biden only needs one of Pennsylvania and Georgia. If he gets only one of these he'll be just over 270; with both of them he'd be up at around 290, but with the way this night has gone Biden would be extra lucky to get both.

Or, put another way, Trump needs to win Georgia, Arizona and one of Michigan, Wisconsin or Pennsylvania. He's not going to win Arizona so therefore he needs Georgia, Pennsylvania and one of Wisconsin and Michigan, a tall order.

Going to bed tonight it looks like it's all but settled in the US election aside from the legal challenges the Trump campaign will attempt to mount in the courts (seeking recounts in the states he's lost or losing in and seeking to stop the counting in the states where he's presently ahead! — the grotesque absurdity of these people appears to be inexhaustible), and indeed these bogus legalities may not even go ahead if Trump fails to hold Georgia, North Carolina and Pennsylvania.

In order to win at this stage Trump needs to hold all three of these — which will provide him with 268 ECVs — and then have the counts in Wisconsin or Michigan or Arizona or Nevada overturned by way of recounts or by some other means. And by no means is it certain he can land all three of these — Georgia, North Carolina and Pennsylvania — not to mind getting the courts to overturn the counts in Wisconsin and/or Michigan, or the counts stopped in any of the states where he's currently in the lead. All of what the Trump campaign people are saying is preposterous, the sooner we can stop talking about Trump and his absurdities (and his absurd representatives) the better it will be all round.

More than likely Biden will win Arizona, Nevada, Wisconsin and Michigan which will put him on 271. Indeed Michigan and Wisconsin are already called for Biden by most news outlets based on tallies.

So Biden doesn't need any of Georgia, North Carolina or Pennsylvania, nevertheless he is still in the running in all of them and he's very likely to win at least one of them (Pennsylvania) by all accounts which will put him on 290 at least which, while far from convincing, is clearly respectable — in 2016 the EC score was 306 for Trump to 232 for HC. And there's still some chance that Biden gets to 306 — if he wins Georgia, say — which will mirror the end result in 2016 which would have a pleasing symmetry.

Georgia is 94% counted right now; as things stand its Trump 50% and Biden 48.8%.

North Carolina is 95% counted right now; as things stand its Trump 50.1% and Biden 48.7%.

And Pennsylvania is 86% counted right now; as things stand it's Trump 51.5% and Biden 47.2%, however the remaining 14% to be counted is believed to favour Biden disproportionately, as indeed is the remaining in all 3 of these states because the remaining is either from big urban areas or mail-in ballots both of which trend Democratic.

Saturday, 7 November

US television networks have finally called it for Joe Biden — including Fox News — giving him Pennsylvania and Nevada: 279 ECVs.

Georgia and Arizona still counting. There's going to be a recount in Georgia, however as I write Biden ahead by c. 7,500 votes with 98% of the valid ballots counted, and experts in such matters say recounts are unlikely to shift so many votes, unless there's been massive and systematic fraud which, in GOP-controlled Georgia, is unlikely — indeed any fraud or gerrymandering in Georgia more likely to come from the Republican side, witness the purging of the voter rolls in the 2018 election cycle for instance. Biden ahead by over 20,000 votes in Arizona, however apparently Trump is chipping away at this, but at a rate that, with 97% of the votes counted, is not going to be enough to take the state from Biden. Most now predict that Biden will end up with 306 ECVs.

Ironically enough 306 ECVs is what Trump achieved in 2016.

No concession from the orange-faced buffoon, needless to say.

In other news out of America, apparently 127,000 new coronavirus cases in the US yesterday, another record-breaking day. And another thousand corpses: 1,149 deaths reported. At the rate things are going there could be 200,000 new cases a day by Thanksgiving.

Monday, 9 November

Lead story today is that Pfizer and German partner BioNTech are the first drug-makers to show successful data from a large-scale clinical trials of a vaccine. They say the experimental vaccine was more than 90% effective at preventing Covid-19 (93% apparently).

We shall see. Even if everything claimed for it proves out it's going to be a long time before it's on the high street in Skibbereen.

One has to have two injections, apparently, about a month apart and one is not fully immunized until about a week after the second of these.

No word about how long that immunity lasts, at least nothing I've seen so far.

Pfizer plan to apply for emergency use authorization once they've processed all data from the trials. Trials took place in the US, Germany, Turkey, Brazil, Argentina and South Africa, 43,500 people in all. If approved they say they could have 50 million doses ready to go before the end of the year and 1.5 billion by the end of next year.

Presumably it will be given to health workers and other essential personnel first and then maybe to people in the most vulnerable groups.

A lot of excitement. Stock markets up about 8 or 10 points today on the news. Stock in airlines and the like especially whose share values were down to pennies. Leisure industry stocks spiking too.

Bet you Trump is fuming: "Why in fuck couldn't they have made this announcement 10 days ago?" he'll be asking, suspecting — correctly in all likelihood — that it's just because they don't like him and didn't want to do anything to help him get re-elected.

Tough row to hoe being an unlovable race-baiting, pussy-grabbing, obnoxious ignorant asshole. Donny No Mates.

Wednesday, 11 November

The Republic of Ireland is now a net-contributor to the EU budget. This is primarily because of the number of Big Tech and Pharma corporations headquartered here for tax purposes. The presence of the like boosts turn-over figures for Ireland's economy by a significant percentage — not sure what that percentage is but I'm fairly sure it's more than 20%.

I learned of this in the course of a radio discussion about the probable impact of Brexit. It is expected that Ireland's net-contribution to the EU budget will increase now that the UK is out. Everyone will need to stump up more to fill the hole where the UK's contribution used to be. The Withdrawal Agreement secured the fact that the UK would honour its commitments to the existing EU budget which is due to run to 2021 so the extra will be in the next budget round onward, which is almost upon us; indeed, it's being negotiated and put together right now which is why this story on the radio at the minute.

UK news disgustingly smarmy this morning with the story that Boris Johnson and Joe Biden had a friendly 25-minute phone conversation yes-terday — a BJ-JB exchange of pleasantries — the Brits actually preening themselves on the strength of it, purring nauseatingly. They really are such small and sickening people. The phone call — which is just a routine courtesy call because clearly Biden spent a good part of yesterday return-ing world leaders' congrats calls, one of whom was to Boris Johnson — he also called the Taoiseach yesterday afternoon, for instance — is actually *front page news* in several of this morning's newspapers (Times, Express & Telegraph) and it's one of the lead items in the radio news broadcasts on the BBC, and presumably on the television news broadcasts too. 'Johnson speaks to Biden before EU leaders' the headline in the Telegraph. The pettiness — and smarmy self-satisfaction — of it is repulsive. 'Phone call boosts trade deal hopes' says the Express front page, so deluded too because anyone with any wit knows that that phone call makes no odds with respect to a US-UK trade deal one way or the other — my guess is there will be no US-UK trade deal worth a spit while Biden's in office — however at the UK's grovelling insistence they might do some kind of ha'penny deal to do with scrap metal and shoelaces but that'll be about the size of it, something for a few headlines to placate Johnson who needs to show something, even if he has to repackage existing trading arrangements into a boosterish 'Great New Deal for Britain'.

I'm struck by the photo that's been put out to accompany this Biden-Boris phone call story too, Johnson's piggy face with a big porcine grin on it, landline phone to his ear and snout, apparently on the phone with the president-elect, Union Jack identifiable in shallow-depth-of-field background, as though the fucking story would not have made sense unless accompanied by a photo of porky Boris on the blower. Moreover, my guess is that the photographer was not in the room when that Boris-Biden phone call happened, which is to say it's just a generic Boris-on-the-blower photo, or maybe it was a photo shoot organised afterwards for the purpose of putting this story out for mass consumption this morning. As indicated the key element of the story as far as mass consumption is concerned is the bit about Britain being First among *Un*equals.

Theresa May made a total fool of herself 4 years ago attempting to do this same story (which is tiresomely predictable because the Brits do it with every president), indeed she actually got on an aeroplane and flew over there in early February so as to be the first world leader to visit the then new president.

Clearly seeing her as appetizing as a forgotten auld buttered scone with dog hair on it, Trump didn't fancy her — she didn't make his manly juices flow and she didn't enhance his standing — clearly disrespecting her. In addition to which he disrespected her because she so totally threw herself at him, and she (poor thing) being so inexperienced at showing a flash of thigh in so flagrant a fashion: one thing Trump does know fairly well is the dynamics of interpersonal power — who has leverage — and with the way May behaved he could see he had all the power and she had none, so he had nothing but poorly disguised contempt for her.

And that initial event having gone so poorly they thought they'd try again, only this time they'd have Trump to England on a state visit, a summertime in England effort — get out all the state silver and hang up some bunting and impressive looking flags and get the household cavalry to shine their breastplates and polish their high-top boots and prance around the courtyard and so on, all that circus-act showboating they do which looks more and more preposterous and pathetic with each after-the-Empire's-over generation. Things went better in terms of optics in England — the whole thing an elaborate ad for Britain and old timey British heritage — but still May got no trade deal, indeed Trump snubbed and insulted her several times more, clearly preferring that the much-more-fun-seeming blonde Boris was prime minister, no rapport whatever with the humiliated, flat-footed May. (Poor old Theresa couldn't even give it away. Watching it, I was embarrassed for her, and she means nothing to me.)

No doubt at all that Johnson is better at this kind of stuff — Johnson is a good man to read a room too (as all confidence-tricksters need to be) — but that doesn't change the fact that the UK's got little to offer in the modern world, not much other than castles and flags and bunting and polished breastplates and the like. Of course they vow to always slavishly follow the US in all it does in the name of the "special relationship", even to the point of self-destruction as Tony Blair did. As I say, they're smarmy, needy, snivelling, nauseous little parasites, shamelessly attempting to ingratiate themselves with the more powerful and manly strongmen of the world.

Vladimir Putin is executing his enemies on the streets of cities in England — and in the course of so doing leaving traces of radioactive substances and military grade nerve agents in hotels and trains and airports and nightclubs and football stadia and so on — and narly a peep out of anyone in Whitehall about it.

The UK does have the capital markets of the City of London of course, however that's not something Westminster has much power over; if anything the political elites work to serve the City barons, and in return the City of London doesn't care all that much for Westminster; they coexist is what it is, Westminster and the City, the latter being the preeminent of the twin cities.

As I'm sure I've written before, if you had a character on stage or in a film behaving as the UK does with respect to the rich and powerful, while — when it can — bullying those they feel they can bully and abusing those they think they can abuse, that character would be both comic and horrifying. Rupert Rigsby in *Rising Damp*, Basil Fawlty in *Fawlty Towers*, David Brent in *The Office* and Steve Coogan's Alan Partridge are all excellent representations of the essence of Britishness in my view, each of whom embodies exactly what I'm attempting to characterize here. Fucking tossers.

Donald Trump is now barricaded inside the White House effectively, indeed a former FBI guy on one of the politics shows — a fairly senior guy in the FBI, a former head of counterintelligence and someone who has been involved in briefing previous presidents-elect during transitions — characterized Trump as 'a barricaded subject' essentially. Aside from going in and out of the White House to go golfing at the weekend, Trump has not been seen since last Thursday evening when he gave an unhinged briefing in the press briefing room, a briefing which even Fox News cut away from because it was so filled with lies and misinformation and wild and unsubstantiated allegations. He's had no events on his schedule for 5 days now, all he's been doing, aside from golfing and sulking, is tweeting — most of his tweets in all caps and all of them totally divorced from reality.

'WE WILL WIN BIG' he tweets a week after the election in which he's been decisively bettered to the tune of over 6 million votes.

Apparently Trump has instructed all departments in the executive branch not to cooperate with Biden's transition team and to do nothing whatever to recognise the transition team as having any standing aside from its own self-appointed standing as 'Office of the President-elect.' So Biden is not getting presidential daily briefings as he's supposed to do, nor is he getting any recognition from the GSA (General Services Administration) who provide the funding for the transition team's personnel, offices and activities.

People from Biden's transition team ought to be seconded into all the departments of state right now so they're ready to seamlessly take up the reins of power on the afternoon of the 20th of January next year. None of this is happening.

Yesterday Secretary of State Mike Pompeo was asked about this present stand-off situation with Trump and Biden and his answer was to say that the State Department was doing everything to ensure a smooth transition to a second Trump administration!

Afterwards Pompeo supporters said this was an instance of Pompeo's dry wit, but bunkered in the White House President Sulk didn't interpret or understand it in any such manner, immediately tweeting the clip approvingly, stupidly saying that it showed why Pompeo graduated top of his year at West Point which makes no sense at all.

Imagine if all this was going on in another country — in Egypt or South Africa or Russia or Argentina, say — the foreign minister and the president carrying on as though the election result was the opposite of what the whole world knows it to have been, imagine how we'd sneer and feel superior, more developed/advanced.

Even more bizarre, VP Mike Pence met with the GOP leadership group at Congress yesterday for a meeting about priorities for a second Trump term! This is Alice Through the Looking Glass type stuff. The Trump presidency, absurd from start to close.

Either they — Trump and a section of the Republican Party — really are planning a coup or they're simply going through the motions in an attempt to placate the toddler-in-chief who's bawling a tantrum and throwing pudding at the expensive wallpaper in his rooms, he who must be placated.

If proper procedure followed the phone calls Biden made yesterday to the president of France, the chancellor of Germany, the prime minister of the UK and so on ought to have been patched through the State Department and officially noted, but, as I say, it's not. All the courtesies and facilitations the Obama people did for the incoming Trump admin not being reciprocated. Quelle surprise. Biden's strategy is to make like none of this petulant toddlerdom stuff matters in the end, they can get on with the transition just as well without Trump's cooperation. Hence the read-outs on the courtesy phone calls with world leaders, highlighting the fact that while Biden is speaking to Merkel and Macron and Johnson and Ursula von der Leyen there are no calls incoming to the White House — unless Trump is communicating with Putin or Bolsonaro, neither of whom have yet recognised Biden as president-elect — and there are no foreign leaders queueing up to visit the barricaded subject in the White House, indeed, as is clear from the White House schedule, which is a published government document, Trump has no appointments or events or visitors whatsoever, nor has he had any for 5 days now. Nothing, nada, zero, zip. A null set. Crickets.

Meanwhile Biden is putting together a taskforce to deal with the coronavirus pandemic and to architect the logistics of the rollout of the vaccines that'll be available next year, and he's briefing packed media events — doing daily briefings now it looks like (doing so in front of [and behind] the seal of the Office of the President-elect) — and he's doing readouts on his calls with world leaders, and in follow-ups talking fluently about Brexit and the Good Friday Agreement, issues to do with Ukraine and Hong Kong and Taiwan and economic recovery and so on, which is to say, looking and sounding like a president of the United States.

Yesterday Mitch McConnell repeated his scripted lines about how Trump has every right to challenge the results and ask for recounts and have irregularities investigated and so on; as far as he's concerned, he said, until the Electoral College meets and votes in December nothing is finally decided. Which tells you how things are likely to go for the Biden admin it seems to me; Mitch is going to continue on where he let off with Obama in 2016. And why not, I suppose, have they not just mobilized over 70 million voters behind the strategies they're pursuing? And has he not held onto the Senate and made gains in the House with such strategies? True, over 76 million people voted for Biden but, I suppose, their thinking is 'Will the Dems manage to turn out 76 million again?' which is indeed a moot point — Trump being a once-in-a-lifetime rallying figure for the Dems. Maybe the GOP leadership feel that with Trump as barker-in-chief maybe they can mobilize most of their 70 million again. And indeed it's true: GOP people far more likely to vote; they're a minority in the country as a whole, but credit where it's due very often they're a majority at the polling places. (By the way, commentary saying that Mitch McConnell doing what he's doing now — sticking with Trump, or at least appearing to do so, regardless of how absurd Trump's claims & charges — with a view to those two run-off elections in Georgia in January: score in the Senate right now is Dems 48 and GOP 50, so he's going all out to win these Georgia run-offs, one of them at least, and to do that he's going to need that Trump base onside, willing to show up at rallies and vote.)

Nevertheless, despite Biden's pretence of nonchalance, there is in fact a limit to how much he can really do without the cooperation of the existing admin, which is why there's talk of going to court to get the courts to force the Trump admin to do the things it is supposed to do to facilitate a smooth transition of power (several elements of which are law-governed), however I suppose none of this can get going until results are certified in a sufficient number of states and most states still counting the last dribs and drabs. It is not going to be a smooth transition at this stage no matter what they do but they must at least be allowed into the buildings and get briefed by officials and so on so they can get up to speed with what's going on because the executive branch of the US government is a vast, multi-dimensional operation. In the middle of a surging pandemic wherein nearly quarter of a million people have died, not to mention all the national security issues, the new admin cannot spend months 1 & 2 reading their way into their briefs. America paid the price for that before with 9/11 when, because of the court battles to do with the disputed 2000 election, the incoming admin had a much foreshortened transition period, as a result of which the political nation decided that the like would never happen again, which is why the Bush-Obama handover is regarded as the gold standard for transitions so that, even though Obama came into office in the middle of a global financial meltdown, few of Obama's difficulties in 2009 stemmed from anything to do with the hand-over by the Bush administration.

Friday, 13 November

Lead item newswise this morning is that Dominic Cummings is to leave his position in Downing Street at Christmastime.

There's been ructions and rumblings in the back offices of Downing Street all week. People in the know say these tensions have been building for months it's just that in recent weeks they've come out into the newspapers and blogosphere, people briefing against one another &c.

Apparently there are two clear groupings in Downing Street: the Vote Leave crew, 8 or 9 of whom sailed into positions in Downing

Street in the wake of Cummings going in there with Boris Johnson, and then there's a more traditionally Tory party crew, a 'chumocracy', a grouping not unlike what used to be referred to as 'the Notting Hill set' in the Cameron-Osbourne regime, these — the chumocracy — centred around Carrie Symonds, BJ's latest ladyfriend, who it turns out is a bit of a power player.

The appointment of Allegra Stratton as press secretary is a Symonds initiative, apparently. Previously Stratton served as Sunak's director of comms; Stratton's husband is James Forsyth, editor of The Spectator, and Sunak and his wife — Akshata Murthy, daughter of Indian billionaire N. R. Narayana Murthyare — are godparents to the Forsyth-Stratton children, and, conversely, the Forsyth-Strattons are godparents to the Sunak children, so that Symonds, the Forsyth-Strattons and the Sunaks constitute one political and social set, the chumocracy, a grouping of genuine modern-day Conservatives in opposition to the laddish machismoism of Cummings & Co, which is largely made up of chip-on-the-shoulder grammar school types, misfits and weirdos as Cummings himself put it.

Cummings' ally, one of the Vote Leave alumni, Lee Cain, Downing Street Comms director, objected to Stratton's appointment, however Johnson wouldn't budge; Cain said he couldn't work with Stratton so Johnson offered him another position, chief-of-staff, so that he wouldn't need to work directly with Stratton if he really didn't want to.

Carrie Symonds then objected to Cain becoming chief-of-staff, as did several others, including cabinet ministers, reflecting audible rumblings on the backbenches already unhappy at the extent to which the Vote Leave crew have taken over not only Downing Street but the whole government, several of whom not even Party members — Cummings' Spads are widely seen as more powerful and influential than the ministers they're supposed to be serving — and Johnson withdrew the offer. Cain then resigned. Cain resigned on Wednesday — he will continue in his present position until the end of the year — but it was the big news item yesterday, not so much for Cain himself — who most people (myself included) had never heard of — but for what it is believed to betoken viz the power-play going on behind the scenes in Downing Street, Cain ultimately being but a frontman for Cummings and his increasing dissatisfaction with the tide of things in recent months, which is flowing away from his desk and towards the sofas and kitchen counters where the chumocracy chatter and conspire.

So that along with reports about Cain resigning yesterday there was much speculation about the security of Cummings' footing within Number 10 going forward. This was a power-play and the Symonds-Stratton-Sunak faction appeared to have come out on top.

I'm not too concerned about any of them, let me be clear, they're all repulsive vipers as far as I'm concerned (although I feel Cummings more repulsive than the others — I can never forgive those lying cynical Brexiteer motherfuckers — however, in fairness, at least Gove and Cummings were and are true believers, and you've got to respect people who've really thought about a subject and honestly and genuinely come to a different conclusion, whereas Johnson believes in nothing at all except his own career and his own ego — famously writing two publishable articles for his absurdly well-paid Telegraph column, one arguing for Brexit and one for the Cameron-Osbourne plan of campaign before finally plumping for the former because it best suited his knight's move on Downing Street), what's important for me is that all this may indicate that Johnson has decided to sign up to a deal with the EU, that he wants to put all this trade deal mess to rest. I wonder if this is what's at the root of it all? (Yesterday evening there were rumours that David Frost, the guy negotiating with the EU's Michel Barnier to do an EU-UK trade deal, was also on the cusp of resigning.)

Apparently Symonds and Stratton want the government to go a different route to the one charted by Cummings, a softer more environmentally friendly route, a softer line on the Union — not just repeatedly saying 'No' to the Scots' demand for another referendum, softening up and promoting the Union instead of simply being hostile and intransigent, or at least seeming to come across this way — and, most important of all, a route which is friendlier and more cooperative with respect to the Tory rank and file and backbench MPs. Indeed, they would like to see Johnson appoint a Tory MP as chief-of-staff, even a former MP. Sajid Javid's name has even been mentioned in connection with the position.

Interesting, I think, that Symonds and Stratton both women while the Vote Leave people are nearly all male and seriously laddishly males at that, not that they like beer and football and coke & ecstasy & titty bars at the weekends and so on, no, not at all (although some of them might do so, however Cummings would have zero sympathy for the like), laddish in computer-geeky big data sorts of ways, I mean, and in the way they embrace conflict and confrontation and exude a keyboard warrior kind of machismo, while Symonds and Stratton want to be modern-day Tories, which is to say they want Boris to embody and convey this type of softer, subtler Toryism, not conduct a right wing Bannonesque type revolution (both Stratton and Symonds would have been perfectly comfortable working in the Cameron-Osbourne administrations, for instance, whereas for Cummings Cameron is the enemy). In many respects Cummings is the British equivalent of Steve Bannon in the Trump administration, who also had the goal of deconstructing the existing administrative state and who also didn't last too long within the governing system, not least because he too attracted too much press interest, whereas Symonds and Stratton more Jarvanka like.[3]

By the bye, it gives a sense of the toxicity of the workplace environment, I think, to report that Cummings & Co referred to Symonds as 'Princess Nut Nuts' and, according to the increasingly bitter briefing and counter-briefings, some days Cummings would be subjected to 20 and 30 text or WhatsApp messages from her upstairs giving her views on different aspects of various policies or news stories, sometimes dozens of them in the space of a morning. Cummings & Co say that Johnson was an impossible ditherer — which sounds credible because the same was said of him when he was at City Hall, and, famously, he wrote two publishable pieces on Brexit for his Daily Telegraph column, one arguing one position and another presenting the opposite argument — however

---

[3] Apparently at one point Symonds and Stratton sat BJ down for lunch one day and in the course of it asked him whether he wanted to continue on with his Buccaneering Brexiteer persona which pleased half the country quite a lot while seriously alienating the other half or whether, in fact, he was more at home with the sort of persona that brought him such success as mayor of London, clever, charming, roguish, funny, successful, loveable, and, of course, he expressed a preference for the latter. By the bye, commentators have noted the timing of these ructions viz the change of regime in Washington, the end of Trump and Trumpism and the dawn of the Biden-Harris era, hence the shape-shifting in snivelling obsequious lapdog-like London, and such observations noteworthy. Boris will have a shake-up and then he and his people will say that he was never like what we saw him as back then, that in fact he has always been lovely and clever and funny and centrist, all the nastiness was Cummings and his people and they're all gone now; they were a bad influence on a good man.

Johnson's people say that what Cummings says is 'Johnsonian dithering' is just Johnson not doing what Cummings wanted; they say Cummings would come in on a Monday morning with some new notion or enthusiasm — having spent the weekend composing a 6,000-word blogpost on the subject — and expect it implemented all across the government bureaucracy by Friday afternoon, which is not how such complex systems work. Cummings may be a genius campaigner but campaigning is not governing.

All this while over 50,000 corpses accumulated in the streets and cities and territories beyond Downing Street and Whitehall, and that's according to the government's very favourable counting methods; the total is closer to 70,000 if one goes with the count of the National Statistics Office, for instance, people who know a thing or two about a thing or two when it comes to counting.

And indeed a good amount of the present-day power of the chumocracy must come from the fact that much of this year has been a pigging disaster for the government, especially for Johnson personally, and the thing Johnson wants more than anything else is to be loved, to be the popular, charming, high-achieving loveable Etonian good fellow, whereas now after 15 or 16 months of Cummings' stewardship he's seen as a bumbling idiot at best and a despicable four-faced liar at the other end of the swing. His approval rating is headed for the toilet, the government has spent untold billions this year, and is committed to spending as much more again, altogether the bill for this pandemic could come to a trillion dollars — Johnson could go down in history as the PM that spent more than any other PM (including premiers who piloted the nation through wars) and got booted out of office after only two years: he's so unpopular at present he could very well lose his footing at the top of the shitheap if he has another 12 months like this last 9 or 10, and smiley Rishi Sunak — 'Dishy Rishi' as the tabloids have dubbed him — is right there close beside him waiting to pick up the crown if Johnson should stumble and lose hold of it. Cummings was a great success for about 8 or 9 months, the latter half of last year and the early part of this, a success from Johnson's pov, I mean — getting Brexit done and winning an 80-seat majority in the general election — but since this coronavirus pandemic seeded & enrooted itself in the island he's been the opposite, a comatose hooker to which Johnson's found himself handcuffed following a great night out, most especially embodied in that episode in early summer when Johnson spent a lot of political capital defending Cummings when it emerged that Cummings had driven from one side of the country to the other with someone he knew to be covid-positive at a time when all the rest of the country was being asked to stay at home, save lives and protect the NHS. However it turned out that them rules didn't apply if you were Dominic Cummings and you were Downing Street's political wizard. Johnson went into the red in terms of political capital standing by Cummings then.

I said at the time that it would cost Johnson and so it has proved. It has cost Johnson and it has cost Cummings too ultimately. The whole thing of saying Cummings did nothing wrong was clearly unsustainable and now, 6 months on, it is the view universally held that Cummings not only contravened the spirit of the laws and regulations in force at that critical time but the letter of them too, and Johnson would have been well-advised to have let him go back then.

Obviously the pandemic cannot be laid at Cummings' door but these are the things that happen when you're in government: 'Events, dear boy, events.' But what he can be held accountable for is that whole mess of driving to Durham in the midst of a national lockdown, and then being so arrogant about it, and that in turn meant that Johnson and his government have never since had any credibility when it came to enforcing restrictions (whereas here in Ireland, for example, there is still a strong sense of national solidarity with respect to the restrictive regs, ditto in Scotland for example where Sturgeon sacked her chief medical officer — a friend of hers — for driving to her holiday home during the lockdown, and here in Ireland we showed Phil Hogan the exit — a fucking *EU Trade Commissioner*, a fucking EU Trade Commissioner *in the midst of a godalmighty rumble with the UK to do with a post-Brexit trade deal* — and these things play no small part in the preservation of the 'we're all in this together' spirit in this country and, as I say, likewise in Scotland).

I wrote the above this morning. It's now just after 6pm and the news breaking in the last hour is that Cummings and Cain will not continue working in Downing Street until Christmastime but leave with immediate effect. Indeed Cummings photo'd coming out the <u>front</u> door of Downing Street carrying a box of his stuff in the past hour. There are at least half a dozen ways of getting into and out of the Downing Street complex, several of which are quite discreet and one or two of which guarantee that someone will not be photo'd or observed by the press so, clearly, Dom Cummings wants this picture of him coming out through the famous doorway on a winter's evening carrying a box of his gear from his desk to be the front page picture of every newspaper tomorrow morning, which it most certainly will be, just as it'll lead every news broadcast this evening. For someone who is supposed to be painfully shy he's made a lot of headlines and this is more of his shy-boy-showboating. To my mind the photo is reminiscent of Michael Heseltine walking out of Margaret Thatcher's government in 1986 or whenever it was. Cain chose to go out the back door or one of the side doors but not Cummings, who, as I'm suggesting, clearly thinks of himself as on a par with a cabinet minister. And that right there is the whole fucking problem: a critical lack of proper perspective.

Tuesday, 17 November

Should have reported yesterday that a second pharmaceutical company, Moderna, says a vaccine they've developed is over 90% (94.5%) effective in preventing Covid-19, based on interim data from late-stage clinical trials.

Wednesday, 18 November

Liam just phoned to say that uncle Kevin died this afternoon, in the past hour, if I heard right. He'd had a stroke and was in a bad way as a result (organ failure &c), as I've recorded previously; he's been in hospital for a few weeks now, somewhere up in Dublin. He was in the Bons in Cork but at some point for some reason he was transferred to another place in Dublin.

Angela in Castledonovan now the last of that Queensfort family.

Jo, Theresa (Tottie), Eileen, Paddy, Freddie, Jonas, Bill, Chris, Angela, Breda, Kevin & Alfie (these not in correct birth order, I'm simply attempting to remember them all and these are as many as I can recall right now, 12 of them).

The other noteworthy thing Liam said is that Denis Callanan, our grandfather, died in 1952. Because of a story Mum once told me I always had it in mind that he died in the 1940s, during the war years. I think I must have muddled up the few stories she told me about him; it was difficult to get her to talk about the past which discouraged clarificatory questioning.

Kevin & Alfie, who were twins, born in 1940. They were sent to Rochestown College, and aged 12, after his father's funeral, Kevin refused to return to the school. Alfie did return, of course, and went on to do well there and career-wise afterwards, while Kevin became a farmer, renting land at first and afterwards over the years piecing a farm of his own together one purchase/acquisition at a time.

Thursday, 19 November

Kevin's death notice on RIP.ie (published Thursday, 19 November):

> Callanan (Newcestown) on November 18th 2020 peacefully in the excellent care of The Beacon Hospital, Dublin, surrounded by his loving family. Kevin, dearly beloved husband of Mary (nee Keegan, Tullamore), "Cummer House" and adored father of Deirdre (Castlerea), Kieran

(Australia), Emer (London), Fiona (Florida), Brian (Drogheda), Fergal (Bandon) and Ronan (Newcestown) and loving grandad to James, Kate, Rory, Aóife, Dylan, Evan, Caitlin, Ciara, Grace, Ben and Lily.

Sadly missed by his loving wife, family, sons-in-law Myles and Richard, daughters-in-law Kelley, Ann-Marie and Jenny, sister Angela, sister-in-law Maura, nephews, nieces, good neighbours, relatives and many friends.

In accordance with Government and HSE guidelines, Kevin's funeral will take place privately. Condolences can be left on the 'condolence' link below.

HOUSE PRIVATE PLEASE

Friday, 27 November

Frosty this week, first proper freezes of the winter so far. Not too severe, however, no more than -2 in the night and highs of circa 4 to 8 during main part of the day. We've had 3 nights of frost now (only one of which was sub-zero, the other two were zero and no more) which has made for a nice sunny week — with bright moon- and star-lighted nights — most of the days have been sunny anyhow, winter sun, low in the southern sky, not even warm enough to dry the melted frost drops off the grass. Still, it's nice, beats rain and gloomy relentless mizzle. When it's clouded-over in these short 7- or 8-hour days it makes things quite glum-looking, poorly lighted. At least when one gets 6 or 8 hours of blue skies and sunshine, be it ever so weak, one feels like there's been a proper day, three quarters of a day anyhow.

Cycling in these frosty mornings as the sun is coming up is a real treat, the ineffable treasure trove of the first light of a new day in a place where one is content, happy, settled. I do 50 rounds of the church almost every morning before opening up — I do so every morning unless conditions are too awful, which has happened only once so far when we had a storm. I did 75 cycles this morning which speaks to the extent to which my capacity is building up. I mostly do 50 in the morning and another 50 in the afternoon.

> Today Cabinet approved a plan that will see all retail outlets, hairdressers, museums, libraries and gyms open next Tuesday, 1 December.
>
> People will also be able to attend religious services and play golf and tennis again from that day when the country returns to Level 3 restrictions.
>
> Then on Friday, 4 December, restaurants and pubs that have a kitchen and serve food will reopen. Hotels can also reopen their dining rooms to the public from that date.
>
> 'Wet pubs' will only be permitted to serve takeaway drinks.
>
> On Friday, 18 December until 6 January, people can travel around the country. Also from 18 December, up to three households can gather.
>
> The Government is going to advise that people wear masks in crowded outdoor areas during the Christmas period.
>
> The National Public Health Emergency Team has warned of the risks of reopening the hospitality sector, but the move has now got the green light from Cabinet.

And so ends our second lockdown. I'm sorry to see it go; like the first one — even though it's been much less quiet compared with the one in March and April — I've enjoyed it. Lockdowns become me, it seems, or at least being locked down here does.

		Population	Infections	Deaths	Tests/1m pop
1.	USA	330,806,424	13,383,321	266,873	579,476
2.	India	1,378,604,014	9,431,691	137,139	100,681
3.	Brazil	212,405,664	6,314,740	172,833	102,728
4.	Russia	145,928,315	2,295,654	39,895	520,004
5.	France	65,259,187	2,218,483	52,325	313,959
6.	Spain	46,752,999	1,628,208	44,668	468,695

7. UK	67,859,075	1,617,327	58,245	626,246
8. Italy	60,470,472	1,585,178	54,904	361,021
9. Argentina	45,244,432	1,418,794	38,473	85,357
10. Columbia	50,919,972	1,308,376	36,584	125,085
11. Mexico	128,844,230	1,107,071	105,655	22,004
12. Germany	83,757,235	1,053,869	16,248	332,072
13. Poland	37,833,389	985,075	17,029	164,207
14. Peru	32,932,217	962,530	35,923	152,566
15. Iran	83,921,387	948,749	47,875	72,031
16. S. Africa	59,316,193	787,702	21,477	90,295
17. Ukraine	43,649,444	722,679	12,213	102,312
18. Belgium	11,605,601	576,503	16,547	505,697
19. Iraq	40,417,268	550,435	12,224	85,164
20. Chile	19,105,644	550,430	15,356	276,061
21. Indonesia	274,219,048	534,266	16,815	20,587
22. Czechia	10,715,215	519,723	8,138	285,370
23. Netherlands	17,146,915	518,273	9,336	235,763
24. Turkey	84,244,944	494,351	13,558	217,388
25. Romania	19,188,803	471,536	11,193	213,605
26. Bangladesh	164,802,127	462,407	6,609	16,647
27. Philippines	109,902,061	429,864	8,373	52,032
28. Pakistan	220,673,722	398,024	8,025	24,593
29. Canada	37,872,563	370,278	12,032	301,291
30. S. Arabia	34,776,977	357,128	5,884	273,336

DECEMBER 2020

Tuesday, 1 December

The following idea came to me over the weekend as I was cycling round the church: publishing the pandemic diaries as a 'Journal of a Plague Year' type production. 'Publishing' might not be quite it but at least take a look at the diaries for 2020 with a standalone production in mind (I have not looked back at any of the diaries for this year as yet, except when going back to check on something specific — I have not read a whole month through is what I mean — much less the whole year or any block of months).

Of course I'd need at least some of 2021 with it, i.e., the end of the story, the coming of the vaccine &c.

The Virus Diaries — all of 2020 and maybe 5 or 6 months of 2021 but the core of it is the 12 or 14 months that go from early springtime 2020 to late spring/early summer 2021.

As I say, I might not attempt to 'publish' them exactly — as in go to a book-publisher and pitch a book proposal (which wouldn't fly anyhow, not for a nobody like me), or even self-publish something that I'd attempt to get into bookstores in Cork and west Cork — maybe only put them up online in blog form, a made-for-purpose website perhaps, or maybe bring them out as an ebook (retailing at €4.99 or some such)? And maybe afterwards, if it seemed to me that there might be a market for them, do a small print-run.

Wednesday, 2 December

The final tally for deaths in the US yesterday was 2,669, today's is 2,883, along with 203,737 new confirmed cases of infection. The situation is spinning completely out of control over there. At the close of business this evening the cumulative death toll for the US is 273,827 deaths, with over 14 million people having been infected with the virus (14,314,265), and these are lab-confirmed cases, goodness knows how many out there with the virus that are not known of and may never come to the attention of the authorities. Yesterday, for comparison, India reported 500 deaths, Brazil 697, Russia 569, France 466, Spain 442 and the UK 603, so one can see the situation in the US is way out on its own — America's No 1!! — in no small part because the country has a president who is the principal source of so much disinformation about the pandemic — undermining public health messaging designed to mitigate the worst effects of the surging virus — a president who has just harvested over 70 million votes for re-election. Which is to say, about half the country refuses to take the situation seriously, thinking it weak and un-American to do so. They've got guns and ammo and opioids and Jesus so what fear need they have of the morrow or any microscopic critters?

Also apparently in almost every county in which Trump held a rally in October infection rates are up: numbers up in 25 out of 30 counties in which he staged rallies — report on the BBC World Service.

Comical Kayleigh did a presser yesterday in which she was as bombastic and aggressive as ever, beginning the briefing by listing off all the *achievements* of the Trump administration with respect to combatting and managing this virus crisis (getting her retaliation in first) — the administration especially seeking to take credit for the work of scientists and drug companies in developing vaccines so speedily, plus, she says, the US has a testing regime which is the envy of the world (or some such expression), whereas in fact *no one envies the US with respect to any element of its handling of this whole virus crisis,* certainly not any developed country anyhow.

She's becoming increasingly like that Comical Ali guy in Baghdad during the US invasion of Iraq in 2003, the so-called Information Minister and his incredible statements in the face of undeniable contra-evidence, at one point denying there were American forces anywhere near Baghdad even as the American war machine shivered the studio in which he spoke his comical lines.

Friday, 4 December

Letter of condolence to Angela in Castledonovan. I've been meaning to write this for a couple of weeks now but only today (and a little bit of yesterday too) finally got round to actually sitting down and doing so, which I've dispatched along with a Christmas card.

Church Meadow
Bridge Street, Skibbereen
Co. Cork

4 December 2020

Condolences on the loss of Kevin, Angela; I feel sure the loss of him is as keenly felt by you as it is by his wife and his children; after all you've known and been close to Kevin longer than anyone. This is not to disparage Mary's great loss or that of her children, of course, not in the least — the loss of a good husband or the loss of a loving and loveable father are enormous losses to be sure — it's just I wanted to let you know that watching the funeral service online on the day, my thoughts were with you every bit as much as with the folks in the front row pews.

Additionally, not a day has gone by since wherein I have not thought more of you, what you must be feeling these bleak winter days. Knowing you as I do I have a sense of how keenly you'll feel this as much as any loss, partly because Kevin embodied so many precious virtues, but also because Kevin's passing makes you the last of the children of Queensfort and I have a sense of how this will resonate mournfully with you. 'The Last of the Children of Queensfort' might sound like the title of a fable or ancient epic but I know only too well how you will not be mindful of the romance or epic potential of the situation. I can only imagine what it must feel like and what I imagine is sorrowful indeed, you have my sincerest sympathy on account of it.

Kevin's funeral service was wonderfully done, if I may say; I found it moving and dignified and authentic and so much more of the like. As I say, I watched the service online on the day but I've watched it through again since then, and it surely is the greatest honour to be so loved and admired that one of the principal sentiments communicated in the funereal solemnities is gratitude at having known the person and for having had the opportunity to be part of his good and wholesome life. Lovely and loving things are always said about people at their passing, of course, but this is not what I mean; to my mind what is standout about that service is the power and authenticity of the feelings undersurging the words spoken — so clearly and movingly evident in Mr Galvin's foreword, in the priest's eulogy, and in the readings, particularly those by Deirdre and Emer, but also in the admirable dignity of the procession of mourners and the turnout outside the church despite the pandemic lockdown restrictions.

In empathy and sympathy and with fondest regards,

I am, your nephew,

Perry O'Donovan

Wednesday, 16 December

Today, this morning, I dispatched the last of the Christmas stuff I've planned to dispatch this year, which — with 9 days to go to Christmas Day (8 if today not counted) — is quite impressive; impressive by my standards anyhow.

I've a couple of things to go to Angela and Don but they will be collected on Christmas Day when Angela says she'll swing by here on the way to Liam's and drop some stuff off for me — Christmas pudding and homemade custard and one or two other seasonal goodies — she and Don at Liam's for Christmas Day. I was invited but declined; the risk with children and folk coming down from the city and the parade of callers at Liam's place over the holidays too much for my blood (pandemic or no pandemic Liam and Mary will have half a dozen callers between Thursday and Sunday, guaranteed, and each or most of these callers will tow a string of childer after them, covid restrictions befuckingdamned in the foothills of the mountains north of Dunmanway where it's as much as they can do in terms of rule-following to drive on the right side of the road, which of course is to say, the *left* side of the road). Cognisant of the non-covid-preserve that is Church Meadow — and presumably not wanting to get stuck in a sticky chat when on route to somewhere else — Angela says she'll drop the stuff for me in my front porch which is where I'll leave my stuff for her which she can collect, all of which suits me just grand & dandy.

So I will be on my own for Christmas this year, which is perfectly fine; I've had one other Christmas on my own here and, honest to goodness, it was one of the best Christmases I ever had — that one where I listened to that radio play about the actor who played all the women's parts in Shakespeare's plays in the 1590s and early 1600s who, by the time of the drama, is a very old man in the 1660s and outside his dingy little rooms in wherever he is in London the Great Fire of 1666 is burning furiously and obviously headed his way but he feels he's too old to be running from the like anymore because all he'd be running towards is homelessness and pennilessness in pitiless Restoration London, the Pickleherring part — for that was the character's name — played by Jim Broadbent (a one-man show, although there were flashback bits in which other performers spoke, not least the actor-cum-playwright himself in a tavern courtyard wherein Pickleherring and the playwright first encounter one another), which was on Radio 4 — a radio adaptation of Robert Nye's *The Late Mr Shakespeare* (1998); I cannot remember what I ate that day but I remember after supper sitting beside an open fire in this room — then a rather empty looking 'front room' — listening to that radio drama and being blown away by how good it was, best radio drama I've ever heard in fact — and I hope and trust this year will be just as good as I'm in great form at the minute, I'm happy to be able to say.

I was also invited to Tim & Laurence's, however, like I say, I'm actually looking forward to my little Covid Christmas in this house, also I think it important not to get carried away with Christmas this year because there's a lot of winter to go as yet and the rollout of these vaccines might not happen for most people for a long while, which is to say, not if Mr & Mrs Cockup have anything to say about it (and they have something to say about most matters), so there will be a lot of people infected between now and when I get vaccinated, and a lot of deaths resulting from these infections I'm sorry to say. Indeed, I think it quite likely the Republic will need to do another lockdown 100% because of this foolish Christmas relaxation, just as the US is now paying for their Thanksgiving romp at the end of November.

Saturday, 19 December 2020

The big news about the virus in these parts today is yet another volte face by Boris Johnson. Only a couple of days ago he was saying that he didn't want to be the prime minister who 'cancelled Christmas' however today effectively he's cancelled Christmas for millions of people.

> British Prime Minister Boris Johnson has announced that London and the south-east of England are to be placed into a new higher tier of Covid-19 restrictions because of the spread of a more infectious variant of the virus.
>
> The move comes after scientists on the British government's New and Emerging Respiratory Virus Threats Advisory Group (NervTag) concluded that the new mutant strain of the virus identified by Public Health England was spreading more quickly.
>
> "It may be up to 70% more transmissible than the old variant, the original version of the disease," Mr Johnson told a news conference this afternoon.
>
> "This is early data and is subject to review, but it is the best we have at the moment and we have to act on information as we have it because this is now spreading very fast," said Mr Johnson.

However, Mr Johnson said there is no reason to believe the new strain is more dangerous or is resistant to vaccines.

Mr Johnson announced that, from tomorrow, areas in the south-east of England currently in Tier 3 will be moved into a newly created tier, Tier 4, effectively returning to the lockdown rules of November.

Non-essential shops, gyms, cinemas, hairdressers and bowling alleys will be forced to close for two weeks, while people will be restricted to meeting one other person from another household in an outdoor public space.

The rest of England will also see the Christmas 'bubble' policy, allowing up to three household to meet up over the holiday period, severely curtailed, applying on Christmas Day only.

Mr Johnson said nobody is to travel outside Tier 4 areas, unless for a specific reason, such as work.

Under the new "stay at home" order, which covers around a third of the population of England, people in Tier 4 will be told they should not stay away from home overnight and people from outside will be advised not to visit Tier 4 areas.

Earlier, England's Chief Medical Officer said the UK has informed the World Health Organization that the new variant coronavirus can spread more rapidly.

Prof Whitty said: "As a result of the rapid spread of the new variant, preliminary modelling data and rapidly rising incidence rates in the south-east, NervTag now consider that the new strain can spread more quickly.

"We have alerted the World Health Organization and are continuing to analyse the available data to improve our understanding.

"Given this latest development, it is now more vital than ever that the public continue to take action in their area to reduce transmission."

Alert Level 4 restrictions will be brought forward to apply across Wales from midnight, First Minister Mark Drakeford said this afternoon.

Mr Drakeford said the pattern of transmission in London and the south-east of England is "remarkably consistent with the rapid acceleration of transmission in Wales" in recent weeks.

In a statement, Mr Drakeford said the latest evidence suggested that the new strain is present "throughout Wales" and said this required an "immediate response".

"The situation is incredibly serious. I cannot overstate this," Mr Drakeford said.

"We have therefore reached the difficult decision to bring forward the Alert Level 4 restrictions for Wales, in line with the action being taken in London and the south-east of England.

"These new restrictions will come into effect from midnight tonight instead of during the Christmas period."

Scotland's First Minister Nicola Sturgeon has announced a "strict travel ban" between Scotland and the rest of the UK.

"In order to reduce the risk of more of the [coronavirus] strain being imported into Scotland, we intend to maintain a strict travel ban between Scotland and the rest of the UK.

"Unfortunately, and I am genuinely sorry about this, that ban will remain in place right throughout the festive period.

"We simply cannot risk more of this new strain entering the country if we can possibly avoid it.

"That means people from Scotland not visiting other parts of the UK, and vice versa.

"Cross-border travel for all but the most essential purposes is not permitted," said Ms Sturgeon.

Sunday, 20 December

A number of European countries — Italy, Netherlands, Belgium, France and Austria — have ordered a suspension of passenger flights from the UK because of this new virus strain which is believed to be much more transmissible. Germany and others expected to follow suit.

Update: Republic of Ireland has now joined these other countries in suspending passenger flights and ferries.

Must be horrendous chaos for people on their way home for Christmas and for people who work in the UK but live in Ireland which quite a number of people do.

Monday, 21 December

Mayhem and carnage at the ports and airport gateways leading to and from the UK. Just about everyone's piled on to the ever-growing list of countries issuing British passenger ban now — Russia, Bulgaria, Turkey, Kuwait, Hong Kong, even Canada, 40 countries so far. The French have gone one step further and stopped the movement of freight as well as passengers.

Yesterday the British health secretary, Matt Hancock, acknowledged that they'd 'lost control of the situation' with respect to this new strain of the virus.

MPs grumbling about the fact that that info — the info that made the PM change the regulations for Christmas and create this new Tier 4 in the English system of restrictions (which is effectively another lockdown without having to use that politically pejorative term) — was known a week ago, back when Keir Starmer was forcefully pressing the PM to look again at the regulations for Christmas, saying the situation was unsustainable, and the PM had great fun mocking him as the man who wanted to cancel Christmas, but the PM delayed going public with the intelligence until parliament had gone off on Christmas recess. If this turns out to be true it will be quite damaging for the PM, I think, playing politics with people's health and welfare and travel arrangements for Christmas just because the PM didn't fancy an awkward afternoon at the Dispatch Box.

And they *did* know about this new strain of virus before last week, Hancock made a statement about it in the Commons for goodness sake, and you may be sure questions about it would have been well-researched before that statement was made. Indeed, given how widespread it is in London and the South East it may be that they've known about this new strain since the early part of the month. However, the PM's spokespeople saying the fact that it's up to 70% more transmissible is the key point, this is the new fact that emerged last week and this is what led to the PM doing that sombre presser on Thursday evening or whenever it was in which he did a volt face and cancelled Christmas for 17 or 18 million people — and that's just the folks in London and the SE, the Christmas of millions more may well be impacted too.

All the newspapers this morning going with headlines such as 'Christmas Chaos', 'Europe Closes its Doors on the UK', 'The Sick Man of Europe' — the latter from the Daily Mirror in conjunction with a picture of the PM in a Union Jack woolly hat looking crumpled and exhausted and dishevelled in the back of a car following his morning run in the grounds of Buckingham Palace. I'm surprised none of the newspapers went with some play on the old theatre show which used to run in the West End for years and years (all the years I was in the UK anyhow) 'No Sex, Please, We're British', something such as 'No British, Please, You're Infectious Scum and We Don't Want You Here' which is the sort of thing I'd have gone for if I was a newspaper editor.

Can't help feeling there's a Brexity tinge to what's going on, certainly that French ban on cargo as well as passengers is very much a 'Fuck you and the Brexity horse you rode in on' in my view. There were already kilometres of tailbacks on motorway slip-roads at all the ports with businesses attempting to stockpile in case of Brexit troubles in the early part of 2021, but now this on top of all that at Christmastime in the middle of a pandemic — and with the prospect of a no-trade-deal with the EU looming — is just the most thunderous Johnsonian omnishambles.

They've not done a post-Brexit trade deal as yet, however, as I say, they're still talking so it may be they will do so before the post-Brexit transition period comes to an end on 31 December. After that — without a trade deal — it'll be trade on WTO terms and conditions, which, in the PR-infused lingo of the Brexiteers, is styled 'an Australia-style' trading arrangement, 'Australia' sounding quite palatable see. However I believe the opposition parties have missed a trick in not co-ordinating talking points so that they speak of 'a Somalia-style' trading regime every bit as much as Johnson and the Tories mention 'Australia', the palatable presentation of the situation, because Australia/Somalia it's all the one, they're just terms for the same thing — attempting to trade with the EU on bare bones WTO terms & conditions, which means tariffs and trade barriers and folders of paperwork, permits and declarations and certificates (with certified translations of same).

I don't think there's going to be a deal at this stage (if I had to guess), not unless the Brits capitulate which they're not going to do, I believe, they've made it impossible for themselves politically. The EU play appears to be to let the Brits see what life is like without a trade deal and sooner or later they'll come knocking on the EU's door, cap-in-hand, seeking deals. The EU is one of the largest and wealthiest trading blocks on the planet and Britain is an island at its backdoor, and about 60% of all the business the UK does is with the EU. All these shit-penny trade deals they're doing with Columbia and Singapore and wherever else aren't going to amount to a hill of green beans compared to the business it does with the EU and the business it is going to want to do with the EU. Global Britain my ass.

Tuesday, 22 December

Government announced today that the country will be returning to Level 5 restrictions from Christmas Eve until Tuesday, 12 January (with a review of the situation in the week before 12 January), in an attempt to level off and reduce precipitous upsurge in coronavirus and covid-related numbers in recent weeks. Certainly if they failed to do something and there was the usual Christmas and New Year shenanigans (in Temple Bar and such like), even if it was only among a proportion of younger people, the numbers would become totally unmanageable — they're threatening to become unmanageable as it is not to mind a couple of weeks' partying and intergenerational socialization in the depths of winter when almost everything happens indoors, the very best conditions for transmission.

I thought we'd need to return to lockdown at some point in the new year having poured fire fuel on the situation over the holidays but I was thinking mid-January. A good lockdown in mid-January and through February would take us all the way through to spring and we'd be vaccinating people all the while and by early summer we'd be out of the woods in terms of the worst of it.

And maybe that's how it will go too in the end. I didn't expect this more decisive and hard line action over the holidays, effectively cancelling the holidays except for Christmas Day itself. However I fear quite enough damage has already been done in the run-in to Christmas, shopping and socializing and so forth.

People who've travelled to be somewhere for Christmas can travel home again after Christmas Day and such like, and I believe non-essential retail can stay open, however, they've been asked to hold off with New Year Sales until after the 12th of January.

The ban on passenger flights and ferries from the UK has been extended until the end of the year, as most people thought it would be — initially it was just for 48 hours.

Thursday, 24 December, Christmas Eve

To my surprise the EU and the UK have finally agreed a post-Brexit trade deal. I'm surprised because the rhetoric on both sides had become quite strident in recent weeks such that I thought it increasingly unlikely a deal would be agreed. The rhetoric has always been quite strident on the Brexiteers' side, of course, talk of 'vassalage' and so on, but recently the EU began squaring up to the Brits in ways they hadn't done hitherto. So much so I began to believe that it was EU policy to let the Brits go out into the wilderness for a few years, see how they like it, because the UK was always going to have to come back and knock on the EU's door at some point seeking trade deals — one really big one or, more likely, 3 or 4 littler ones over the course of a decade or two. It began to seem to me that the policy was to knock them back into in their rightful place — outwith the fruits and privileges of union membership — soften their cough.

And then yesterday afternoon and evening the whole picture changed quickly: rumours and reports began chattering that a deal was close to being finalized — 95-97% of stuff already agreed by autumn but that final 3-5% was all the hard stuff, the unresolved, outstanding issues. Indeed at one point it even looked like they might make the announcement yesterday evening. In the end the announcements came this afternoon (at around 3pm).

It's the largest EU trade deal ever apparently (which I'm surprised by), nearly a trillion euros worth of business per year (£668 billion according to British spin; and they have yet to agree a deal on services — this present deal deals with goods as distinct from services — and, after all, by far the biggest proportion of the UK economy is the services sector, financial products and services in particular, and they still need to agree on a number of other big departments, issues to do with data compatibility and all such like — which in terms of detail, hygiene, interoperability and all such like is as complicated as the food and agriculture sectors — work which will begin in the new year presumably; and my guess is it will be quite a few years before all these deals will be done). However this one is the most important insofar as — in conjunction with the Withdrawal Agreement of 2019 — it forms the framework and constitutional outlines of all that will follow.

Friday, 25 December, Christmas Day

Just finished my Christmas dinner. Fantastic, one of the best Christmas meals I've ever eaten; best meal I've ever prepared for myself, I feel: perfectly cooked (deboned & stuffed) Skeaghanore chicken (cooking the chicken with stock is the key to getting perfectly moist chicken meat — the stock & cooking juices then the base for gravy afterwards — that and having good quality chicken to begin with), roast potatoes and gravy done the Jamie Oliver way (videos on YouTube), spiced red cabbage with sliced pear from Kalbo's (along with plump sultanas marinated in pepper sherry) and then spinach with crispy bacon bits along with a bottle of that sparkling apple drink from Spain. Everything simply delicious.

Spent most of the day on it — preparing and attending to the cooking of it — sat down to it at 5:30. Worth every minute and every cent. Ate a large plate of stuff, almost two plates of stuff in fact because I went for seconds of everything. Couldn't possibly eat the Christmas pudding &c from Angela — homemade Christmas pudding and homemade custard — not just yet anyhow; see how I feel in a couple of hours.

Angela gifted a box of Christmas stuff: spiced beef, ham with a mustard and apricot sauce, the Christmas pudding and a Mason jar of homemade custard and, as if all that wasn't enough, a gift box of Hugo Boss stuff out of Brown Thomas.

It's been a really lovely day. It *is* a really lovely day I ought to say because there's still a good stretch of it to go: I was up very early this morning — childishly excited — went out walking after breakfast; home again before 8am, the hour at which most folks just getting up. Weather lovely these two days, cold but sunny (frost last night/this morning).

Another storm — or at least stormy weather — tomorrow, coming in tomorrow night. We've had lot of weather in just one week this week: sunny days, wet days, frosty days and two middling-force storms (which is to say, 40 to 60kph blows with 60 to 90kph gusts). The variety enjoyable.

Saturday, *26 December*

Apparently the EU-UK trade deal is 1,245 pages of text, along with 800 pages of footnotes and appendices.

Writing in *The Times* today Michael Gove acknowledges that the whole business of Brexit has been ugly and moreover that he himself has been responsible for many errors and misjudgements during the course of it all, but, he says, it's time for us to put all that behind us now and begin to pull together again and re-forge friendships. Easy candyfloss for him to puff out, for myself I'd like to see him, Cummings and Johnson dance the hangman's dance from lampposts in Parliament Square, perhaps then I'd be willing to talk about beginning anew. That crew will never be forgiven for what they've done and as a consequence they will never get the country to pull together again. A new generation of leaders will need to come into being before we can rear-view all this, if ever the like can be achieved, by which I mean people genuinely feeling 'What's done is done; let's begin a new chapter'. Gove and his fellow travellers think the story's over, not a bit of it, I feel sure: Brexit is but one Act in the drama. I believe that in my lifetime we'll see the break-up of the UK as we've known it and we'll see what remains of it (the rump UK) at war with itself; and though they'll seek to deny responsibility for it, most people will hold these guys — Gove, Johnson and Cummings — responsible for the final break-up of the British union and for fuelling-up and spark-ing-off the town and (inner) city strife to come (and while these things have been long in coming for all sort of reasons, in truth Brexit *will* be the proximate cause of all that's to come; Brexit simply would never have happened without The Three Amigos: Farage & Co would only ever have been a sideshow, a sideshow that would have taken voters away from the Tories, to be sure, but left to their own devices never would they have gotten anywhere near Whitehall, let alone Downing Street).

The other thing that struck me about that weasel's article is that he says the EU and the UK will have 'a special relationship' going forward. I've written about this previously: what is it with these people and their need to have 'special relationships' all the time? Special relationship with the US — which folks in Washington openly laugh at, mock anyway (i.e., British neediness, their need to have each POTUS say the words asap) — special relationship with the EU, with India, with South Africa and southern Africa, with Kenya and east Africa, with Nigeria and west Africa, with Israel and Palestine, with India, Pakistan and Bangladesh, with Australia and New Zealand... I could go on (I really could — they claim to have a special relationship with Portugal, for instance, and with Canada and Antarctica and the Falklands and with a good number of the islands in the Caribbean and with Hong Kong and so on and on). Tossers: if everything is special then nothing is special. And, like I've said previously, if you had a person conducting himself (or herself) in a like manner in the community you'd avoid him/her like you'd avoid the Mocks of the Marsh Road.

In fact they're all out this weekend in various outlets, Johnson himself and Frost also — the UK's negotiator in the EU-UK trade deal talks — all singing from the same hymn sheet, all saying 'Let us now turn the page, let bygones be bygones, the new year ahead a moment for national renewal...'

They won't get themselves off the hook so easily as that! singing sweet songs in harmony from winter holiday boughs. Slimy poisonous vipers.

Tuesday, 29 December

Over 40,000 new cases of infection reported in the UK yesterday (41,385), the highest one-day total so far.

3,493 deaths in the UK in the past 7 days.

21,286 people in hospitals in the UK right now, 1,529 of them on ventilators.

71,109 dead overall in the UK according to the official way of counting covid-deaths in the UK — death within 28 days of testing positive — but closer to 100,000 deaths if all deaths where covid is one of the factors mentioned on the death certificate are counted.

On a more positive note, over half a million vaccinated in the UK already — 616,933 as of this morning — which is quite impressive given that only today will we here in the Republic of Ireland see the first people get the vaccine — the UK medical authorities approved two of the vaccines 2 or 3 weeks ago, so they've had a good head start on everyone else; and the so-called 'Oxford' vaccine is due to get approval this week so they will have a third in the new year (next week), and the Oxford/ AstraZeneca one doesn't need extra-cold storage so in terms of logistics it will be able to penetrate out into communities much more considerably; UK authorities hoping to be administering up to one million jabs a week by the end of January; here in Ireland they're talking about 10,000 a week, or 20,000, depending on who you listen to; that's the plan, the actuality might be something else altogether — this is likely to be like the roll-out of testing in March and April where there was a tidy step between the PR guff from Cabinet ministers and chief scientists speaking at televised pressers in Government Buildings on Merrion Street Upper and the reality in rain-soaked Ballymuck on any given Wednesday.

Wednesday, 30 December

Today — in one day's business! — they plan to take the legislation giving effect to the EU-UK trade deal that was finally agreed last week through all its stages in both the Commons and Lords and have it on HM's desk for signing first thing tomorrow morning. In my naiveté I was under the impression that legislation of such magnitude would be under scrutiny for 3 days of this week at least, and in my opinion even that would not be sufficient: after all, what's being enacted here is — broadly speaking — the equivalent of the Treaty of Lisbon or the Treaty of Nice or the Treaty of Amsterdam or some such.

These flight-in-the-night proceedings will come to be regretted. If the UK really is the great power that it claims to be in its bombast then this is no fit and proper way of proceeding. You reap what you sow.

Thursday, 31 December 2020

Very nearly 4,000 covid-related deaths in the US yesterday — 3,744 — and nearly the same number the day before. Now fast approaching 20 million cases of infection in the US overall, along with 350,000 dead (342,312 presently but if they're clocking up 3,000 and 4,000 deaths a day it's not going to take more than a few days to get to 350,000; may even ding that 350,000 bell this weekend).

British papers simply writhing in nationalist euphoria this morning; almost every paper has a front-page picture of BJ signing the recently concluded EU-UK trade deal, BJ seated at a desk in front of an array of Union Jacks. On behalf of the EU Commission and the European Council, Ursula von der Leyen and Charles Michel signed the huge leather-bound tomes in Brussels earlier, the documents were then flown to London where BJ put his piggy signature to same.

175

Combining the news of the Oxford-AstraZeneca vaccine's approval for use in the UK along with the passing of the legislation that gives effect to the no-tariffs trading regime that will prevail from tonight onwards, aside from the Guardian and the Mirror, all the newspapers have headlines such as 'New Dawn for Britain' (Daily Mail), 'One Giant Hope for Mankind' (The Sun), and 'Our Finest Hour' (The Daily Express). The broadsheets — The Times and The Telegraph — are nearly as bad.

A thousand people dying a day, over 50,000 new cases of infection a day, hospitals in London and the southeast at and above capacity such that people on ventilators are being shipped to places such as Southampton and Cambridgeshire, the reopening of schools postponed, three-quarters of citizens in the highest level of pandemic restrictions, government borrowing at an all-time high for non-war times, and the country has just been taken out of one of the most important and successful trading groups on the planet on the basis of lies, deliberate misrepresentations and nationalist codology, and yet the papers (and many other outlets too) parroting the PM's line about how the country will 'prosper mightily' and the future is bright for GB now that the shining helmet of sovereignty has been liberated from the orc-like EU overlords and Britain's best days are ahead of it, along with every species of such patent propaganda.

I really don't think I've ever seen so much stupid shit in all my life, pure propaganda, alienating ugly nationalist propaganda. The country is in serious crisis — in real danger of coming apart at the seams, and this sort of lying nationalist propaganda is more corrosion on the ties that bind the union together because I'm certain sure many Scots are seeing what I'm seeing too and having the same reaction, which is to say, revulsion — and it seems to me the worse the crisis gets the more rabid the nationalism and detached-from-reality the propaganda-machine's output.

JANUARY 2021

Saturday, 2 January

3,394 new cases of infection notified to the Department of Health today. And four more diagnosed with virus have died.

Now 96,926 confirmed cases of infection in the Republic of Ireland, and a cumulative death toll of 2,252.

In Northern Ireland, the health department reported 3,576 cases in the past 48 hours along with an additional 26 deaths.

This upsurge in virus numbers has been predicted for weeks so it oughtn't surprise, yet it does: I feel shaken by these numbers, shocked and frightened in a way I have not been since March and April.

"It is really important that vulnerable and older people do not leave their homes unless absolutely essential", says the Chief Medical Officer.

If one has ears to hear this is full scale crisis talk. I'm panicking a bit because I'm reflecting on how lax I've gotten about everything compared to how I was. March to May/June I was fully serious, and although I prepared seriously for winter in terms of stocking up on stuff, and mentally preparing myself for 6 or 8 months of siege, truth is I was never as serious again as I was in those early months — which is to say, frightened, therefore serious.

For example, although I get c. 75% of my groceries delivered, in addition to stuff I get from Kalbo's and from NeighbourFood, sometimes I still do walk-in trips to Fields.

The things I go and get for myself are small things — grapes, avoca-does, sheep's cheese, the quince I like… maybe 6 or 8 or 10 items — and in so doing I aim to be in and out of the store in 5 or 10 minutes (I pick times and days to facilitate this). I don't actually time myself but I'm super-conscious of the fact that the air in Fields must be the most con-taminated air in Skibbereen because just about everyone in Skibbereen and district, and more importantly everyone *visiting* Skibbereen and district — staying here in holiday homes or self-catering apartments or some such — will be in there at some point during the week, partaking of the air and contributing virus-laden micro-droplets to it.

In fairness to Fields — unlike Lidl and Aldi, for instance, which are sealed boxes with air-conditioned ventilation systems — they do as much as they can to get flow-throughs of air, leaving the front and back doors open, for instance, in addition to the regular supermarket air-condition-ing of course. But, even so, the footfall in Fields is simply extraordinary. I did not go in there Christmas week — even without a pandemic Fields is to be avoided in the week leading up to Christmas, no exaggeration I'd rather do without stuff over the Christmas period — making do with what I could get hold of elsewhere in town — than go into Fields in the week leading up to Christmas.[4]

But I did go in there on New Year's Eve, for example. For some reason I didn't think everything would be closed New Year's Day — I've gotten

---

[4] This a lesson learned long ago, and it's amazing how others fail to learn it for it's the same every year: at max capacity Fields has about 12 checkouts, and at Christmastime — especially the week leading up to Christmas — I've seen queues of 8 and 10 and 12 people queuing at each of these checkout units, each customer with a trolley groaning with festive provisions; no exaggeration, it would take the best part of an hour to go from the back of one of these checkout queues to the front, and this after the bumper-car chaos in the aisles with nauseatingly saccharine Christmas muzak on the sound system peppered with interruptive and unappealing entreaties to avail of special-offer brandy butter and mince pies or frozen pork sausage rolls, 'entreaties' just short of shouted at you by some shit voice-over 'artist' paid to attempt to sound festive and jolly and upbeat but failing to do so, instead sounding demented and incompetent. Indeed, even to get a trolley in the first place, I've seen conga-type queues 30 and 40 strong snaking out onto the December-lighted street outside, which you shuffle your way along as a primary school choir dressed as elves sings Silent shagging Night into your fucking earhole (shivering plastic buckets populated with good-cause coins in an effort to make em sound like sleigh-bells in the snow and, of course, to remind you that they're not singing for the fun of it), which — altogether — must be one of the most unChristmasy things one can do at Christmastime because it's just mad consumerist excess tarted-up with tinsel and fake snow and plastic reindeers, all on a base bedding of pre-digested sentimental codology.

so used to everything being open all the time now, one forgets there are still a couple of days in the year when everything shuts down, Christmas Day and New Year's Day being two of them; maybe Easter Sunday too but I'm not even sure about that anymore. Anyhow at some point during NYE I realised I needed a few things and so went to Fields in a bit of a scramble — which was in the middle of the day, admittedly, but I had to go because once I realised they were closing for NYD I realised there was some chance they'd close at 6pm, maybe even earlier, as opposed to 9pm, the usual shut-up time (they shut at 6pm on bank holidays, for instance). On NYE I wanted only 3 or 4 things. That said, I've just picked up the receipt from the kitchen table and it seems I'm mistaken because there are 7 items itemized on it — however, in fairness, I only went for 5 items, the two extras were impulse pick-ups.

But also I went into Fields today — Glenstal salted butter, sheep's cheese, and more grapes — so that's twice in one week. In fairness I don't think I do that very often — once a week is gamble enough for my blood — but what a week to do so! These 2 or 3 weeks are the worst weeks in terms of diseased out-of-towners staying in their coastal holiday homes, aside from the heights of summer of course.

Actually, today and NYE not too bad in Fields, nothing like Christmas week, indeed today and NYE more or less like normal days. Actually about 25% busier than normal days, I would say, however that 25% clearly out-of-towners.

I don't go to cafés or pubs or hotels or cinemas or gyms or hairdressers or beauty parlours or anything else — all of which are not open in any event — but, as I say, I do also go to Kalbo's once a week, and not only is Kalbo's small — 4 or 5 people in there is crowded — it is also a honey-pot for out-of-towners who know what's what in this area. And the ventilation in Kalbo's is poor (as I would judge). Food excellent, of course, which is why I go there.

I don't think Kalbo's as potentially dangerous as going into Fields, nevertheless that's me going into two places a week, and, as I say, I think one of these a genuine gamble. That said I'd rather be going into SuperValu in Skibbereen than in Kinsale or Carrigaline, say, which I wouldn't venture into at all — the closer to the city the more risk it seems to me.

And I did bits and pieces of Christmas shopping of course — albeit that was in early December: Peter O'Sullivan's toyshop, Designs, the bookshop… and the post office to post a few things. Which is to say, in December I've been into places I would never normally set foot in — in fact, I was in more places in December than all the preceding 8 or 9 months combined.

Of course I wear facemasks everywhere I go, and gloves. I never have coffee or anything else when I'm out and make it my business not to need to go to the loo when I'm away from the house. I pay for everything using a card and, for example, I never take my phone with me when I'm out shopping because of the danger of it ringing and, out of instinct, taking it out and looking at it and without thinking feeling 'O, I must take this [call]' and with that you've your gloves off, and maybe you pull your mask down so as not to sound like you're in the middle of some sort of kinky sex act, and, as you talk, you shift the groceries from one hand to the other or any of a score other little risky things that one might do without thinking (à la Kate Winslet's character in *Contagion*). So I leave the phone at home, let callers leave a message or else I'll see the missed calls when I get home and call them back.

Also I tend not to do several things at one time, for example, go to Kalbo's, then the post office, then Fields and then the hardware store on the way home, because, as with the phone, in attempting to do too many things in one outing one is liable to get flustered and do things one wouldn't do if more mindful. I might combine Kalbo's and Fields if I'm not getting too much from either place maybe, but often as not even these I'll break up into two separate outings.

NeighbourFood I don't worry about at all. (I don't go to any of the other stalls in the market.) Because if you're going to get infected picking up stuff from the NF stall — an open-air stall in an open-air market — then there's no protecting oneself: the goods are paid for online and I'm gloved and masked when I go out to there, and afterwards I wash-up once I've stowed the produce in the fridge/freezer/cupboards.

And I'm careful with stuff that comes into the house, especially from Fields. I don't give everything a wipe down with a disinfectant wipe — which I did do back in March and April — but I do avoid them for 24 hours at least, and often 48 hours.

And of course I use gloves when stowing away the groceries I bring into the house, or are brought to the house by the Fields' delivery person.

And I don't reuse facemasks or gloves: if I wear a facemask or use a pair of gloves I won't touch them again for two days afterwards, at least. I've a plentiful supply of all such like.

The post I do not open for a day or so, and even then I'll wear gloves. Another thing the CMO says is 'assume you're infectious'; because of those two emersions in the air-pool of Fields, today and on the last day of 2020, for the next 10 or 12 days I intend to assume I may well have been in contact with the virus. Hopefully not enough to have been infected but I'm sure it must have been in the air I breathed.

Monday, 4 January

Aunt Angela in Intensive Care in Bantry Hospital which I've just heard from Liam (telephone conversation). She's been depressed since Kevin's death and since Christmas she's deteriorated altogether. Apparently its nothing physical especially — I mean nothing outside the normal wear and tear of a woman in her 80s who's lived most of her life hillside farming on a small farm in the foothills of the uprises north of Drimoleague — she's just given up the ghost, lost the will to go on. It's an indication of how serious things are that Una is with her right now. Denis has just finished doing the few night-time jobs in Castledonovan and is on his way down there. The country is in Level 5 lockdown and one is not supposed to travel more than 5kms from one's place of residence unless for work or for medical or other essential reasons, and, aside from staff and supplies and services, Bantry Hospital is in total lockdown — i.e., no visiting or outpatients whatsoever except in emergencies and in extremis — yet they're allowing Una and Denis to be with Angela, which suggests we ought to be on standby for that call — that call that informs us of her last.

Before going down to Bantry, Denis phoned Liam to bring him up-to-date. Liam said Denis was in an awful state, weeping helplessly.

I'm not too surprised at the news; it could have been predicted — I expected something of the like at some point in 2021 and if not this year then very soon after it. However I'm surprised by the rapidity of it. Liam said Denis says she's simply lost the will to go on, deciding to die almost.

One doesn't need to be especially perceptive to recognise that of all the children of Queensfort Angela is the one who would have been least able for the 'Last of the Children of Queensfort' mantle. Mum, Chris, Alfie, Kevin… any of them would be better suited to surviving a while with that unhappy distinction, accepting it (to some extent anyhow) and soldiering on, but for all her bluff bravado Angela not at all.

Worse — far worse in my view — is the news that Liam and Mary feeling quite poorly with flu-like symptoms at the minute, so poorly that earlier today they went and had themselves tested at the testing place in Ballinacarriga. Please God the results will be negative, and if not then have them come through without requiring hospitalization.

As I've acknowledged I myself have gotten a bit slack with my pandemic regime in recent months, and my regime is about 10 times more rigorous than Liam's — Liam still doing those fucking minibus school-runs, for instance! (Not right now obviously because schools closed but if they were open he'd be doing so.) Add to that hosting a couple down out of the city for Christmas, not to mention all the callers that called to the house (as I'm very sure happened — cannot see Mary's sisters not calling up with presents, for instance, and spending about 2 hours giving and receiving and nattering), and then there's the people Liam and Mary would have called on: Liam called to Mary in Bantry for one, for example; did he go into the house when he called? Did they wear masks when conversing? I fear the answers to such questions.

All that said, there's still a fair chance that it's just a chest infection, there's a lot of it about (I'm sure) as there is every year during the long west-of-Ireland winters. Some form of regular cold or flu infection.

I was speaking to Pat Hughes today for instance — she was supposed to reopen Ilen River Playschool this week but decided not to because of the way the coronavirus numbers have suddenly exploded; she will not do so for a few weeks she said, not until things begin to come back under control again — and she said that in the Skibbereen area (by which I suppose she means the postal area, which is about 25,000 people) only 48 people infected, which in fairness is a tiny fraction of the community. I've heard of very few cases myself among people I actually know: Donal

Duck the only one, in fact. I do not know how reliable that 48 figure is —
I didn't think to quiz her for provenance — but if correct, and if the same
or similar is true for Dunmanway and district, then there's a fair good
chance that, as I say, Liam and Mary just have a normal winter bug of
some species. I dearly hope so anyhow; with all Liam's underlyings, and
given the obesity of the two of them, I wouldn't fancy their chances if they
developed serious covid. How really foolish of them to take the chances
they've been taking during this pandemic with two infant children! I
didn't say any of this to Liam, of course, I'm sure they'll be self-lacerating
quite enough as it is without me coming along with my little pinches of
salt and lectures about lessons to learn to make things even more painful
for them.

6,110 confirmed cases of infection reported today, along with a further
6 deaths.

This brings the total number of deaths to 2,265, and the overall number of cumulative cases since the pandemic began to 107,997.

776 people hospitalized, 70 of whom are in intensive care; 92 additional hospitalisations in the past 24 hours. (881 the largest number of
hospital patients recorded in the Republic during the pandemic, reported
on April 15th last.)

In Northern Ireland, a further 1,801 cases of infection reported today;
12 more deaths also recorded.

Things bad and getting dramatically worse not only here but also in
the UK: Scotland and England have gone back to March and April type
lockdowns — Wales is sure to follow soon — back to square one again —
because suddenly the fear is that if things continue as they are presently
the whole health system will be overwhelmed — apparently over 80,000
positives in labs in the UK on 29 December alone!

Nearly 60,000 news cases of infection reported in the UK today.

In a televised address to the nation Boris Johnson says the whole
country is to go to Level 5 restrictions from midnight tonight. Scotland
already moved to top level lockdown restrictions earlier today, announced
by Nicola Sturgeon in the Scottish parliament.

Scottish lockdown is due to continue until the end of the month at
least, at which point things will be reviewed. Commentators talking of
the lockdown in England continuing until mid-February.

We are already in Level 5 lockdown here in Ireland, however schools are due to reopen on Monday next (11 January) — which itself is a postponement from 6 January. Cabinet sub-committee meeting tomorrow which will be followed by a full Cabinet meeting on Thursday morning and the expectation is that schools will be instructed to remain shut until the end of the month at least, which is to say, we ourselves will also return to a full scale stay-at-home-and-bolt-your-doors March-and-April style lockdown too — first we were told we would be returning to Level 5 lockdown restrictions as soon as Christmas Day was done, however, back in mid-December that was described as 'Level 5 minus' — schools would reopen after the holidays, for instance, and non-essential high street shops could remain trading too, however they were asked not to get involved in New Year sales campaigns until after 12 January — however after Christmas, as soon as it became undeniably clear that things were getting dramatically worse very quickly that 'Level 5 minus' guff was deleted and replaced with full Level 5 lockdown; now, as I say, it's 'Level 5 plus,' back to stay in yer dwellings and don't venture forth without good cause, which is to say, essential workers and essential services personnel only, and these not 'requests' or advisories, these public health regulations are law and the law will be enforced, legislatively underpinned and policed on the high streets and highways.

A little while ago I was thinking maybe I'd edit and publish my diaries for the pandemic, something akin to Defoe's *Journal of the Plague Year*; at the time I was thinking of the diaries for 2020 along with maybe 3 or 4 months of 2021, just to conclude the story — up to when I got the call to go and get vaccinated, say. I've been reading the diaries for January and February 2020 and I'm surprised to find no mention of the virus at all, even though I know I was concerned from February onward at least — I spent nearly €100 on industrial type ppe in Drinagh Hardware in the last week of February, for instance, and that week also I went in search of diving goggles in CHMarine, eventually getting good quality swimming goggles in the sports shop on North Street, and I spent about as much again on Pharmacy stuff, and, of course, I would have been reading about the oncoming pandemic for at least a week before that, maybe a couple of weeks — it was already a hot political issue in the US by mid-February.

I've not looked at the diaries for March and April as yet but — at least as far as my diaries go — the virus story doesn't begin until March 2020.

Now with this return to a March-and-April type lockdown the wheel has turned full circle so maybe — if I did decide to do the like — my story could go from March 2020 to March 2021 (or March-April 2020 to March-April 2021), in any event, loosely speaking, a year such that maybe the diaries could have the following title: *A Year of Living Cautiously*, which is not too bad a title, I feel — for certain someone somewhere is going to use it at some point.

I ought to add I've no idea whether there's a good read in these coronavirus diaries. I'm just saying it's not like I think I'm onto 'a winner' here or anything. Also it may be that when we get out of all this people will never want to hear about 2020 and the first half of 2021 again, much less read about it, and pay out hard-earned money to do so too! Not much of a commercial proposition, is it?

Wednesday, 6 January

Text message from Liam first thing this morning (I'm still at the breakfast table when it pings in): 'Aunt Angela RIP 8 10'

What a few years it's been for us, the last of two whole families skittled: Alfie, Mum, Kevin and Angela, and, on the O'Donovan side, John & Mary Long and Lily.

It may be that seven or so funerals is par for the course when you get to this stage in life — Maurice of Mallowgaten must be into his 60s by now, he's at least as old as Angela and Mary, if not older, and Angela and Mary certainly into their 7th decade, Maurice's brother, Vincent is older than that again (Vincent may even be into his 70s), and Anthony in Somerset also into his 60s, and of course his brother John already gone from us — John was at least 10 or 12 years older than Anthony.

On the other side of the tree Margaret of Gortanure is an OAP as she told me herself recently, which means Tim must be up near the 65 mark too, and so on; indeed, it won't be too long now until I myself am also into my 7th decade — I'm now the age my father was when he died. And of course we're all are grandparents now, which is to say, my sisters and cousins and myself are 'the old folks' now.

Somehow seems more dramatic or profound — meaningful (symbolic anyhow) — when them that's falling away are the last of a whole generation.

Although we oughtn't to speak of them as 'one generation': Lily, Denis, Dad and Kathleen, and Jo and Eileen from Queensfort, were born in the first quarter of the last century, whereas all the others were born in the second quarter. There's only 15 years between 1940 and 1925 but culturally someone born in 1940, say, is a world away from someone who first drew breath in 1925.

Think of the differences between someone born in 1945, say, and someone born in 1960. Or, similarly, the differences between someone born in the 3rd quarter of the last century and someone born in the 4th quarter (people born between 1950 and 1974 — as Mary, Angela, me and Liam were — as opposed to people born between 1975 and 1999 — as Donal, Cal, Claire and Cathal were, people for whom Richard Nixon and Watergate is part of old archive news, just as Anthony Eden and the Suez Crisis is for me and people of my generation, the Before Times; whereas for us, my generation, Watergate, Nixon, Ford and Carter, and Ted Heath, Harold Wilson, T-Rex, ABBA, Jack Lynch, George Best, Muhammad Ali are all part of lived life.

In replying I asked Liam whether he'd had his test results as yet. No, he says; he's expecting to hear from them at some point today, after noon.

At about 2pm got another WhatsApp message from Liam: he tested negative but Mary's tested positive.

What a fucking mess, a totally avoidable mess. It matters not a fuck that he tested negative because they drove to the test centre in Ballinacarriga together and home again afterwards. And they've been sharing mugs and plates and a bed and child-rearing duties for the two or so days since. Plus, given they both feel really rotten with flu-like symptoms — which is why they were both sent for testing — it's likely that his is a false negative — i.e., more likely than her's a false positive, I fear.

As may be detected from the above there's a little tinge of anger in my reaction, which I know is not helpful but, nevertheless, there it is. I'll do my best to keep it buttoned down. Mary works in Bantry Hospital, on the admin side but even so. Because of where she works (and because of the way Bantry is) she was always the point of vulnerability.

But it's Liam I'm most worried about: in addition to obesity, he's in a much more at-risk age group and he's got a range of underlying conditions, serious ones, diabetes &c.

I don't mean to suggest I blame Mary or anything of the kind. Liam has continued to drive that fucking school bus, for instance, and you could just tell he didn't take things too seriously — he only wore a mask going into shops because one is required to do so, when he's not in a shop or any other form of indoor setting, he pulls the mask down, either under his chin or down below the nose at the first opportunity; and he has a big wild hairy beard, for goodness sakes, wearing a paper mask over a big wild-man-of-the-mountains beard is like using a woman's stocking for a condom. The beard was gone when he dropped down that Christmas stuff he dropped down to me (we conversed at the front door) but he certainly had a Donal Murphy type beard for most of 2020, up until uncle Kevin's funeral at least for I saw him among the gathered in the churchyard when I watched Kevin's funeral service online.

And that's another thing: going to fucking funerals during a pandemic, in spite of public health restrictions, like a west Cork cunt. Nothing on God's green earth would keep him from going to Mary Long's funeral, for instance, or Kevin's. It wouldn't surprise me if he goes to Angela's too, and does so this week or whenever it is, despite the fact that he lives with someone who has tested positive for the virus. "O shure, I kept well back" he'll say, just as he says "Ah shure, I wear the auld mask" when I ask him whether he really needs that school-bus money so badly — which is not really a question at all, of course, if he had ears to hear, rather a protest, albeit it a weak-assed one. (Only too well do I know the kind of mask-wearing Liam does as he drives that fucking bus.)

I've no idea what they're going to do. I sent back a reply with conventional expressions, asking him to tell Mary I'm sorry for her troubles and wishing her well &c but have heard nothing more from him or them since. Really nothing to do. They must presume they're both positive now and go into quarantine and wait it out, hoping they don't get too sick with it. There's no point in Liam isolating or isolating Mary or any of the rest of it because they wouldn't do it right and it'd be the same as doing nothing at all. Waste of time and effort. I did suggest that Liam go and get tested again but there's not really much point in that either, is there? If Mary really is infected then it's almost certain that he is too at this stage.

The United States has broken its own record for the number of daily deaths recording 3,936 fatalities in 24 hours, according to the Johns Hopkins University tally.

The previous record for deaths in one day was set six days ago, with more than 3,920 deaths.

Also 250,173 new cases recorded which brings the US to more than 21 million confirmed cases of infection and 357,067 deaths since the onset of the pandemic.

The number of people hospitalised is also at its highest since the beginning of the pandemic, with more than 131,000 patients occupying hospital beds due to Covid-19, according to the Covid Tracking Project.

The only good news out of the US today is that it looks like the Dems have won those two run-off Senate seats in Georgia. One of them, Raphael Warnock, pretty much for certain, and the other one, Jon Ossoff, looking good too. Still counting in the Ossoff-Perdue race, but Ossoff ahead by a reasonably good margin in a tight race — about 16,000 — and the votes remaining to be counted are from Dem-friendly districts. People in the know say it's now likely that not only will Ossoff win but he will win by more than 0.5%, the margin which would allow Perdue to call for a recount.

If Ossoff and Warnock both win, the US senate will be balanced 50:50 so as president of the Senate VP Kamala Harris will have the casting vote if things tie up 50:50 (which they're likely to do, repeatedly), which means Biden will get his cabinet picks through, most of them anyhow, he'll have a reasonable chance of getting his legislative programme through, most of it anyhow, and they'll manage to do some of the long-overdue reforms and Trump-admin rollbacks that need doing.

Thursday, 7 January

I could have mentioned this yesterday evening but I didn't want to get into it then because it's far too big a subject for a handful of end-of-entry paragraphs.

Yesterday in joint session the US Congress was set to congressionally certify the voting numbers sent in by the Electoral College: 306 for Biden and 232 for Trump. The college formalized its results back in December after the results had been certified by the governors in all 50 states. Moreover, since the election, 60 or so court cases have been instigated to challenge some of these results, or some aspect relating to the proceedings which led to these results and all but one — a minor detail — have been rejected and/or dismissed, including by Trump-appointed judges, even including the conservative-dominated Supreme Court which refused to hear attempted proceedings for want of either standing, jurisdiction, credible evidence or genuine points of law.

Yesterday, at the time Congress was gathering to formally certify the election results, Trump and his Storm Trumpers held a 'Save America' rally down near the White House where they were addressed by a succession of Trumpist crazies culminating in the commandant-of-doolally himself, *il presidente*, Benito Trumpolini, who concluded his insane address by telling his amped-up and conspiracy-crazed supporters that in America only shows of strength work, "You have to fight like hell", he said "And if you don't fight like hell, you're not going to have a country anymore" — inviting/directing them to march on the Capitol to give grunt to the brave men and women in Congress who'd signed up to challenge and frustrate the congressional certification of these "fraudulent election results" — i.e., Ted Cruz, Josh Hawley, Jim Jordan, Marjorie Taylor Greene, Lauren Boebert & Co, 'the Sedition Caucus' as they've been dubbed.

Trump finished his mad speech to this massive aggregation of aggrieved proto-Fascist clownboy Trumpers yesterday by saying "We're mad as hell and we're just not going to take it anymore"—i.e., we're not willing to stand by and accept this stealing of what is rightfully ours, meaning the election in the first instance, but also more broadly 'our' country, the government of it in particular; as with the Brexiteers 'Take Back Control' is a common theme/meme/T-shirt/tattoo/placard slogan, often also 'Take Back Our Country' / 'Take Back Our House' / 'Take Back Our Democracy', which is to say, take these things back from the blacks and the coloureds and the feminazies and the homos and the queers and the Muslims and the immi-grants and the communists and east and west coast libtards, book-readin' quiche-eatin' college campus some bitches... — consciously or otherwise echoing Howard Beale's car-crash exasperation in the 1976 film *Network*. Need to go back and check on this to be 100% sure, but what I heard him say seemed to me to be almost a direct quote of that famous Howard Beale line, something I haven't heard anyone else pick up on as yet — probably because yesterday's drama already too much to chew through; however historians and others with more time to work with won't miss out on such illuminating cultural fragments, you may be sure.

Like the Electoral College meeting in December, the congressional cer-tification of election results is normally simply a pro forma or ceremonial affair, however repeatedly and aggressively Trump has refused to accept the election result. He says he believes the election was stolen from him, that Georgia was stolen — despite the fact that Georgia is run by Trump-supporting Republicans, both in the governor's mansion and in the state legislature are seriously right wing Republicans, *Trumpist* Republicans, people not a bit shy of purging voter rolls in Democrat-leaning areas and every other species of common or garden political shenanigans, peo-ple less likely to be part of a Democrat plot to steal an election victory from Trump it'd be hard to find — so too was Arizona stolen from him, another traditionally reliable Republican sunbelt bastion, along with Pennsylvania, Wisconsin and Michigan, the upper mid-west 'blue wall' captures that gifted the WH to Trump in 2016, which this cycle returned to the Democratic fold. Trump alleges a vast left-wing conspiracy and he says Joe Biden is an agent of communist China, the moon is a spher-ical presentation of hard blue cheese, and America is being stolen from its true owners — which is to say, obese, non-college-educated, white trash... — there is almost no level of absurdity or crazy one could go to in characterizing what Trump and these Trumpists allege, and apparently believe, which would be too much; I heard one Trump supporter in one news report say that his 'commander-in-chief' was 'Donald Trump and Jesus Christ'!

Meanwhile, as I reported yesterday, the Dems have taken those two run-off senate seats in Georgia which (effectively) gives the Democrats control of the White House, the Senate and the House of Representatives.

Trumpists, of course, allege that these Warnock and Ossoff victories also stolen. Warnock is the first black person to be elected to the Senate from a former slave state — indeed he is only the 11th or 12th black person ever to sit in the upper chamber — and Jon Ossoff is Jewish, only 33 years old, so he'll become youngest member of the Senate since Joe Biden back at the end of the last century; Trumpists say 'How in fuck is it possible that the good ole boys of Georgia would elect a Negro and a Jew? Give me a fucking break already!' and lots other of the like.

One of the really damaging things in the run-up to the run-off polling day on Tuesday was the release of an audio recording of a Donald Trump phone call — a call from the White House with Mark Meadows, Trump's chief-of-staff, and several other administration officials also on the call — to Georgia secretary of state, Brad Raffensperger, in which Trump attempts to charm, bribe, cajole, threaten, bully, bamboozle, entice, flatter... — it's an hour long phone call in the course of which Trump cycles his way through all of the above — into 'finding' 12,000 votes for him which would flip Georgia out of Biden's column, seeing as Biden won the state by just 11,779 votes. 'Just say you've recalculated', Trump urges.

It's an astonishing recording clearly showing that it is *Trump* who wants to steal the election. If you listen to the whole recording you'll be struck by three things: how stupid Trump is, how totally unpersuasive this *Art of the Deal* negotiator is — how desperate-sounding and deluded he is — and, finally, how like a low grade wannabe-mobster boss he sounds. To give a flavour of what I'm saying, the following is extracted from the Washington Post's transcript of the recording:

> **Trump:** [...] We *have* won this election in Georgia based on all of this. And there's nothing wrong with saying that, Brad. You know, I mean,

having the correct — the people of Georgia are angry. And these numbers are going to be repeated on Monday night. Along with others that we're going to have by that time, which are much more substantial even. And the people of Georgia are angry, the people of the country are angry. And there's nothing wrong with saying that, you know, that you've recalculated.

Raffensperger: Well, Mr. President, the challenge that you have is the data you have is wrong.

[…]

Trump: […] what's the difference between winning the election by two votes and winning it by half a million votes. I think I probably did win it by half a million. You know, one of the things that happened, Brad, is we have other people coming in now from Alabama and from South Carolina and from other states, and they're saying it's impossible for you to have lost Georgia. We won. You know in Alabama, we set a record, got the highest vote ever. In Georgia, we set a record with a massive amount of votes. And they say it's not possible to have lost Georgia.

And I could tell you by our rallies. I could tell you by the rally I'm having on Monday night, the place, they already have lines of people standing out front waiting. It's just not possible to have lost Georgia. It's not possible. When I heard it was close, I said there's no way. But they dropped a lot of votes in there late at night. You know that, Brad. And that's what we are working on very, very stringently. But regardless of those votes, with all of it being said, we lost by essentially 11,000 votes, and we have many more votes already calculated and certified, too.

[…]

Trump: […] you can't let it happen, and you are letting it happen. You know, I mean, I'm notifying you that you're letting it happen. So look. All I want to do is this. I just want to find 11,780 votes, which is one more than we have because we won the state.

And flipping the state is a great testament to our country because, you know, this is — it's a testament that they can admit to a mistake or whatever you want to call it. If it was a mistake, I don't know. A lot of people think it wasn't a mistake. It was much more criminal than that. But it's a big problem in Georgia, and it's not a problem that's going away. I mean, you know, it's not a problem that's going away.

[...]

Trump: So what are we going to do here, folks? I only need 11,000 votes. Fellas, I need 11,000 votes. Give me a break. You know, we have that in spades already. [...]

Raffensperger and his lawyer recorded the phone call for their own protection — in the event of Trump misrepresenting the content of the communication exchange, which, within hours he did do, so Raffensperger released the actual audio recording.

I'm not sure what the exact figures are but both Ossoff and Warnock won their respective run-off races by small margins. Partly this was down to the Dems getting their people to vote in these elections (in run-off elections Republican turnout holds up reasonably well but Dem turnout often plummets — many of the people likely to vote Dem have more on their minds than who sits in those plush upholstered Senate seats — however Trump's obnoxious personality is an amazing rallying klaxon, on both sides of the political divide) but partly it was also down to quite a few people who might have been disposed to voting Republican staying at home, either staying home because they were strongly pro-Trump and they believe the president when he says the voting system is rigged and so they may have concluded 'What's the point? If the thing is rigged then the Dems are going to win anyway', or they were Republican-leaning people and they heard that audio-recording in which it is undeniably clear that *it is Trump who wants to 'find' votes by one means or another, not excluding criminality and conspiracy*, and so (like Raffensperger) they decided they wanted no part of anything of the like. (By the bye, bear in mind that Raffensperger says he voted for Trump twice, in 2016 and again in November 2020. Raffensperger, and Kemp, the governor in Georgia, are genuine Trumpers, however they're not outlaws, and they want no part in overturning a legitimate US election and, by so doing, participating in a coup d'état, which is to say, being traitors to the US Constitution they vowed to uphold, protect and defend when sworn into office. And credit to them, in fairness.)

So anyway the riled-up Trump mob descends on the Capitol buildings following the 'Save America' rally yesterday, breaching the security barriers and then breaking windows and forcing open doors before cascading down the corridors and hallways of the citadel of representative government in America — 'Give me Liberty or Give me Death' some of their placards read, and of course, 'Make America Great Again', 'Q Sent Me' and so on along with Trump flags, Q-Anon flags, Confederate flags and various far-right militia group flags and emblems aplenty. Armed, covid-riddled Trumpist crazies occupied the Senate chamber (the frightened legislators scuttled out of the chamber wearing gasmasks kept under their seats in case of another 9/11 type attack on the capitol), mob leaders sat in the Speaker's chair in the House of Representatives and they smashed their way into the Speaker's office, violating it, rifling through the paperwork there, trashing it and pocketing keepsakes...

It was a total breakdown of law and order by people who deludedly believe themselves to be law-and-order advocates: many of these right wing nut-jobs believe themselves to be auxiliary policeman and paramilitary defenders of the Constitution and American Liberty.

Meanwhile over in the White House surrounded by family members Trumpolini was reported to be watching these scenes of mayhem and anarchy on TV. In his rabble-rousing speech earlier in the day Trump said he'd be marching to the Capitol along with his unwashed followers but of course this was a total lie. First daughter Ivanka tweeted that the hoards marching on the Capitol were 'patriots'; she deleted the tweet as soon as things began to get ugly-looking, evidently not recognising that things had been seriously ugly-looking for some time already. It's been ugly-looking for months now. The stench is coming from inside your father's administration, darling, indeed a good measure of it comes from inside you. Several reports say that WH staffers scarpered altogether yesterday as the wheels finally came of the Trumpolini clown-car — several formal WH resignations-in-protest submitted yesterday, others just left their desks and went home — so that the West Wing is now virtually empty anyway, none but the royal family and the most loyal of the palace guard remaining, watching it all on television just as everyone else in the country was doing, and around the world too, including me here in west of Ireland.

O and by the bye, over 4,000 Americans died of Covid yesterday; meanwhile the president is eating potato chips while watching a riot he instigated play out on several television screens. Pure fucking Hunter S. Thompson, HST on steroids.

Acting like a president ought to do, President-elect Biden did a televised address to the nation yesterday afternoon (4pm Washington time; about 9pm Irish time) — Biden's speech carried by all the networks — in which he described these events as an 'insurrection' and called on the president to come out and call off his mob-dogs and put a stop to the riotous outrages he'd instigated.

Yesterday most of the Republican leadership — including sheepish VP Mike Pence (a sheep in sheep's clothing) — openly split with Trump; most dramatic of all Senate leader Mitch McConnell — Trump's main enabler on Capitol Hill for the past 4 years — who said that to overturn an election based on false and baseless allegations of 'fraud' would be to see the Republic go into a 'death spiral', the whole country would never again accept the result of an election, he said, every 4 years would be a no-holds-barred scramble for power. (Best speech I've ever seen McConnell give, in fairness. However, it was little enough, and far too late, so in the final analysis he gets no credit for it.)

The rest of the leading Republicans — Ted Cruz and Josh Hawley in the senate, for example, (cynical fucks who don't give a fig for Trump, they just want the support of Trump's white hot base for their own WH bids in 2024) along with over 100 GOP members of the House — sought to disrupt and delay the congressional certification of the election, the business of which resumed after order had been restored and the Capitol cleared of rioters. What the Sedition Caucus want, so they say, is a 10-day delay so a bipartisan commission can look into these allegations of fraud and poll-rigging and all such like in Georgia, Arizona, Pennsylvania, Wisconsin and Michigan. (Odd, isn't it, how there are allegations of irregularities only in those states that Trump lost; apparently everything kosher in all the states Trump won; and interesting too, is it not, that when the Dems were masterminding this vast multi-state power-play they only did so with respect to the presidential election, they didn't do so down ballot, with the result the Dems lost seats in the House and failed to pick up target seats in the Senate. However, no surprise to learn that the conspiracy spinners have amendments accounting such apparent anomalies.) As McConnell said yesterday, these self-serving people —

Cruz, Hawley & Co — can indulge in their political antics safe in the knowledge that their colleagues will fulfil their constitutional duty and congressionally certify the election results as they ought to — because the last thing Ted Cruz wants is another 4 years of Donald Trump, or any Trump for that matter, or Trumpist.

Congress reconvened late last night and listened to these bullshit objection from Cruz and the rest of these cynical fucks and then went ahead and certified the Electoral College returns, as they're supposed to do because the whole thing's really only a ceremonial procedure (which they're constitutionally mandated to do on the 6th of January), and so Joe Biden will be inaugurated as the 46th president of the United States at noon on 20 January, as was always going to happen as far as anyone interested in real world is concerned.

However, the fallout from all this will be considerable. Trump's a busted flush now. Utterly toxic. He may well be a source of serious toxicity in GOP affairs for the next 4 or more years but effectively he ceased to be president of the United States yesterday. He was only a lame-duck president anyway, but now he's a legless, flightless and friendless duck — a DINO, a duck in name only.

Even so, the damage is done. The scenes yesterday reminded me of nothing so much as the climatic scenes in Robert Harris' trilogy on the life and times of the Roman lawyer and statesman Cicero, specifically the scenes portraying the chaotic and self-destructive Clodius Pulcher administration in the second volume of the trilogy, *Lustrum*, the radically populist administration of a princeling turned tribune of the plebs.

However, yesterday wasn't a stand-alone event, yesterday has a long tail, going back to the Tea Party and Sarah Palin and Michelle Bachmann at least, and back before that too, to Newt Gingrich in the 1990s, and maybe even back before that.

It's been a long time coming, but this is not the beginning of the end for the American experiment — the experiment in self-government Lincoln spoke of in his Gettysburg Address — it feels to me more like we're somewhere in the middle of the end of the America we all thought we knew.

Imagine how yesterday's scenes were viewed in Beijing and beneath the onion-domes of the Kremlin! And in Teheran and in the mountains of Afghanistan, and in the badlands of northern Pakistan. For all such like it must have been the best television to come out of the US since the collapse of the Twin Towers in September 2001.

A house divided against itself cannot long stand, Lincoln said; I believe we're seeing the structure crumbling before our eyes right now, certainly the ground on which it stands is juddering and shuddering and structural cracks are evident for all to see, frieze statuary crashing onto the marbled floors as frightened senators run before an aggrieved, inarticulate, unwashed angry populace.

75% of Republican voters believe there was massive, widespread fraud in the election in November. Over 70 million people voted for a second term for the utterly incompetent and clearly cracked clown-prince Trumpolini, so that's tens of millions of citizens believing that the presidency of Joe Biden is not legit. And this is something that's not going to calm down and get better with the application of soothing lotions and grand, finely crafted speeches, in my view, the like can only fester and worsen.

Not only do folks on both sides of the political divide have their own facts, they have their own news channels — Fox, Newsmax, OAN, Breitbart — their own Facebook, WhatsApp and Parler groups, their own churches and gerrymandered districts, their own narratives and their own priorities, and, so far as I can see anyhow, ne'ar the twain shall meet.

And they won't meet because they don't want to meet. Both sides are spoiling for a fight, a proper set-to. Yesterday only a capture-the-flag rampage into the other's territory, a bit of fucking fun. The real fight ain't even kicked off yet. Groups who genuinely seek proper set-tos usually get them, and will never be satisfied until they do. It seems to me that the surest cure for what ails em is the letting of some blood. And *there will be blood*, I feel.

Just wait til they attempt to prosecute Trump and his associates, which most assuredly they will do now. And if they go after Trump and his enablers (and I feel sure they will — Merrick Garland is to be the new AG, remember him? Obama's nominee to the SC following the death of Antonin Scalia in February 2016, who Mitch McConnell refused to give a Senate confirmation hearing to) there will certainly be incarcerations. Trump is correct about one thing: there's been massive criminality like you wouldn't believe. His phone call to Raffensperger and the call to the president of Ukraine which led to his impeachment are two calls that came to light; imagine all the other calls that have been made over the past 4 or 5 years! Imagine all the folks who didn't have the firm grasp of right and wrong that Brad Raffensperger and Alexander Vindman have showed themselves to have.

And even if the new AG doesn't posse-up for some Trump-hunting, there are plenty of state-level prosecutors who will do so — to be the person that cuffs a president (especially this guy) is not only career-making, it's *history*-making. Trump may well attempt a self-pardon as his last act before walking out of the Oval Office 13 days from now and fight it out in the SC as to whether the president has the power to self-pardon, but whichever way it goes in that SC fight, a presidential pardon does not protect you from state-level prosecutions. My guess is that Trump is going to have to fight like a junkyard dog to keep his tail out of jail. Prosecutors in NYC are set to RICO his ass if reports are to be believed. Indeed, my prediction is a royal family night-flight — clutching as much treasure as they can grasp hold of — to some friendly oasis in the Middle East — Israel or the UAE or Qatar or some such. If I'm correct about this then it'll emerge that setting up this oasis has been one of the main foreign policy objectives/achievements of this administration. This is what Jared Kushner has been working on (Kushner has disappeared off the scene altogether since November: *Whatcha working on there, Jared?*).

Either that or Trump will need to plead dementia, or some other form of cognitive codology — brain spurs, perhaps, to go with the 'bone spurs' that got him off the Vietnam draft.

The extent to which both sides of the American political divide speak of 'civil war' is noteworthy, and to my mind speaks darkly of times and tides to come. It feels like we're in a pre-Civil War situation. We've been in a Cold War for a generation or two now (going back to the Ken Starr hit on Clinton), and as I say maybe even more than that, maybe going all the way back to Watergate — certainly Roger Stone, Roger Ailes, Donald Rumsfeld, Dick Cheney and others continued to be sore about all that Nixon stuff for decades, traumatic wounds carried for 40 years and more

— but this cold war is hotted up quite a bit now as events yesterday amply demonstrate.

One last point and I'll leave it alone after this because, honestly, I could spend all day writing about these subjects: Watching the coverage on various channels on YouTube yesterday evening I was struck by something Van Jones said on CNN: imagine if thousands of Black Lives Matter protesters did what these Storm Trumpers did yesterday — force entry into the Capitol wielding weapons and blinding cops with bear-spray wearing militia uniforms and sporting other forms of battle gear, trashing Congressional offices and taking selfies in the Speaker's chair and so on — what would the response of the authorities have been?

There were 50 arrests yesterday. Just 50! Admittedly there will be others going forward, especially after January 20th, but had they been BLM people can anyone seriously doubt that there would have been 50 dead black people on the steps of the Capitol yesterday afternoon? And maybe 500 of em.

Or imagine if it had been Muslims. There'd be fucking internment camps before Memorial Day. 100% there would be. And maybe public executions for the ring-leaders.

No way could one look at those scenes yesterday and look at the way BLM protests are policed, for instance, and say that all are equal before the law in the United States.

And he's absolutely correct. It's a perfectly valid point. An important point. There's pictures of cops posing for smartphone selfies with these mobsters in the halls of Congress!

As I say, the radioactive fallout from yesterday will send thousands of toxic splinters in many directions, creating centres of toxicity far and wide for years and years to come.

People often talk about 'inflection points' — especially American media output — well, boys and girls, I think we can safely say that we had ourselves an inflection point yesterday.

What happened yesterday is right up there with 9/11 and the like — Pearl Harbour, and the assassinations of JFK, MLK and Robert Kennedy, that's how serious it feels right now.

American Carnage forsooth.

This morning the WH put out a statement calling for calm and committing to a peaceful transfer of power. Too late for that, pal; at this stage we already do not have a peaceful transfer of power; *this* is what a non-peaceful transfer of power looks like!

And, secondly, by the time that WH statement was put out law and order had already been restored, thanks to a curfew order in DC and thousands of National Guard personnel in SWAT team get-up (units scrambled out of neighbouring Maryland and Virginia), and no thanks to Trump or any of the folks in the WH — indeed, as I understand it, the WH chain-of-command had to be circumvented to get these National Guard units onto the streets and order restored.

And, finally, putting out a press statement in the wee hours — by this time Trump had been locked out of his Twitter and Facebook accounts for the simple reason that the president was spreading misinformation and inciting an uprising against the lawfully elected government of the United States — tells you something about what must have been going on in the WH: no sleep, no clue, no exit strategy. And so now they're panicking a little bit, concerned about their legal and political exposure.

There's talk of invoking the 25th, where the cabinet led by the VP deems the president unfit to perform his duties, due to illness or any other form of incapacity. Perhaps with this promise to be a good boy going forward Trump is attempting to forestall the 25th Amendment play.

I don't want them to do so because if they did Pence would be under immense pressure to issue Trump and some others pardons, and, like Ford's pardon of Nixon in the 1970s, a Pence pardon would stand up, I believe. Pence would do so to protect himself as much as anything because if it did emerge that there was massive and widespread criminality — which I'm fairly sure there has been — he'll be implicated as much as anyone, in so far as said activity went on in an admin in which he was one of the chief executive officers.

Let Trump attempt a self-pardon, I say, and we'll fight it out in the courts. Meanwhile the state prosecutors can be proceeding with their state-level prosecutions.

Additionally I'd like to see Trump in office but quite out of power for a couple of weeks, a figure of ridicule and contempt, an untouchable. I want to see his exit from the WH grounds on the 19th or the morning of the 20th, or the weekend of the 16th/17th or whenever it happens. I want to see him in that WH fish bowl, somewhere where he cannot hide, shamed and reviled. I do not want to see him get a spare-his-blushes pass. I want to see him too ashamed to show his face at the inauguration of his successor. My fear, however, is that Pence *will* act: better to be president for 10 or 12 days than never be president at all he may calculate.

Friday, 8 January

Text from Liam yesterday evening in response to me asking how he was feeling, and how Mary was doing: Mary quite sick, he says, but he seems to be OK, so far anyhow.

I'm not going to start in on the whole subject of the situation in the US again other than to say that there's been cabinet resignations — transport secretary and education secretary — and other WH staff and admin people hightailing it for the exits. And Trump himself has done a hostage type video — very like the one he did in the wake of the Unite the Right rally at Charlottesville — saying all the right things, namely that the mobsters who ran amok in the halls of Congress on Wednesday were a disgrace and ought to be prosecuted to the fullest extent of the law, that wasn't what he meant at all… blah blah blah, all lies, all insincere, all written for him by lawyers and advisors which — as in the Charlottesville episode — he read off an autocue in a way which clearly indicated he's reading a script, like a troublesome schoolboy made to read out an assignment he's composed under the stern supervision of a teacher determined to get him on the right track.

To my way of thinking such a performance only adds to the offences. 5 dead as a result of Wednesday's hooligan fiesta.

Dems threatening second impeachment if Pence doesn't make moves to put Trumpolini out of office and take the steering wheel for the last few days of this shameful administration, however it looks like an empty threat for while I'm sure the House would vote for impeachment, there's a whole procedure to go through before one gets to the point where such a vote could be lawfully staged, and there simply isn't time I don't think.

Plus I believe the new admin would prefer to be seen focusing on the coronavirus pandemic and the vaccine rollout, not on impeaching a guy that has 11 or 12 days left in office.

And the 25th Amendment is not so straightforward either, certainly without the president's cooperation. Presumably the two cabinet secretaries that've walked would've voted for invoking the 25th, so now Pence is two votes less than he might have had around the cabinet table, so I don't see that happening either.

(Trump's cabinet have been a study in shameful cravenness; there's sickening video of them — one after another — offering puke-inducing testimonials about how wonderful Trumpolini is, and what an honour it is to serve in this historic administration, all while *il presidente della repubblica* sits at the cabinet table solemnly soaking in the perfumed exhalations. The kind of thing you'd expect to see in North Korea, or in Saddam Hussein's Iraq, but not in the United States or in any serious, grown-up polity. *That* cabinet is never going to abandon him; they nailed their colours to the mast long ago, they're going down into the briny deep with Ahab and the Pequod, no question about it.)

And — belt & braces, and maybe to protect himself in the event of any attempted prosecutions — Trump is attempting to make it more difficult for Pence by making a hostage video in which he promises to be a good boy from now until the end of term. It was those out-of-town ruffians who befouled our temple of democracy, he says. What a selfish sewer rat he is!

(Pro-Trump media and the underworld of right-wing craziness already saying that it was Antifa activists dressed up as Trumpers on Jan 6th, and they did all these terrible things just to make the wonderful Trumpolini look bad. Like I've noted before, there's no keeping up with these conspiracy-crazed loons.)

Sunday, 10 January

Notice for Aunt Angela on RIP.ie:

> On January 6th 2021, peacefully surrounded by her loving family in the tender care of the staff of Bantry General Hospital, Angela, Castledonovan, Drimoleague and formerly of Queensfort, Bandon. Beloved wife of the late Jackie, adored mother of Denis and Úna. Sadly missed by her family, son-in-law Seamie, cherished grandchildren Darragh and Leah, sisters-in-law, nephews, nieces, relatives, neighbours and friends.

> Under HSE and government guidelines, a private funeral will take place. Angela's funeral cortège will leave her home in Castledonovan at 1.15pm on Friday and proceed to All Saints Church, Drimoleague (via Castledonovan old creamery, Quarry Road and Main Street) for requiem Mass at 2pm and burial afterwards in the adjoining cemetery.

Watched the livestream of the funeral service yesterday and was really angered to see Liam at it! Liam who is living with someone who has tested positive for the virus — a PCR lab test, no less. And although he tested negative himself I'm fairly sure that result is a either a false negative or else he's contracted the virus from Mary since seeing as he's nursing her (she's quite sick apparently, however Liam himself is OK). In any event he ought to presume his test result is a false negative, and presume that even if it isn't a false neg he's likely to have contracted the virus since they were tested on Monday, which is seven days ago.

Not only was he at the funeral and in the church he was *an active participant in proceedings*, shouldering the coffin in and out of the church, for instance (opposite Maurice Hurley; also shouldering were Denis, Seamie [Una's husband], Eric from Queensfort I think it was, and one of Kevin's sons, Kieran?, the one who works in Musgraves); also bringing up one of those symbolic 'offerings' people parade up to the altar in modern-day funeral services, gardening gloves for her love of gardening, her camera for her love of photography, a wooden spoon for her love of baking or whatever the fuck it happens to be. Liam brought up one of these symbolic 'offerings' during the service, handing it (ungloved) to the aged priest — i.e., it's one thing to go to the funeral and stay outside in the graveyard several yards away from everyone else but it's another matter altogether to go indoors and participate in proceedings.

And he (Liam) didn't even wear a fucking mask! The priest did wear a facemask but it was pulled down below his jaw most of the time. He — Liam — had a woollen scarf pulled up over his mouth and nose, which was useless anyway but the scarf kept slipping out of place so that, even if it might have been 10% useful in terms of protection, that 10% was wiped out every time the scarf failed to stay in its designated place (which, when they were shouldering the coffin, was every second step).

I'm so angry I daren't trust myself to speak to him.

[My sister] Angela angry about it too, so she says, but she was there and (evidently) agreed to keeping quiet about Mary's positive test result.

She says she protested but 'Liam prevailed.' No way she could have genuinely protested because Liam doesn't prevail if you go to the priest or the funeral directors or the principal mourners and alert them to the situation, which you're duty bound to do I feel; and not duty-bound because it's the law or any public health regulation, this is just common fucking sense, a sense of commonwealth; Liam does not get to make such a determination. This is not a matter of opinion or of manners — you have your public health standards and I have mine — this is life and death! Thousands on this island dead already — more than died in 30 years of the Troubles in Northern Ireland, more than all those who died in the War of Independence — and thousands more seriously ill. And the state billions in debt as a result of what I consider to be a really decent effort by the authorities to cushion us from the worst effects of it. It's not about want Liam wants or how he feels! There's no such thing as Liam prevailing if you're serious. There's no negotiating in this circumstance and no prevailing.

And Angela tells me that there were at least 100 people at the funeral. I don't know if there were a hundred people *in* the church, she just said there were 'at least a hundred at it'. One cannot see from the single livestream camera, which faced up at the altar area only, taking in the first few principal mourner pews at most. And while the church had sealed off every second pew so as to give the appearance of complying with public health regulations, in the pews people were allowed to occupy the congregation were sitting *shoulder-to-shoulder* so far as I could see.

And, as indicated, that priest — someone who is supposed to be such a good friend of Liam's — must be in his 70s at least.

Goodness me, if he or anyone else at the funeral comes down with the virus in the next couple of weeks!

It's all too dreadful to think of. Go to the fucking funeral if you feel you must, but wear a fucking mask at the very least, and keep well clear of everyone else. *Give me something*!

It's not even something theoretical or conceptual Liam needs to grasp here: the mother of his two children is home in bed seriously sick with this thing! Does she need to die before he takes this shit seriously? Would he even do so then?

The one really good part was Denis' oration, not because it was a wonderful oration — although in fact it was quite well-composed — but because he's such a good skin, something which irrepressibly shines through such that he could have read out a letter from the ESB and it would still have been a moving tribute. He's a genuinely decent bloke, and that's what comes across.

Monday, 11 January

Daytime temps expected to be 8 to 10 today, which is to say, back to normal for the time of year. It's been cold for about 3 weeks now, severely cold for about 10 days — severe by our southwest-coast-of-Ireland stan-dards anyhow. It started to get cold Christmas week, however the really serious stuff was last week and the week before when it was near zero or sub-zero almost all the time, some nights as low as minus 4 and 5. Up the country minus 6 and 8, and in Scotland and the north of England temps as low as minus 12 and 15; indeed it's cold all over Europe, snow in Madrid this weekend, for instance, 8 to 10 inches of it, and freezing temps as in minus 8 and 10; lots of coverage of the snowfalls in Spain in the British and Irish media because, of course, it's a better story insofar as Spain is where we go to for sunshine so the story's more striking, like getting snow in Florida; for us Spain = sunshine, ripened oranges on orange trees, lukewarm wine and olive groves in dusty terracotta-coloured hillsides, such that it's bizarre to see people skiing and sledging in Puerto del Sol.

Nearly 1,500 people in hospital in Ireland (RoI) right now with covid-related issues, and the pressure on the hospital system is such that you may be sure none of them would be occupying hospital beds unless they absolutely needed to. 127 in ICU facilities.

The state has again done a deal with the private sector to spill over into their facilities if needs be, and it looks like need there is going to be from here onwards.

Lead story for many news outlets this morning is patients being triaged in ambulances outside the main hospital in Letterkenny, sorting out who most needs to go into the few beds available — and presumably sorting out the covid sheep from the non-covid goats, although no doubt right now they'd need to treat everyone as potentially infected.

All across the north and all along the border counties in the south it's emergency stations.

Over 700 people in hospital with covid-related issues in Northern Ireland.

Another eight covid-related deaths reported to the Department of Health today, bringing the total number of deaths in the Republic of Ireland to 2,352.

A further 4,929 new cases also reported, bringing the total number of cases [in the Republic] to 152,539. 1,582 Covid-patients currently in hospitals. The number in intensive care is up by 21 to 148.

Wednesday, 13 January

63 more Covid-related deaths reported to the Department of Health today.

And 3,569 new cases of infection.

133 people with the virus hospitalised in the last 24 hours, taking the total number of patients in hospital to 1,770.

172 in intensive care, up 14 from yesterday.

The national 14-day incidence rate per 100,000 people now 1448.8.

19 deaths reported in Northern Ireland today along with 1,145 new cases.

1,564 deaths in the UK today, the highest number of deaths in one day since the pandemic began, bringing the total dead in the UK to 84,767 according to the UK's health department count (Dept for Health only counts deaths within 28 days of testing positive; go by other counts and it's over 100,000 dead; indeed according to Office of National Statistics figures to do with excess deaths which came out earlier this week, the UK hasn't seen this level of excess deaths in one year since WWII).

Also nearly another 50,000 new cases of infection reported in the UK today (47,525).

The US recorded over 4,000 deaths yesterday (4,281), bringing the US death toll to 389,621 according to the WorldMetersInfo website. At this rate it's likely the body count will go over the 400,000 mark before Trump leaves office next Wednesday. And very nearly 25 million infected.

They're voting to impeach him in the House of Representatives right now as I write these sentences. Almost certainly it'll pass. Even Liz Cheney, Dick Cheney's daughter, who is No 3 in the Republican Party hierarchy in Congress, has said she will be voting to impeach him. Like other establishment Republicans her preference would be for him to resign and fuck off to Mar-a-Lago and play jerk-off golf but, failing that — to borrow from one of the so-called Squad — 'Impeach the motherfucker'.

The drive-shaft has dropped off the Trumpolini clown car now. Banks and every species of corporation punting away from the Trump Organisation, the brand is toxic. The PGA has pulled out of having their tour event at Trump's Bedminster club in New Jersey due to happen later this year. He's been banned from Facebook, YouTube, Twitter, Reddit and just about every other mainstream social media platform. Right wingers have been flocking over to Parler (the redneck Twitter) however everything Parler does is hosted on Amazon's AWS servers and Amazon has evicted Parler in toto, shutting down the operation (this after Apple and Google outcast the app from its app stores).

Trump spent yesterday in Alamo in Texas doing a photo-op at a section of his Great Southern Wall. This is what the WH plans to do between now and the end of his term, a photo-op royal tour of what they see as the great achievements of The Wonderful Trumpolini.

However yesterday was a disaster: in typical Trumpolini fashion he emerged out of the WH for the first time since last Wednesday's attempted insurrection counterpunching: he did nothing wrong, impeachment is the greatest witch hunt in history, the mainstream media… blah blah blah. No words of apology, no acknowledgement of the magnitude of what happened — one branch of government launching a riotous assault on a co-equal branch in an attempt to overturn a lawful election and reinstall the existing, rejected president for another term of office.

Indeed he doubled down on things yesterday, warning Dems that his supporters were 'very angry' with these impeachment proceedings which are totally got up because he's done nothing wrong, he says. Which is to say, again he threatens the political nation with the wrath of his cornhole supporters.

It played badly. It played well with his radicalized supporters, of course, but it played badly with establishment America, corporate America, and the establishment GOP. Mitch McConnell, the party leader in the Senate, let it be known that he's glad Nancy Pelosi and the Dems are going ahead with impeachment, seeming to indicate he'd consider voting to convict when the subject comes over to the Senate. Clearly the party old guard has had enough and want to take this opportunity to amputate this mutant limb from their organisation once and for all.

However it's a high stakes game of brinkmanship because Trump is still wildly popular with the Republican base. If anything they support him more now than they did this time last year. I've seen several reports from suburban America where you have middle class people saying the most incendiary things, stuff which is rooted in total falsehoods — particularly about the legitimacy of the recent election — and where they even openly say they want Trump to continue in power whether he won the election or not. They don't want democracy, what they want is a strongman leader and they want that leader to be Donald J. Trump. What Trump has succeeded in achieving is he's created a Putinesque type political base, and he's cuckooed himself into the Republican Party so as to be able to mobilize and manipulate that base (in the recent election the party didn't even have a party platform document — party policy was literally whatever Donald Trump said it was, even if he said contradictory things on opposite sides of the same week: the policy is whatever the Dear Leader say it is, even if it changes from Monday to Sunday).

According to polling 75% of Republican voters believe Trump was cheated out of his election victory by a conspiracy of mainstream media, international corporations and Big Tech. China and Venezuela also involved somehow.

50% of Republican voters believe that Trump did nothing wrong last week and if anything wrong was done it was Antifa and BLM provocateurs with Joe Biden and his coloured ladyfriend egging them on.

Many of them are alarmingly radicalised. And they're armed and angry. And stupid. So much so I'm minded of that Voltaire quote about how if you can get people to believe absurdities you'll get them to commit atrocities.

Lots of Trump supporters turned up at the president's event at the Wall yesterday, many armed and in combat gear. (The choice of Alamo — The Alamo — no random choice, of course.) The FBI and the DA in Washington staged a DoJ press briefing at the same time Trump was doing his grievance ramble in Texas, which cannot have been an accident — the counter-scheduling. All the MSM outlets went with the DoJ briefing — the first formal press briefing by law officers since the events of last Wednesday, and, in it they did not shy away from terms such as 'sedition' and 'insurrection' — while Fox and other right wing outlets continued with the inflated and aggrieved Oompa Loompa in Texas, which, by the bye, was not a presidential speech at all, not even a little bit, it was wholly a campaign speech.

I believe we'll see counter-programming like this every day between now and when Biden is sworn-in: every time Trump uses taxpayers' dollars to stage what is a Trump 2024 event, Biden or someone else on the other side will do some counter-programming and MSM outlets will carry the not-Trump event. Now that Trump is off all social media all he's got is television and the TV networks seem determined not to give him airtime. If he does something they'll cover it but only in edited packages afterwards, no more live coverage. This is war, full scale campaign manoeuvres.

Meanwhile Trump's supporters in Congress making speeches about the need for national unity and healing now — while at the same time attacking the Dems as divisive — but such self-serving speeches from people who themselves were making the most divisive speeches just a couple of weeks ago — Yeehawdists calling for a Trumpist Jihad — only serve to ratchet-up the irritation and hatred even as they speak of unity & healing.

Both sides really spoiling for a fight, which to my mind seems increasingly inescapable.

Thursday, 14 January

Trump impeached by the House of Representatives yesterday, and (importantly) the vote to do so bipartisan, 232-197 — 10 Republicans voting with the Dem majority. Not a lot to be sure but significant nevertheless; it would be a few more but for the fact that members of the House have re-election campaigns in 2022 and do not want to be primaried by MAGA loons, the primary campaigns for which kick off 12 months from now; that said, there are at least 100 members of the House who genuinely belong in the Sedition Caucus, which is to say, people who believe that the election was stolen from Trump and, even if it wasn't, Trump should continue as president because Making America Great Again is a work in progress and that takes precedence over some old timey constitutional nit-picking by book-learned non-patriots.

Difficult not to see the GOP splitting into two parties — it's split into two groupings already — the traditional conservative Republican Party and the populist Trumpist party, which is to say, the radical authoritarian Putinesque party (the ReTrumplician Party) under the leadership of Trumpolini himself in the immediate future but, later on, perhaps it'll be that coked-up pipsqueak Don Jr attempting to do a Marine Le Pen, or maybe Ivanka giving it some kind of Eva Perón performance, or maybe Josh Hawley, Jim Jordan or Ted Cruz will pick up the flag-staff and have MAGA loons beat drums for their candidacy. Might even be Kayleigh McNasty, she's ambitious enough. Or the pig-headed Huckabee-Sanders?

Which way does Nikki Haley go, traditional Republican or the Trumpist way? Or will she continue to attempt to stand astride the growing divide? Tellingly we haven't heard a peep out of her this past week — one of the most significant weeks in modern American history and in her own selfish interest she's MIA — which tells you everything you need to know about her, I feel. In fairness to Chris Christie, for instance, he's fixed his colours to the mast — for the traditional party side — saying that Donald Trump ought to resign on foot of what's happened, as I believe all the quality candidates will do, i.e., stay with the mothership because unless you're crazy you ought to be able to see that nothing but more and more crazy lies the Trump way, craziness and corruption, beyond-the-pale stuff. I believe Nikki Haley will go this way too (the traditional conservative route) when she's pushed to a fork in the road; for now, however, with smoke and teargas clouds puffing up from the Capitol compound, she's still weighing up her options, trying to figure out what'll be most advantageous for her career progression. A study in present-day character and principle, or lack thereof. And which way will Sarah Huckabee-Sanders go? These are the kinds of people that will determine which side prevails. If they stay with the mothership the whole Trumpist thing will burn itself out fairly quickly, but if enough quality people go with the Trumps and their 74 million voters (and I'm guessing that about half of these voters will stay with the Trumps, for a few years anyhow) — a dozen or so, say, a dozen or so top-line names, but 20 or 30 people of genuine stature, enough to look like they could staff a cabinet, this whole Trump thing could have legs. For what it's worth, my guess is that it'll burn out and collapse in a mess of legal wrangling, corruption and recrimination like everything else Trump has ever attempted to manage his whole life.

Extraordinary pictures on the front pages of the newspapers this morning: 20,000 troops in the US capital right now, more troops than are presently in Syria, Iraq and Afghanistan combined, and that part of Washington where the White House is, along with the Capitol buildings and the Supreme Court &c, now inside a ring of 2-metre-high steel fencing such that it's beginning to look a little like the so-called Green Zone in Baghdad; troops in combat camouflage and carrying AR15s (or whatever type of rifle it is US troops use) everywhere. Pictures on the front pages of newspapers of US congressmen and women walking down corridors in the US Capitol with — on either side of them, left and right, sleeping on corridor floors — off-duty service personnel, who presumably are doing 3-team 8-hour shifts, something like that. Also pics of troops sleeping in Statuary Hall. Looks like an army of occupation.

O how those war birds come home to roost. When you need 20,000 troops on the streets of the capital to have a transfer of power from one party to another, what you have is a polity self-evidently in crisis.

As one commentator aptly commented, 'Thanks, Mr Trump, you've managed to turn Washington into a Banksy picture.'

Tuesday, 19 January

First sentence in the first diary entry for January 2020: 'Wish I could begin with perky, upbeat look-forward but I'm just coming out of dreadful week of illness from flu, the weather's awful (storm blowing outside and another more serious one due on the other side of the weekend), the toilets are blocked, I'm about to turn 56, I've no friends and I've wasted my fucking life on stupid hopeless worthless bullshit sociology and would-be literary fiction, a nice how's yer father on the doorstep of 2020, a new year and a new decade, my *7th* decade, by the bye, if one counts the 1960s as my first, which I do.'

I've begun editing the diaries for 2020, the Virus Diaries; I don't mention the virus or the alarm surrounding it until March, so March is the month I'll begin with, which means, unfortunately, I cannot include this comic-novel-worthy exasperated expression of unwellness, unachievement, desperation and frustration.

93 Covid-related deaths reported today along with 2,001 new cases of the disease. 713 new cases reported in Northern Ireland along with 24 more deaths.

> Britain reported a record number of deaths from Covid-19 today with 1,610 people dying within 28 days of a positive coronavirus test, exceeding the previous peak set last week.

The number steeply up from the 599 deaths reported in Monday's official figures. There is often a lag in reporting new deaths after the weekend.

33,355 new cases recorded in the UK today, down from the 37,535 reported on Monday.

UK government figures showed that so far 4,266,577 people had received a first dose of a Covid-19 vaccine.

The UK is hoping to vaccinate 15 million high-risk people by the middle of February.

Meanwhile, latest figures from the UK's Office for National Statistics' Covid-19 Infection Survey show that an estimated one in eight people in England had had Covid-19 by December last year, up from one in 11 in November.

Antibody data on infection in private households suggests that one in ten in Wales had also been infected by December, alongside one in 13 in Northern Ireland and one in 11 in Scotland.

The figures come from the ONS in partnership with the University of Oxford, University of Manchester, Public Health England and the Wellcome Trust.

Last week, the Medical Research Council Biostatistics Unit Covid-19 Working Group at Cambridge University said it believed the proportion of the population who have ever been infected was 30% in London, 26% in the North West and 21% in the North East.

This dropped to 13% in the South East and 8% in the South West.

Nearly 40,000 people in hospitals in the UK at present with covid-related issues (37,946). 3,789 on ventilators.

And, cumulatively, nearly 3.5 million confirmed cases of infection in the UK (3,466,849).

91,470 dead according to the Dept for Health count (death within 28 days of testing positive). The unspun figure is well over 100,000.

Wednesday, 20 January

Yesterday, on Donald Trump's final full day in office, the US clocked up 400,000 covid deaths. What an appropriately awful milestone for this disgraceful administration.

Like a maladjusted child Trump will not attend the inauguration of his successor today, first time in about 150 years an outgoing president will not do so; he and his family skulked off to Florida on Airforce One this morning, leaving Washington a militarized camp — 25,000 regular troops and National Guardsmen in the city, along with trucks and Humvees and a 2-metre high ring of steel around all the key centres of government — not what could be termed a peaceful transfer of power, another miserable first for The Tumpster.

He leaves office with a 34% approval rating according to the latest Gallup poll. In 5 years — since first announcing his candidacy — he never once achieved 50% approval or anything above it, the only president never to have done so since polling began. Lots of presidents have left office with low poll ratings, of course, but the point is at some time during their presidency they had 50% approval ratings or better, even if only for a few honeymoon weeks when first elected; Trump never even achieved it at the time of his election in 2016.

Mitch McConnell, leader of the Republicans in the Senate, and now the most senior elected Republican in the country, said yesterday that Trump egged on the mob the day of the Epiphany mayhem — or attempted insurrection or whatever it comes to be termed — which, if that's a harbinger of spring, summer and the rest of this year is a most ominous development for Trump. Trump will be facing trial in the Senate at some point in the next few weeks — whenever Nancy Pelosi sends the Article of Impeachment which passed in the House of Reps last week over to the upper legislative body.

"The mob was fed lies," said McConnell on the Senate floor as it met for the first time since the attack. "They were provoked by the president and other powerful people."

It's not even whether or not he's convicted in the Senate trial — although I'd love to see him convicted and therefore denied all the status and many privileges of an ex-president — it's that what McConnell says may speak to the way the wind is blowing among establishment Republicans and, presumably, among establishment Washington generally (reflecting the will of corporate America), all of whom may feel that the Republic has gone right up to the edge of the abyss in recent weeks, looked over into that abyss, and having done so now wants to pull back and get away from there. This is the best case scenario. If so, Trump's fall could be precipitous; because he's still surrounded by liveried servants and marines in dress uniform saluting him and so on, perhaps he doesn't fully realise how quickly he could become a hunted figure, a fugitive from justice, with all that that entails. And if I was him (or part of his entourage) I wouldn't lean too heavily on his so-called friends in the Middle East, people who'd imprison their own brothers and mothers for ransom. The world is never so harsh as when you're tumbling from pedestaled grace and grandeur, outstretched hands aim at taking your wallet or your fancy jacket or your jewellery, these outstretched arms might hold you in place for a little while but only to hold you steady until they relieve you of your valuables.

My guess is that from here to the end Trump's story is going to be like *The General in his Labyrinth* [the Gabriel García Márquez novel] 'a story that explores the labyrinth of Simón Bolívar's life through the narrative of his memories, in which despair, sickness, and death inevitably win out over love, health, and life as they troop through hostile or uncertain territories to get to the coast — in hopes of getting themselves out of the Americas and into what they hope will be exile and safety abroad.'

Thursday, 21 January

Sun shone for Joe Biden's inauguration yesterday, albeit winter sun, nevertheless, the day was bright and fresh looking under a beautiful blue sky featuring only picturesque cotton-ball clouds, like a day after a fairly serious storm. If I remember right it was overcast and spitting rain for Trump's inauguration 4 years ago; Trump later denied that it had rained on his parade-day — a partner lie to his more famous lie about the size of the crowd at his inauguration — as came to be his way with basic facts along with anything else little or large he perceived as sleight or shade viz his mythic standing.

Everything went well for Biden and Harris, I think, and the split-screen of the great and the good of Washington gathering on the West Front of the Capitol on one side of the livestream pictures and sore loser Trump with his bronze-face make-up accompanied by his Slovenian escort-wife stepping down from Air Force One in Palm Beach airport played badly for the latter, I feel.

Before getting on Air Force One and flying down to Florida, Trump took Marine One from the White House lawn just after 8 AM to Andrews Air Force Base where what's left of the Trumpolini people had organised a little farewell-to-the-chief event, which was pathetic, forced, fake; he went up the steps to Air Force One to the sound of Frank Sinatra's 'My Way' belting out on loudspeakers, shlocky to the last. His candidacy for the role of president began with a rent-a-crowd event in the lobby of Trump Tower — the cheering crowd paid $50 a head for showing up and cheering on cue at the event, which is a well-sourced story, not just anti-Trump fake news — and, correspondingly, it ended with an event for which his people had to round-up a crowd: invitations were +5! which is to say, each invitee could bring up to 5 others, and the invites went out to all and sundry, even Anthony Scaramucci and John Kelly got emails inviting them to apply for tickets to the event — Kelly and Scaramucci used to work for the Trump administration (chief-of-staff and director of comms, respectively, but they've since become critics of Trump and his administration, indeed both now saying he needs to be impeached and convicted for his part in the January 6th attempted insurrection). They even had a military band at this event at the air base and a 21-gun salute, all to make Trumpolini feel presidential, something he could never do without such props, feathers, brass buttons and gaudy baubles. Even a red carpet for him going from the White House doors over across the lawn to where Marine One waited to take him away. Embarrassing, real Joffrey Baratheon type stuff. No amount of carpeting or gold leaf or flunkies in dress uniform could ever make him feel what he desperately sought to feel — powerful, important, significant, masterful, commanding. Everything simply disappeared into the black hole at the centre of his being leaving him always feeling empty, lonely, unloved and worthless. (By the bye, they say narcissism is a coping mechanism for self-loathing, and with Trumpolini this is clear to see.)

Pence played his part in Biden's inauguration ceremony, fair play — the way Pence has conducted himself these couple of weeks has redeemed his reputation a little, I feel, he's still massively in the negative overall, of course, but he ought to get some credit for his conduct since the turn of the year — as did Mitch McConnell and Kevin McCarthy — even Ted Cruz and Josh Hawley were in attendance for goodness sakes — but Sulky Trump's bruised ego wouldn't allow him to, despite the fact that the symbolism of the inauguration ceremony is important to the project of the United States. Plenty other presidents and candidates have felt bitter and angry in defeat, yet they attended because not to do so would be to put your ego above the good of the Republic; even HC did it 4 years ago despite the fact that she must have been suffering from a great many still-weeping wounds, and you have to admire her for it because doing the like must be unimaginably trying; similarly George HW Bush was seriously upset with Bill Clinton following the 1992 campaign, yet he too manned-up for the occasion, as did Al Gore in 2001 and just about everyone else going back to the Civil War years, but not Donny the Sulk. Actually, it was better he wasn't there: to have had him there glowering from the sidelines would have been bad energy on what was a happy and hopeful occasion.

A young black poet, Amanda Gorman, stole the show, I think, reading/performing a really good slightly rapish-sounding poem (The Hill We Climb) which both spoke to the serious moment of the occasion — not only the moment of the inauguration ceremony yesterday but all the events of the past few weeks and months: the attempted coup d'état, the attempts to overturn a lawful election led by the nation's chief executive, the cascade of stupid and destructive lies, the coronavirus death-pile, the deaths of George Floyd, Ahmaud Arbery, Breonna Taylor &c &c and the Black Lives Matter demos — but was also uplifting; it was the kind of thing Obama might have written if Obama had been a poet rather than a pol; and her performance was as striking as Obama's keynote speech to the Dem nominating convention in Boston in 2004, except she did what she did in a 3rd of the time it took Obama to say more or less the same thing 16 and a half years ago. Beautiful looking person too — Amanda

Gorman (beautiful on the surface but also the more striking kind of beauty that comes from within, the beauty of grace) — and a performance that in my opinion put the showboating of the hundred-million-dollar performers Lady Gaga and Jenifer Lopez in the poorer quarters.

The sun shone in an azure sky under which it was windy — nicely windy, making all the flags flutter picturesquely — and cold (everyone gloved and scarfed) but all went well, it was the kind of event that made you feel everything's going to be OK, everything can be repaired, renewed and rebuilt, and built back better too, which no doubt is exactly what Team Biden were aiming for.

One last point for now: when Biden and Harris took their oaths of office the words of the oaths seemed more meaningful than I remember these seeming previously, which no doubt is because Trump so clearly disrespected the oath he took four years ago, the spirit of it and the letter of it.

As Jimmy Kimmel put it in his opening monologue on the eve of the inauguration: the day marks the end of an error (i.e., the Trump era/error).

Tuesday, 26 January

The UK went past the 100,000 dead mark today, and that's the Dept for Health count which only counts people who die in hospital and die within 28 days of testing positive for the virus — by other counts the UK passed the 100,000 dead mark some time ago; another 1,631 deaths reported today taking the official count to 100,162. UK figures by far the worst in Europe, worse than France or Spain or Italy or Russia, and not just a little worse, much worse — only circa 70,000 deaths in Russia, for example; France is quite bad too but, at c. 74,000, not nearly as bad; and nearly 55,000 dead in Germany, for example.

By the bye, I don't think I reported that at one point during this wave — which is to say, earlier this month — the UK had over 40,000 people in hospital with covid-related issues, circa 4,000 of them on ventilators. Hospital numbers have come down since then but it's still around 37,000, still immense when you consider that each one of the 37,000 must require the attention of at least 3 members of staff you'd have to guess — care 24 hours a day, and not only medical care and attention but also catering and admin and everything else that needs doing in hospitals.

And over the weekend the US went past the 25 million mark for infections just as the whole world went past the 100 million mark, two other noteworthy milestones. At present, just over 2 million Covid deaths worldwide.

And while on the subject of milestones, today the Republic of Ireland went past the 3,000 deaths mark.

A further 90 deaths reported today along with 928 new cases of the disease.

The death toll since the beginning of the pandemic now stands at 3,066, and 189,851 the total number of confirmed cases.

1,750 patients with Covid-19 in hospitals around the country, 216 of them in ICUs.

Chief Medical Officer Dr Tony Holohan said six additional cases of the variant first identified in South Africa have been confirmed here.

Dr Holohan said the decline in the daily incidence rate of Covid-19 has begun, but he said the volume of disease in the community remained very high. "To date we have reported 96,000 cases in January 2021, which has already passed the total of 93,500 cases reported in 2020."

The 14-day incidence rate of the virus is 721.1 per 100,000 of population.

550 new cases reported in Northern Ireland today along with 16 more deaths.

The other thing that happened in Ireland today with respect to this pandemic is that the government announced that the present lockdown regime would continue until 5 March — bringing the Republic into line with what's already been announced with respect to Northern Ireland — no great surprise as it's been widely trailed that this would happen.

And speaking of milestones, let it not go unnoted (uncelebrated) that the Republic has come below the 1,000 new cases a day mark today; I'm not sure when it was that we were last below that mark (which for almost all of 2020 was our high-water mark) but it feels like it was a long time ago. I was genuinely and properly shocked when the daily numbers went up to several thousand a day — 3,000, 4,000, 5,000, 6,000, and even more than that because we had over 8,000 one day — for a while there it seemed like we might lose all control of the situation, like a fairly rickety vessel at sea in a proper North Atlantic blow.

The next milestone now is when we come below 1,000 new cases a day for the whole island because the island's the thing, not the 26 counties or the 6 counties in the north; silly to be speaking of the like in such a situation — it is certainly an invisible border as far as this virus is concerned, or any virus for that matter.

The 6-week extension of the present lockdown is to get us back down towards somewhere near a hundred or 200 new cases a day, obviously, but also (simultaneously) to see if we can motor some more with respect to the vaccine rollout. Also there's concern lest any more of these new variant strains seed themselves on this island; the UK variant already has done so and now it's the dominant strain here but there are others, the strain identified in South Africa, for instance — which is also now here, I believe, but contained, we hope — and another in Brazil (which I don't think has been identified here as yet), and of course there may be others not yet identified. All these new variants are almost like new pandemics, new pandemics on top of a pre-existing pandemic; this is part of the reason the numbers have so exploded here since Christmas — the UK variant doing its worst — as compared with the surges in 2020, the other part being the amount of testing we're capable of now as compared with 9 and 10 months ago.

The UK may have the worst death rate figures in Europe but they've the best figures for vaccine rollout: nearly 7 million people have had at least one shot, 10% of the population (2 shots is what's advised; the UK authorities leaving 12 weeks between #1 and #2 despite the fact that manufacturers recommending just 3 to 4 weeks, or at least that's what the manufacturer did in the trials that produced such good trial results; a 12-week gap between shots #1 and #2 not trialled; the thinking behind the 12-week gap being that it's better to get at least one shot into c. 30 million people than get two shots into 15 million, which seems reasonable).

The EU, by contrast, has only about 2% of its people vaccinated so far.

A vicious dust-up has kicked off between the EU and AstraZeneca because AZ contracted to provide 80 million doses to the EU by the end of January but now says it can provide only 30 million. The EU not happy about this and especially not happy about the explanations forthcoming for this massive hit to expectations, or *not forthcoming* to be more precise.

Situation not improved by the Brits crowing about the relative success of their vaccine roll-out in the most unseemly way, declaring themselves to be 'No. 1 in Europe' in an almost Trumpy way (the Conservative Party social media output a particular offender in this respect; and, unsurprisingly, the Conservative Party line is echoed in the rabid Tory press). This, they're saying, is Brexit in action: we're swifter and smarter and more focused on our nation's needs outside the cumbersome constraints of the lumbering, ham-fisted, multi-lingual, quasi-socialist, bureaucratic, bloviating EU.

'Vaccine Nationalism' now part of the political lingo.

EU clearly stung by the disrespect shown by AZ — a Swedish company, however with respect to this project it is working with Oxford University, and the project has had lots of backing from the British state — and nettled also by the propaganda coming from the Brexiteer Brits (in fairness it does look bad which is why there are rumblings among the 27 about whether they'd do better to break from the pack and attempt to do their own one-to-one deals too, which of course would suit the drug companies very nicely, having 27 fairly well off countries competing for something now more valuable than gold and other precious commodities, and of course the like — discontent, disharmony, disarray in the EU ranks — is like porn and ecstasy to the jerk-off Brexiteer propagandists). So much so there's talk of the EU putting an embargo on any vaccine supplies manufactured in EU territories leaving the EU until EU contracts are first fulfilled. As I say, the EU are clearly stung by all this; I've never seen them flex their muscles so threateningly, except maybe with Big Tech on a handful of occasions.

Also reports in the German press say that the AZ vaccine offers less than 10% protection to the over 65s in some tests, as opposed to the over-90% effectivity for the Pfizer vaccine and the other mRNA one, Moderna's.

I think we should tell AZ to fuck off altogether and just go with the vaccines that are clearly so much better anyway. Indeed, if I was given a choice I'd rather have the Pfizer or Moderna vaccines, even if I had to pay, however I fear it'll be that second rate shoddy English one I'll be given.

I ought also to say that AZ reject these charges put upon them by the EU; they say the issue is the fact that the UK signed their contracts 3 months before the EU finally signed off on their contracts so they were able to scale up for the UK supply-line much earlier. In addition there's been an issue with some of the ingredients, which have to be cultured into being — i.e., there's a biological process involved in generating part of the ingredients — and some of the culture vats in the EU supply-line have turned out to be not up to the mark, which can happen. They had similar issues with the UK supply-line, they say, but that was a couple of months ago and those issues have now been sorted (with the help of production facilities in the EU apparently) such that they can supply the UK with all its needs.

The story is on-going but my guess is the EU are not going to be plámásed by this, which is AZ's second or third attempt to tell a story that 'explains' the situation and, fact is, all the while the UK is being pro-vided with millions upon millions of doses that are being manufactured in a manufacturing facility in Belgium while the EU is being told to wait until March or April for the 80 million doses that were supposed to be delivered in January and February which it is simply not going to tolerate. Nor should they.

Wednesday, 27 January

Opened the curtains and blinds this morning (and yesterday morning) before 8:30 AM; it was not fully bright at that time but it was bright enough to open the curtains and blinds and go out and do some cycles round the church. And in the evenings it's sometime after 5pm when I draw the curtains to again; indeed it's quite bright now until 5:15 and even 5:20, and half bright from then to nearly 6pm. Point is, the depths of the winter clearly receding. I've never noticed this so much before, I don't think; I always think January as bad as December, they're sisters, siblings anyhow just as November and February correspond and likewise October and March, April and September, August and May, and June and July a pair, however siblings they may be but they're not the same at all because in one — January — one is moving away from the depths of the darkness of the year and in the other — December — one is driving into the very worst of it.

Indeed, I can sense the turn towards spring already, and it's not just a 'sense' of it, quite an amazing amount of growth to be seen about the place: camellias blooming, snowdrops and daffodils, or about to, rose-bushes which I cut back at the end of last summer with new year foliage, magnolia with little candle-like buds containing the wherewithal for Easter blossoms, and, just generally, much more light and life it seems. By the end of next month it'll be curtains open before 8am and not drawn to again until after 6pm. Those are the two watershed times for me: 8am and 6pm. I love it when these are returned to us and so dislike it when the darkness takes them from us.

Sunday, 31 January

As I've written in these diary entries I wanted the EU to be robust with respect to AstraZeneca and the supplies they'd committed to supplying — they'd agreed to supply the EU with 80 million doses of the vaccine by February (which would have been divided up among the EU nations according to population) — but now they say they can only provide circa 30 million doses before March. Meanwhile the Brits have given nearly 8 million people their first vaccine shot and they hope to have 15 million done by mid-Feb, and the jerk-off Brits are crowing about their achievements in this respect in the most intolerable way, wrapping the Brexiteered Union Jack around each of their nationalistic ejaculations.

At the end of last week the EU decided to ratchet things up a little so they instituted a new regime wherein vaccine producers producing Covid vaccines in EU territories had to register what they were producing with the EU and declare where the produce was destined and, if leaving the EU, they needed to get EU approval — the like of this is not that unusual and indeed the legislation under which the new regulations were issued was last used with respect to PPE early last year, i.e., no PPE to leave EU territories without EU approval. Similar emergency provisions exist on the statute books of most national territories.

However as part of this new tougher regime some senseless busybody in the warren of the Commission's offices in Brussels invoked Article 16 of the Irish Protocol to do with Brexit and the border between Northern Ireland and the Republic of Ireland, which allows for either side — the UK authorities or the authorities in the Republic or those in the EU — to institute border checks on the Northern Irish border (which of course is also an EU border now) in emergency situations, which is to say, the EU authorities authorized border-checks if need be as that border is a backdoor into and out of the EU. No consultation with London, Dublin or Belfast, nor any sort of heads-up.

Uproar. Everyone upset, Dublin and London because they were not consulted and forewarned as they ought to have been — indeed the Brexit agreement stipulates that the like can only be done by consultative ways and means — and one half of Ulster because the like means checks on the border which divides the territory of Ireland and the other half because they were told for the past 4 years that under no circumstances should there ever be border-checks on the island of Ireland except in the most dire of circumstances, which is why there is now a trade border down the Irish Sea instead, much to the chagrin of the DUP and other unionists, and yet here we are 29 days into the new post-Brexit era and with the very first EU-UK dispute the EU pulls the emergency cord, and does so with no consultation whatsoever.

Arlene Foster and her colleagues now calling for the UK government to respond in kind on account of the fact that she and people like her are having trouble getting asparagus in Waitrose — which is to say, she'd far rather have a border on the island of Ireland than have any kind of one in the Irish Sea, indeed she'd be willing to have a Trump style wall around the Six Counties than have even the lightest of light-touch regulatory misalignments between Great Britain and Northern Ireland.

Really stupid because the EU could have done what it wanted to do — which is ratchet up the ante with respect to the vaccine situation — without going anywhere near the hornet's nest that is Northern Ireland. There was going to be no fucking vaccine shipments travelling from the Republic into Northern Ireland! Have a bit of fucking common sense!

Within hours the EU Commission had to do an embarrassing U-turn, and in being forced into a U-turn with respect to the Irish situation it was also stampeded into backing down over the whole thing such that now the position is that the EU will not take any action where transports are going to fulfil valid contracts, which in effect is a humiliating back-down. Embarrassing.

It's hugely embarrassing for the Commission, so much so there's even talk of Ursula von der Leyen resigning, which I think absolutely absurd; talk about making a stony hillside into a rocky mountain range!

But it's not just about this mess this weekend it's also about the way the whole vaccine thing has been handled: the Commission taking over the purchase of these vaccines was supposed to be a demonstration of the value of being part of the EU and instead, increasingly, it appears to be a demo of the exact opposite. There were fairly serious anti-lockdown riots in the Netherlands in the past week, two nights of rioting. The health system in Portugal is in serious crisis. And there are elections just around the next time-bend in both France and Germany. Meanwhile (right now anyway) Brexit appears to have been a success for the UK, certainly the country doesn't appear to be any the worst for it that I can see.

And apparently it's the Commission president herself that's been front and centre of all this, the takeover of the purchasing of the vaccines and their distribution. Plus no doubt she has serious enemies who would love to topple her. And I imagine it is these people (UK Brexiteers included) who are flying kites about the 'fact' that von der Leyen might have to step down because of this debacle, which (as acknowledged) is indeed embarrassing. As an EU-enthusiast I'm feeling kind of red-faced myself at the minute. However, like I say, I certainly do not think she should resign, that would be to turn a stupid difficulty into a really serious crisis.

Malign English Tory ragsters having a field day with all this: 'Boris's Double Vaccine Victory Over EU' is the big bold headline in the Mail on Sunday today — and in red ink '8.4 millions vaccinated' — 'Vaccine Victory' trumpets the Sunday People, and 'Britain ready to help out EU on vaccines' condescends The Sunday Telegraph (who are only having a bit of fun of course because they have no intention of helping out the EU at all) and on and on it goes.

At the same time — another big story this weekend — the UK has formally applied to join the CPTPP (Comprehensive and Progressive Agreement for Trans-Pacific Partnership) which is what's left of the stand-up-to-the-rise-of-China trading and cooperation bloc Obama spent so much time crafting during his second term. When Trump came into office with his America First agenda he pulled out of this — he did so partly because of his America First agenda and partly because of his antipathy for all such multi-national constructs and partly because of his antipathy to all things Obama — however the other nations went ahead with a watered-down version of it. It's basically a free trade deal between all the functioning democracies of the Pacific Rim, including Australia, New Zealand, Malaysia, Japan, Vietnam, Chile, Peru, Mexico and Canada.

At first sight it seems absurd that the UK would spend so long attempting to leave one comprehensive trade block only to apply to join another, and one at the other side of the globe too, but, firstly, the CPTPP is not like the EU in that there is no 'ever closer union' in the genome of this grouping, it's just tariff-free trade — strictly business — and, secondly, there's some chance Biden will revivify the Obama-Biden administration's pivot-to-Asia agenda and rejoin, in which event the UK will effectively get it's free trade deal with the US ready-made by way of the CPTPP.

Between this and the EU's vaccine fiasco the flag-waving Brits are cock-a-hoop at the minute such that talk of helping out our benighted European neighbours by maybe giving them some loose change vaccines is just cherry-on-top fun which even anti-Brexit BBC presenters are joining in on.

It's sickening to listen to and live through.

I wanted the EU to toughen up with respect to AstraZeneca, and with respect to the UK too, but to do that they didn't need to get into the weeds about Northern Ireland. No need to go anywhere near that mad mess unless there actually was a specific need to go near it, which there isn't and wasn't.

Indeed my feeling is such that I would seek to see if there's a way to tell AZ to go fuck off with its shoddy product altogether — that we in the EU would go with the good stuff even if it meant taking twice as long to get everyone vaccinated. And if that meant stopping Pfizer shipments going to the UK then so be it.

If you're going to get tough and put the boot in then do so, don't get caught up in some tangled mess about the Northern Ireland border and then back down and retreat back into the Commission building with your tail in the mud. Now we've got the worst of all outcomes, we've got the Brits piping Rule Britannia in our fucking earholes, and factions in the EU hierarchy skelping skin and hair off one another. And — most importantly — we don't have any more vaccines and even when we do get some it's still most likely to be that shoddy Anglo-Swede manufacture which has the least effectivity of all of the vaccine products available so far.

There's even talk of Hungary doing a deal with the Russians for their Sputnik vaccine which I wouldn't inject into my fucking loo. This is Victor Orban thumbing his nose at the hierarchy in Brussels because Brussels give him a hard time about being a jumped-up racist xenophobic and homophobic wannabe strongman but if he goes ahead and does the deal with Putin it'd be difficult to justify stopping him. And of course the Russians would only love to do such a deal, Russian scientists helping out their benighted and all-at-sea European friends and neighbours, Russian know-how and benevolence. Disingenuous and unbearable turds to the right of us and to the left, meanwhile we're stuck in the middle with EU.

FEBRUARY 2021

Thursday, 11 February

Minus 20 in Aberdeenshire last night (minus 21.4 C, in fact). Nowhere near as cold further south in the UK but still a very cold night, somewhere between minus 2 and minus 10 or 12. Cold on this island too, especially up in the northeast, Ulster and the northeast of Leinster.

Been watching the trial of Donald Trump in the US Senate which began Tuesday. House managers doing an exceptionally good job in my view: Jamie Raskin of Maryland and Joe Neguse of Colorado really effective, best legal presentations I've ever seen.

The first day was all about whether or not the Senate ought to go ahead with the trial given that Trump's already gone from office, and particularly in light of the fact that the Constitution says the sanction for impeachment and conviction in a senate trial is removal from office. Trump's defence team — supported by Republicans generally — arguing the trial is not constitutional; a lot of Republican talking heads on television over the past few days urging country to turn the page, put all this unpleasantness behind us and move on, and furthermore arguing that, in fact, it's the *Democrats* who are determined to divide the country with this unnecessary and vindictive trial. The balls on these guys!

Not surprisingly — and quite correctly — Democrats say there can be no 'moving on' until the facts are established and acknowledged, not least the fact that Donald Trump lost the recent election in what was a 4-square and lawful election and then, having lost — by 7 or 8 million votes in the popular vote and by 74 votes in the Electoral College — he attempted to do his utmost to have the election result overturned, legal and illegal manoeuvres, culminating in — when he had run out of all other options — vindictively inciting a riotous mob to storm the Capitol to prevent Congress certifying the election results, the final step in the transition from one administration to another before a new president is inaugurated.

Trump himself along with his courtiers and agents — including many in Congress — still refuse to accept that Trump lost the election, and therefore implicitly regard Joe Biden as an illegitimate president. This is toxic — an abscess which needs to be lanced and drained — a massive unresolved problem at the heart of the system, one which needs to be resolved. Do you stand with Trump and his lies and illegalities or are you with the system as it has always been understood, the system you are supposed to be a steward of, the system which every office-holder has taken a solemn oath to preserve, protect and defend?

Besides the Constitution says an officer of state can be removed from office if found guilty of treason, bribery, high crimes or misdemeanours, and furthermore (by way of the provisions of the 14th Amendment) barred from ever holding an office of public trust again, so these proceeding are not just about removing someone from office, they're also about barring Trump from ever holding office in future, a means of branding him an outcast from the political nation, an untouchable vis-à-vis the government of the United States.

Moreover there are examples — legal precedents — of office-holders being impeached and convicted after they ceased to be office-holders.

The first impeachment was of a senator, William Blount, in the 1790s, who was found guilty of conspiring with the British to sell Florida and Louisiana. First the senate voted to expel him from the senate and *afterwards* (i.e., when he was no longer a senator) Congress impeached and convicted him for the purpose of preventing him from ever holding public office again. At that time most (if not all) of the authors of the constitution still alive and active in politics, therefore there can hardly be controversy about the framers' intent — i.e., the correct reading of the text of the constitution.

The case people have been talking about most, however, is the Belknap impeachment. Belknap, secretary of state for war in the 1870s, was found to be involved in a corruption system to do with War Department contracts. When Congress discovered his corruption it moved to impeach him. However, in the mistaken belief that someone who has already departed the office in question cannot be impeached, before the impeachment vote in Congress, Belknap went to the White House and submitted his resignation to the president (Ulysses Grant), thinking to vanish their fox, so to say. However, not only did the House go ahead with the vote to impeach, afterwards he stood trial in the senate. A majority in the senate voted to convict him, however not the two-thirds majority required so he was acquitted, but, the point is, the principle that office-holders can be impeached — for things they've done, or failed to do, while office-holders — even if they resign or otherwise vacate the office before they're impeached — or if their term of office comes to an end as in the present instance with Trump — is clearly well-established. As the House managers have pointed out, if t'weren't so office-holders would effectively have licence to do their damnedest and then all they need do to protect themselves is resign and scurry out the door with their booty, which would be nothing other than a charter for lawlessness and corruption.

So, not only does a straightforward reading of the impeachment provisions of the Constitution allow for these present proceedings against Trump to proceed but historical precedents support it too, which is to say, this is how these provisions have always been understood, understood by generations of custodians of the American system of government.

Moreover, as Jamie Raskin so effectively argued on Tuesday (Raskin is a former constitutional law professor), not to proceed against Trump in this circumstance would be to create a 'January Exemption' with respect to the impeachment provisions in the Constitution: conduct that would be 100% impeachable in December 2020 would become non-impeachable in January 2021 by virtue of this would-be precedent. It would be a standing invitation to any president to do anything he or she set his/ her will toward on their way out the door, knowing that by virtue of this invented 'January Exemption' they could not be impeached and put on trial once the thing had been uncovered because they'd already ceased to be in office.

Besides, Trump was impeached while still in office — impeached on a charge of inciting a riotous mob which resulted in the invasion and ransacking of the Capitol. Now of course it may be his defence team could argue that he did not *intend* that his supporters degenerate into the worst version of themselves and run riot in the halls and chambers of the Capitol, however it's clear that Trump wanted them to intimidate Congress ("You will never take our country back with weakness" he told his supporters at the Ellipse, "You have to show strength"), intimidate them enough to drive them to reject the Electoral College returns. And we know from the call to Raffensperger in Georgia his intent was to overturn the election result by any means necessary, including, if need be, by simply 'recalculating' the count in Georgia, which is to say, 'finding' 12,000 more votes for Trump: "So look", Trump said to Raffensperger, "All I want to do is this. I just want to find 11,780 votes, which is one more than we have because [you know] we won the state"; "Just say you've recalculated," Trump urged as if the like was no big deal.

In addition to which it seems Trump wanted Mike Pence as president of the senate to reject the certified results, literally read out results other than those handed to him for announcement by the clerk of the Senate, thereby causing confusion, confusion enough to make matters uncertain, and so send the issue back to the state legislatures [which Trump had already squared off onto the coup's side] who could then appoint new slates of electors for a reconvened Electoral College, despite the fact that Pence had no such power or authority, not lawfully anyhow.

And we also know that declaring martial law and having the military re-run the election was also discussed inside the White House, so there is no doubt that Trump wanted action outside the lines, which is to say, by any means necessary.

And he's also liable in terms of what he failed to do, namely call in the National Guard and other forces to protect the Capitol once he learned that the place was under riotous assault by a mob, and call on his Storm Trumpers to quit rioting, which is to say, preserve, protect and defend the Constitution as he's duty-bound to do.

Tuesday was all about these issues, i.e., the constitutionality of the proceedings. At the end of Tuesday the Senate took a vote as to whether the impeachment proceeding was in order or not. The Senate voted 56 to 44 that the proceeding was in proper order, which is to say, Constitutional and lawful.

A smart way of organising the business because several Republicans would have hoped to take cover behind the constitutionality issue when they voted to acquit, which it seems clear they will do no matter what evidence they're presented with — all 50 Dems will vote to convict, however a two-thirds majority needed for conviction, so the House Managers need to flip 17 Republicans, and it seems there's little or no chance of this happening; they might get as many as 10 or 12 but no more. The six Republicans who voted with the Dems on the procedural motion on Tuesday evening were: Mitt Romney of Utah, Lisa Murkowski of Alaska, Pat Toomey of Pennsylvania, Susan Collins of Maine, Ben Sasse of Nebraska and Bill Cassidy of Louisiana. The first 5 of these predictable but Cassidy was something of a turn up; he flipped, he said, because he was convinced by the strong presentation of the House Managers and, by contrast, the really poor presentations by Trump's defence team, which were indeed laughably poor — even people on Fox News acknowledged they were poor (Sean Hannity and Laura Ingraham, no less). One of the Trump lawyers rambled on in a folksy way for 40 minutes (talking about growing up in Pennsylvania — or wherever he was from — in the eternal sunshine and optimism of the 1960s and who'd have guessed — listeners were invited to wonder — that that awestruck little boy in Fartsville, Pennsylvania, would end up pleading a case before the US Senate? it was so poor it was both funny and excruciatingly embarrassing) and the other fellow was a mad angry little Trumpist who argued that all of this chaos and international humiliation ought to be blamed on the Democrats, that the Democrats simply wanted to disenfranchise the 74 million citizens who voted for Trump, egregiously side-stepping the fact that the reason we're here is that Trump literally sought to discount the votes of the even more millions of people — the 80-something million who voted for Joe Biden!!

By organising the business this way the constitutionality of the issue is now settled: these proceedings are constitutional because the Senate has formally ruled they are which is akin to a judge ruling on a motion to dismiss in a court of law. Now senators have to vote on the merits of the facts of the matter relating to whether or not Trump incited that riotous mob on January 6th.

As I say, the vast majority of Republicans will still vote to acquit, no matter what evidence is presented, but let them do so. Get them on the record as so doing, record their names in scrolls of stone.

The case being presented by the House managers is overwhelming; not one of the 8 members of the House team prosecuting this case has been poor, quite the contrary, all have been really good. I've mentioned Raskin and Neguse but let me also mention Madeleine Dean of Pennsylvania, who I found compelling too, Ted Lieu of California, Delegate Stacey Plaskett of the Virgin Islands, Joaquin Castro of Texas, Eric Swalwell of California and David Cicilline of Rhode Island, every one of them an 8 or 9 out of 10 in my opinion (with Raskin and Neguse 9 or 10 out of 10). And here I speak of the content of their presentations but also the delivery, remarkable in my opinion, some of the best public speaking presentations I've ever seen.

And then, in addition, the way they've organised the business: no one speaks for too long: all the presentations are about 30 or 40 minutes at most. In the impeachment last year — the Ukraine impeachment — it seemed to be all Adam Schiff and if you didn't like the self-satisfied Schiff style then tough because that's really all I remember from that impeachment, the rather self-righteous Adam Schiff (I know other House managers spoke too, however, even though I watched that trial I couldn't name any of them now, and I don't believed I mentioned any of them in these diaries at the time, whereas this present proceeding is very clearly a *team* effort, and all the better for it).

However, it ought to be acknowledged, this insurrection charge is a much more straightforward case to make, something we were all witnesses to. Indeed the mosaic of evidence fits together convincingly to such an extent I wonder whether, even if the Senate votes to acquit, the local DA might bring a criminal case on the exact same charge and using the very same evidence: incitement to riot. The evidence is compelling: the incitement wasn't just the speech Trump gave at the Ellipse on the morning of January 6th, he cultured and nurtured and fomented that mob for months, and the House managers have done a really good job at putting together all the pieces (enough of them anyhow) to make a mosaic-like portrait of events which certainly corresponds to what I witnessed, and, as these diaries testify, I was paying attention.

As I've said, it's considered unlikely the House managers will get a conviction (a two-thirds majority of the senators) but I predict they'll pick up one or two or three more flips from across the aisle. I find it impossible to believe that so many could attend to the presentations being made and not have at least a couple of them say 'Look, I'm a supporter of the former president, I voted for the former president (twice), and I felt that this trial ought not to have gone ahead, however the Senate ruled that it could do, so, on the merits of the facts presented, in good conscience I feel I have no choice but to vote for conviction here because Mr Trump and his people clearly *did* incite that mob' and take the political hit back home.

Moreover all the rioters that've been identified, investigated and arrested since January 6th say they were inspired/motivated to do what they did by President Trump, indeed they believed themselves 'deputized' by the president (i.e., authorized). It's simply not worth it — being a senator or any sort of representative — if you have to contort yourself so much in the face of clear and obvious four-square facts if that's the only way you can continue to be a senator or representative. Do something else with your life for goodness sake and preserve your good conscience; no stipend or celebrity is worth the loss of good conscience. As the line in *A Man for All Seasons* goes: 'What does it profit a man if he gain the whole world but lose his soul? But for *Wales*, Master Rich!' Or in this instance, not even Wales, just for Capitol parking privileges.

According to reports quite a few senators ostentatiously *not* paying attention to proceedings: Rand Paul of Kentucky doodling doodles on a sheet of paper — no cameras allowed in the chamber (other than the official Senate television pictures which do not offer audience shots) but there are reporters up in the gallery — Josh Hawley not even at his desk in the senate well, he's up in one of the galleries, feet up, reading, apparently catching up on paperwork, Ted Cruz focused on his iPad and so on. However, there's only about 12 or 15 of these Trump Ultras (they're not even Trumpers anyway, they just want to run for the GOP nomination in 24 and they want the support of Trump's white hot base), there's a middle block between Mitt Romney & the moderates and Cruz & Hawley & the Sedition Caucus, 20 or so who (according to reports) if it were a secret ballot would vote to convict, at least half of this middling group would do so anyhow, so I believe it's not impossible to fish a few flippers out of this pool of shivering spineless cowards. (Also bear in mind its two-thirds *of the senators present* for conviction, not 67 as an absolute number. So, for example, if only 90 senators show up that final day then only 60 votes needed for a conviction.)

Nevertheless, I'm not expecting anything other than a brazen acquittal — like I say, the GOP do brazen more brazenly than any group I've ever seen. However I'll make this prediction: an acquittal of Trump in this so-called 'trial' — despite the overwhelming evidence of his wrong-doing and guilt — will only serve to make criminal proceedings against him (for what happened on January 6th and everything that led up to the events of that day) more likely. There's a fair-to-middling chance that if he was convicted in this senate trial and barred from holding government office ever again that would be the end of it, but, if they acquit him now, 50 or 60% of the country will feel that justice has not been served (quite the contrary) and pressure from below will force the hand of the authorities to act, even if they'd prefer to turn the page and move forward with Biden's agenda. But my sense of it is that the country will not be willing to move on from this without some measure of genuine accountability first.

The House managers know the Senate will acquit, so my guess is that this whole thing is really aimed at the public at home on their sofas and has been from the get-go — the immediate aim being the midterms. About 40 or 45% of the country are hardrcore Trumpers — Trumpers, Super-Trumpers and/or Storm Trumpers — and will stay with him to the end — not even if it emerges that Trump wholly betrayed the country to some foreign entity, not even if it emerges that Trump pimped Ivanka to Valdimir Putin in a Helsinki hotel room, or Eric to Mohammed bin Salman in Saudi Arabia — but that still leaves 55 to 60% of people who can be reasoned with. It is no accident, I believe, that with these House managers — aside from being first class at what they're doing — we have white and non-white, men and women, people of Hispanic and Asian origin, Christian, Jew and non-believer… basically a reflection of what America looks like today, whereas, so far at least, for the Trump side all we've seen is middle-aged, mediocre white men spouting either lies, nonsense or/and angry ejaculations.

And Biden is rolling out a 2 Trillion dollar America Rescue package and he'll surely get most Americans vaccinated before next winter — everyone who wants to be vaccinated at least — and after that America will be on the run-in to the midterms.

Republicans are hoping to do to Biden in '22 what they did to Obama in 2010 — pinch-bar Congress away from the party that has the White House and afterwards block and frustrate everything the administration seeks to do such that Biden can govern only by means of executive orders, which of course can be reversed by the next president — so the Dems wholly focused on ensuring this scenario doesn't replay. And I believe if the House managers do what they're doing right they'll fix Trump's legacy once and for all as the 'Inciter-in-chief', as Jamie Raskin dubbed him yesterday, and as a mobster and racketeering grotesque in the minds of over 50% of the country, and if the Biden administration does the stuff it plans to do, then I believe the Dems will be good for '22, and for '24 too.

Biden and all his WH people staying completely aloof from what's happening in Congress this week. Press secretary Jen Psaki holding briefings in the briefing room every day and Biden is doing presidenty things in the White House, staying focused on the needs of the American people as the Team Biden spin has it — it's as though Capitol Hill and 1600 Pennsylvania Ave are in two different political domains — which is good for the Biden admin (Biden's approval numbers are good, in the middle to high 50s, a 16 and 17 point gap between approval and disapproval numbers, whereas Trump never once got above 50%, not even at the time of his election and inauguration, the only president never to have done so since polling began; and indeed in some polls Biden is up at 60% approval, and even higher than that, 62% approval rating in one poll, but here I'm using the poll of polls numbers).

Moreover, I believe there will be a godalmighty civil war in the Republican Party going forward — it's ongoing already, it's been ongoing for 10 or 12 years now — which is really going to cost it in terms of elections results — we've seen this already, in Georgia just recently in the run-off elections, for example, and in the Doug Jones election in Alabama a while back, and also in Arizona where the GOP internal civil war has clearly cost the party, but I believe it'll get much worse going forward. The war in the GOP will cost it at the polls, either because they select totally loony characters like the Q-Anon advocate Marjorie Taylor Greene or the glock-toting Lauren Boebert from Colorado, or because the GOP vote will be split with pro-Trump and anti-Trumpers standing, or because the moderates leave the party altogether and form an American Conservative Party, which is what I think they ought to do. I think it would be successful ultimately, even though it would probably take quite some time to work through the cycles, the Conservative Party getting only about 15 to 20% of the former GOP vote at first but they could grow that, whereas the Trump Party vote would probably start off with 80% of the former GOP vote but that's an aggregation that'll only decline afterwards, 80 or 85% will be its high-line (30 or 35% of the general electorate).

Meanwhile the Dems will be in power (at the federal level anyhow) for a generation at least. And rightly so too, not because they are wholly correct about everything (goodness knows they aren't!) but because Republicans have shown themselves to be wholly unfit to hold power. They need to clean house and get themselves correct before they're fit to hold office again: Steve Bannon, Paul Manafort, Jared Kushner, Ivanka Trump, Roger Stone, Steven Miller, Jason Miller, Rick Perry, Ben Carson... you cannot be fucking serious! Incite a fucking riot like Tump did last month and you find him not guilty in spite of the presentations we've seen this week? No, up with this we cannot put. Enough already. Go fuck off with yourselves, the lot of you.

Saturday, 13 February

This just in — 21:50 Irish time (16:50 Washington time) — the following taken from the BBC News live text coverage of events in Washington:

> The Senate voted to acquit Trump 57-43, seven Republicans (Sasse, Romney, Burr, Collins, Murkowski, Toomey and Cassidy) joining Democrats on the charge of incitement.

Trump has once again avoided conviction by the US Senate because his fellow Republicans, by and large, stuck by him.

That, at its most basic level, is a win for the ex-president. He is still eligible to run for president again in 2024, if he so chooses.

Trump does not emerge from this impeachment trial unscathed, however.

One of the most memorable portions of the prosecution case by House managers were the new videos of Trump's supporters, wearing Make America Great Again hats and waving Trump flags, ransacking the Capitol.

Those images will forever be associated with the Trump brand. Every rally he holds from here on will evoke memories of that riot.

It may not cost him among the Republican rank and file, but independent voters – and moderates – are unlikely to forget.

Trump's office released a statement just moments after his acquittal (again reporting from the BBC News website, live coverage).

"This has been yet another phase of the greatest witch hunt in the history of our country," it reads at one point.

No mention of the January 6th riot, rather it reiterates the defence team's line that it is the Democrats that are the party supporting rioters and mobs.

"It is a sad commentary on our times that one political party in America is given a free pass to denigrate the rule of law, defame law enforcement, cheer mobs, excuse rioters..."

Trump's statement concludes with a look to the future and a promise to his supporters.

"Our historic, patriotic and beautiful movement to Make America Great Again has only just begun. In the months ahead I have much to share with you, and I look forward to continuing our incredible journey together to achieve American greatness for all of our people."

We were expecting four or five Republican senators to side with Democrats at the end of this trial, and we ended up with seven.

Senator Richard Burr of North Carolina the unexpected addition to the list. Senator Bill Cassidy of Louisiana and Senator Pat Toomey of Pennsylvania slightly less of a surprise as they voted to advance the trial in a procedural vote on Tuesday.

Burr, who is retiring, said in a statement after the vote that he believed it was unconstitutional to impeach a president who was no longer in office, but once the Senate set the precedent that it was within the law, he listened to the facts as an impartial juror.

"The facts are clear," he said. "As I said on January 6th, the president bears responsibility for these tragic events. The evidence is compelling that President Trump is guilty of inciting an insurrection against a co-equal branch of government."

Burr concludes that he did not make the decision lightly, but Trump "violated his oath of office to preserve, protect and defend the Constitution".

As for Cassidy, he kept his statement to the point: "Our Constitution and our country is more important than any one person. I voted to convict President Trump because he is guilty."

Senator Toomey has not issued a statement yet.

Republican Minority Leader Senator Mitch McConnell is delivering remarks now.

Once a Trump ally, McConnell bluntly criticises him for promoting unsubstantiated theories about election fraud, and then for not doing his job "as the chaos unfolded" on 6 January.

"With police officers bleeding and broken glass covering Capitol floors, he kept repeating election lies and praising the criminals," McConnell says.

The veteran Republican adds that Trump supporters who use the millions of votes Trump received in the election as a shield against any criticism, a deflection, is "absurd", because "74 million Americans did not invade the Capitol. Hundreds of rioters did".

After his uncommon attack on a fellow Republican, McConnell gets into why he did not, then, vote to convict.

He says impeachment is a "narrow tool for a narrow purpose".

"If President Trump were still in office I would have carefully considered whether the House managers proved their specific charge."

But McConnell says his understanding of the Constitution is that only the president, vice-president and civil officers can be convicted: "We have no power to convict and disqualify a former office-holder who is now a private citizen".

"If removal [from current office] becomes impossible," he continues, "conviction becomes insensible."

McConnell continues his criticism of the former president: "Trump is still liable for everything he did while in office.

"He didn't get away with anything he did, yet. Yet. We have a criminal justice system in this country.

"We have civil litigation. And former presidents are not immune from being accountable by either one."

Even already the Republican senators who voted to convict are facing backlash from within their party.

The former president's son, Donald Trump Jr posted on Twitter suggesting that there will be an impeachment for the "RINOS" – Republicans in name only – an insult frequently favoured by his father.

Seven Republican Senators crossed party lines and voted to convict. So what awaits them now?

For two of them, the political consequences won't matter very much. Pat Toomey of Pennsylvania and Richard Burr of North Carolina are both retiring.

Three others – Susan Collins, Ben Sasse and Bill Cassidy – were just elected in November and so will have six more years to win back any voters angered by their decision today.

Mitt Romney has less time – he is up for election again in 2024. But as a moderate and long-time critic of Trump, he's never been a favourite of his party's more right-wing voters, and is popular in his home state of Utah.

Lisa Murkowski of Alaska has even less time – she'll face voters again in 2022. But much like Romney, she has long endeared herself to voters there with her moderate approach, and the open primary system in Alaska makes her a strong candidate.

However, for now it's Mitch McConnell's statement that's most intriguing to my mind — after all Trump's acquittal in this 'trial' is an outcome long foretold — containing as it does a finger-pointing direction to go after Trump in the law courts — because justice has not been served, not yet, he says. McConnell does not camouflage the fact that he believes Trump to be guilty of inciting a riot and launching an assault on a co-equal branch of government in an unlawful attempt to overturn an election — attempting to frustrate the will of a clear majority of the people — and, thereby, hold onto power — as the prosecutors said in their presentations, precisely 'the Founders' nightmare' — which is to say, an attempted coup d'état. It is extraordinary how forthright McConnell is in his statement, a statement made on the floor of the Senate right after Senate Leader Schumer's statement which directly followed the reading out of the 'Not Guilty' verdict.

McConnell's position is completely untenable, it seems to me. He says Trump is clearly guilty, and that justice has not been served — not as yet anyhow — however he says he voted to acquit because Trump has already left office and the purpose of impeachment is solely to remove an office-holder from office. First of all, this is contrary to precedents of the Belknap impeachment in the 1870s, for instance, and the first ever impeachment in the US, that of Senator Blount in the 1790s, for another, both of whom were impeached and put on trial in the senate *after* they resigned from office or, in the case of Blount, after he'd been expelled from the senate. But *Trump was impeached while he was still in office* — impeached for what he did and what he failed to do as president; the only reason the trial didn't take place while he was still in office is that the senate was in recess and McConnell — then Senate Leader — flatly refused to recall the upper chamber until the day before the inauguration of the new president! Which is to say, McConnell himself shielded the guilty party until he'd left Washington and now he's saying Trump cannot be found guilty (even though guilty he is) because he's left Washington! Preposterous! Untenable.

Trying to be too clever by half. And my guess is that this redoubt isn't going to hold at all; it's not going to satisfy any side (Trump, non-Trump or anti-Trump), indeed it will antagonise (if not infuriate) all camps outside his own office and leadership group. Nevertheless it's a striking speech, I think, for lots of reasons, well worth viewing (here is link to a YouTube video of it): https://youtu.be/7oTgnwVDQ7I.

And it's a striking contribution not least because while only 7 Republicans voted to convict, in effect I think we can add McConnell to that grouping too because the implication is clear that if this very same trial took place before 20 January McConnell would have voted to convict, so it would have been 8 Republican senators at least. This is already the most bipartisan condemnation of a president ever in an impeachment proceeding, far exceeding the previous record which was one lone voice, that of Mitt Romney in the impeachment of Trump a year ago, the Ukraine phone call impeachment — up until then in all previous presidential impeachments (which is to say, that of Johnson in the 1860s and Clinton in the 1990s) everything went strictly along party lines in every vote, even procedural votes. And, I feel fairly sure in suggesting, there must be two or three others who feel the same way as McConnell says he does. Might even be twice that, which makes for 62 or 63 or 64 votes to convict. Still not enough for an impeachment conviction, to be sure, but, in fact, if Leader McConnell went through the gap I believe at least half a dozen sheep would have followed, and maybe as many as 8 or 10. Moreover, my guess is that there are probably about 85 or 90 senators who actually believe that Trump is guilty as charged, it's just they simply wouldn't give the Dems the satisfaction of condemning their former standard-bearer — they wouldn't do so even if a recording emerged in which Trump was recorded saying "Hey guys, here's an idea: let's start a fucking riot! Scare the bejasus out of 'em!" (they'd say the recording was a forgery, a 'Fake News forgery') — not least because, if they did do so (if they did find Trump guilty), they would thereby be pinning a target on themselves because Trump did not act alone, he was not on his tod over the course of the past 3 or 4 months, nor over the course of the past 3 or 4 years — so better get your game face on, circle the waggons, and tough it out like Gary Cooper and Charlton Heston would do.

And, just for the record, here is the text of the statement Trump and his team put out just after the acquittal was announced, which cannot read well to any Republican hoping to reclaim the party in the post-Trump era — be they establishment Republicans and moderates, or even folks such as Ted Cruz, Josh Hawley, Tom Cotton and Rick Scott, all of whom have their eyes on the White House prize; sure looks like Donald Trump is not planning on leaving the arena any time soon.

> I want to first thank my team of dedicated lawyers and others for their tireless work upholding justice and defending truth.
>
> My deepest thanks as well to all of the United States Senators and Members of Congress who stood proudly for the Constitution we all revere and for the sacred legal principles at the heart of our country.
>
> Our cherished Constitutional Republic was founded on the impartial rule of law, the indispensable safeguard for our liberties, our rights and our freedoms.
>
> It is a sad commentary on our times that one political party in America is given a free pass to denigrate the rule of law, defame law enforcement, cheer mobs, excuse rioters, and transform justice into a tool of political vengeance, and persecute, blacklist, cancel and suppress all people and viewpoints with whom or which they disagree. I always have, and always will, be a champion for the unwavering rule of law, the heroes of law enforcement, and the right of Americans to peacefully and honorably debate the issues of the day without malice and without hate.
>
> This has been yet another phase of the greatest witch hunt in the history of our Country. No president has ever gone through anything like it, and it continues because our opponents cannot forget the almost 75 million people, the highest number ever for a sitting president, who voted for us just a few short months ago.
>
> I also want to convey my gratitude to the millions of decent, hardworking, law-abiding, God-and-Country loving citizens who have bravely sup-

ported these important principles in these very difficult and challenging times.

Our historic, patriotic and beautiful movement to Make America Great Again has only just begun. In the months ahead I have much to share with you, and I look forward to continuing our incredible journey together to achieve American greatness for all of our people. There has never been anything like it!

We have so much work ahead of us, and soon we will emerge with a vision for a bright, radiant, and limitless American future.

Together there is nothing we cannot accomplish.

We remain one People, one family, and one glorious nation under God, and it's our responsibility to preserve this magnificent inheritance for our children and for generations of Americans to come.

May God bless all of you, and may God forever bless the United States of America.

For what it's worth I don't think Trump will run again in 2024. Aside from the fact that the Trump brand is irredeemably tarnished now — at least in terms of winning an election at the national level — but between now and 2024 he's going to get tangled up in too many legal wrangles, one or two of which could be serious. Obviously they'll seek to drag out all such proceedings as long as possible and, even if there are adverse findings, they'll instigate appeals and side-tracking manoeuvres for years and years, but my guess is they'll be enough to make Trump's candidacy effectively non-viable as a serious prospect.

Don Jr might have a go but that twerp is not the character his father is: Don Jr may be raucously popular among yeehawdists in every hickburg from Florida to Oregon, however he's not got what it takes to manage a zero-to-nomination run because, after all, what is he but 'Don Jr', a little Donald, a MinneMe, his father's son; whereas by contrast, like or loathe him the fact is his father has been a cultural icon for 40 years, not only nationally but internationally — I first started hearing of Donald Trump in the 1980s! — and spectacularly the old man has made and lost and regained again princely fortunes, enough to star in the immensely successful Apprentice show in which he played a successful big shot business guru, a ratings-topper for a decade, so much so it spawned imitations and franchise sales the world over, and, reportedly, by one means and another, netted Donald about $400 million. Plus I don't think Don Jr has got the malignant drive the old man has (the wound), he might well be a malignant little bastard but the old man is so much more than that; he is, in fairness, a fucking phenomenon, whereas Don Jr is just a pipsqueak, a little fart of a character.

Ivanka might consider having a go but while I think she would have more to her than Don Jr, my guess is she has a glass jaw. She simply wouldn't be able to take the punches like the old man can. That said, the talk about Ivanka is that she'll first attempt to get elected as a senator — in Florida, presumably, where she and her husband have now moved to, pushing Little Marco out of the boat and taking his seat — which, put alongside her 4 years of WH senior advisor experience, would indeed begin to look like a much better looking résumé with 2028 or 2032 in view; even a seat in congress would do, I suppose, although she'd prefer the more rarefied air of the upper chamber I'm sure, and by then — the second half of the 2020s — she'd be a more formidable candidate. However, even at that I think she'd get caught out with an uppercut or haymaker one way or another eventually, either in the primaries or, failing that, in the general election itself. She seems fragile to me. Aside from which if the Trump Organisation is fully targeted and tarnished, that'll tarnish her shine too as ultimately she's rooted in that toxic soil, aside from having been a senior advisor in an administration that put babies in baby-jails at the southern border and launched a riotous assault on a co-equal branch of government, I mean. Her financials wouldn't bear too much stern scrutiny, I bet.

Also what I get from the Trump statement above is that in order to stay relevant the Trumps will need to stay on the attack non-stop going forward, and eventually this might be their undoing: they'll either punch themselves out such that they simply become background yapping or else the logic and momentum of the positions they adopt in order to make news and keep themselves relevant will inevitably lead to them launching their own party: the MAGA Party — an analogue of UKIP — or the Patriot Party — an analogue of the Brexit Party, which, in my view, amounts to the same thing as punching yourself out effectively because such a project will be seen as an anti-democratic enterprise, an authoritarian, Putinesque vehicle, which undoubtedly will harvest up to 40% of likely voters but, the point is, that's not enough to win elections. And, as the practical effect of such a venture becomes more and more evident — a generation of victories for the Democrats — the party's popularity will wane because I don't see corporate donors getting behind a madcap authoritarian party — the party of Marjorie Taylor Greene, Lauren Bobert, Jason Miller and the like — and I don't see suburban moderates funnelling their votes to it either, not if the events of January 6th are any sort of foretaste of what's to come.

No matter what way things go it'll be bad for the Republican Party, I feel sure. From where things are right now, I cannot see how they are not facing into a generation in the political wilderness — a decade or so at least. They've earned it.

Monday, 15 February

Interesting, I think, that the 57-43 vote to acquit Trump in the Senate exactly reflects where the country is: between 56 and 58% of people think Trump is guilty of inciting the rioters on January 6th and he ought to have been convicted for it and between 42 and 44% of people hold that Trump did nothing wrong at all, in fact he was upholding and defending the Constitution.

The original idea for the Senate was not that it reflect the partisan divides in the nation — that's what the House of Representatives is for — it was supposed to be a higher tribunal, a council of the wise and the learned — above party politics, the Platonic Guardians, the guardians of the system, something on a par with the Supreme Court. Indeed when the Constitution was composed there were no political parties, although the framers were aware that party formations and factionalism were possibilities, however it was presumed that even if parties were to develop the Senate would remain above party politics. And for a surprising amount of time the Senate was quite like this, even unto within living memory, but in the last 20 or 30 years the Senate has devolved into just another partisan arena. Indeed, the situation appertaining now is not co-equal branches of government as was intended by the Founding Fathers but warring factions that have politicized the White House, Congress and even the Supreme Court to such an extent it's utterly banjaxed the whole complex clockwork. Extreme factionalism is a cancer in the system and it's spread to almost all the key organs.

Mitt Romney is an ideal senator, in my view, and there may be a dozen more like him (Joe Biden was another of this type), but in the main the present-day Senate is packed with partisan hacks — some of whom (far from being learned or wise) defiantly abhor book-reading and other forms of highbrow culture and have all the signs of so doing — and quite a few of them see the Senate as nothing other than a springboard for a White House bid.

Wednesday, 17 February

At the weekend, after the impeachment acquittal verdict was announced in Washington, I wrote that in order to stay relevant Trump and his people will need to go on the attack almost non-stop (they cannot legislate, they cannot issue executive orders, they have no policies — 'America First' is not a policy, nor is 'Make America Great Again,' these things simply mean whatever Trump says they mean at any moment in time, and he might well say different things at different times, one being inconsistent with the other, and it wouldn't matter because, as I say, there's no policy foundation there to begin with), so all they've got is the cult of this malign personality, attack, intimidation and menace.

Yesterday Trump launched a full-on assault on Mitch McConnell in response to the statement McConnell made in the Senate following Trump's acquittal, a clear attempt to incite moves to unseat McConnell as GOP leader in the Senate. This is not in the least surprising, of course, it was a matter of when the counterpunch came, not if; McConnell must have known this or something like it would be Trump's response even as he drafted his remarks.

Statement by Donald J. Trump
45th President of the United States of America

The Republican Party can never again be respected or strong with political "leaders" like Sen. Mitch McConnell at its helm. McConnell's dedication to business as usual, status quo policies, together with his lack of political insight, wisdom, skill, and personality, has rapidly driven him from Majority Leader to Minority Leader, and it will only get worse. The Democrats and Chuck Schumer play McConnell like a fiddle — they've never had it so good — and they want to keep it that way! We know our America First agenda is a winner, not McConnell's Beltway First agenda or Biden's America Last.

In 2020, I received the most votes of any sitting President in history, almost 75,000,000. Every incumbent House Republican won for the first time in decades, and we flipped 15 seats, almost costing Nancy Pelosi her job. Republicans won majorities in at least 59 of the 98 partisan legislative chambers, and the Democrats failed to flip a single legislative chamber from red to blue. And in "Mitch's Senate," over the last two election cycles, I single-handedly saved at least 12 Senate seats, more than eight in the 2020 cycle alone — and then came the Georgia disaster, where we should have won both U.S. Senate seats, but McConnell matched the Democrat offer of $2,000 stimulus checks with $600. How does that work? It became the Democrats' principal advertisement, and a big winner for them it was. McConnell then put himself, one of the most unpopular politicians in the United States, into the advertisements. Many Republicans in Georgia voted Democrat, or just didn't vote, because of their anguish at their inept Governor, Brian Kemp, Secretary of State Brad Raffensperger, and the Republican Party, for not doing its job on Election Integrity during the 2020 Presidential race.

It was a complete election disaster in Georgia, and certain other swing states. McConnell did nothing, and will never do what needs to be done in order to secure a fair and just electoral system into the future. He doesn't have what it takes, never did, and never will.

My only regret is that McConnell "begged" for my strong support and endorsement before [going before] the great people of Kentucky in the 2020 election, and I gave it to him. He went from one point down to 20 points up, and won. How quickly he forgets. Without my endorsement,

McConnell would have lost, and lost badly. Now, his numbers are lower than ever before, he is destroying the Republican side of the Senate, and in so doing, seriously hurting our Country.

Likewise, McConnell has no credibility on China because of his family's substantial Chinese business holdings. He does nothing on this tremendous economic and military threat.

Mitch is a dour, sullen, and unsmiling political hack, and if Republican Senators are going to stay with him, they will not win again. He will never do what needs to be done, or what is right for our Country. Where necessary and appropriate, I will back primary rivals who espouse Making America Great Again and our policy of America First. We want brilliant, strong, thoughtful, and compassionate leadership.

Prior to the pandemic, we produced the greatest economy and jobs numbers in the history of our Country, and likewise, our economic recovery after Covid was the best in the world. We cut taxes and regulations, rebuilt our military, took care of our Vets, became energy independent, built the wall and stopped the massive inflow of illegals into our Country, and so much more. And now, illegals are pouring in, pipelines are being stopped, taxes will be going up, and we will no longer be energy independent.

This is a big moment for our country, and we cannot let it pass by using third rate "leaders" to dictate our future!

The Republican Party is now openly and formally at war with itself. 'Where necessary and appropriate, I will back primary rivals who espouse Making America Great Again and our policy of America First.' As noted previously, they've been at war for some time already but now it's fully out in the open.

All 7 Republican senators who voted to convict Trump in the senate trial have now been censured by their state and local parties. We may even see recall attempts because the fury of the folks back home is not to be underestimated. One local party chairman (I cannot remember whether it was a guy from Utah or Pennsylvania, but it matters not because I suspect he spoke for all or most of em, from Maine to Alaska back down to Louisiana) did a television interview over the weekend in which he ended up saying "We sent Toomey [or whoever it was] to Washington to represent us; we did not send him to 'vote his conscience' or 'do the right thing' or whatever it is he thought he was doing with that vote", i.e., they sent their senator to Washington to support the Dear Leader no matter what, even if it's inciting a riotous mob to invade and ransack the Capitol to prevent them fulfilling their lawful duty by certifying the election results!

Aside from holding a scattering of those grotesque super-spreader MAGA rallies, now the only way Trump can stay on the scene like a sex machine is to demonstrate his destructive power by toppling Mitch McConnell and, similarly, going after anyone else who dares to defy or speak out against him — just as he previously drove Jeff Flake from the field, and Jeff Sessions and Paul Ryan and quite a few others; he really does have immense power within the party, and he's not in the slightest bit shy about using it like a thorny stick. As the statement above indicates, he's also got Brian Kemp, the governor of Georgia, in his sights because Kemp stood by Raffensperger and other election officials who refused to put their thumb on the election scales for Trump down in the Peach State.

Romney will certainly have someone up against him when he's next up for reelection and the same will happen to any other renegade up for a reelect in '22 or '24 — indeed it wouldn't be a surprise to see Sarah Palin put herself forward as the Trump candidate in opposition to Murkowski in Alaska. I feel sure Palin would love to have herself some of this here action.

Liz Cheney will certainly have a Trumper standing against her in Wyoming and so too will the other House members who voted for impeachment.

And now there's talk that Lara Trump, Eric Trump's wife, is in the running for selection to replace Richard Burr in North Carolina when he retires next year. And, as I've written before it may be that Ivanka will look to oust Marco Rubio down in Florida (where she's now taken up residence) because while Rubio has made shameful attempts to stay onside, the Trumps know only too well that Rubio is no friend of theirs.

A final word on this for now: aside from the threat to stand Trump candidates against the enemies of Trump and Trumpism, what I'm struck by in Trump's statement is how badly written it is: 'play McConnell like a fiddle', 'a dour, sullen, and unsmiling political hack' and so on. It sounds like the kind of stuff you'd see in a student newspaper in a vicious Student Union campaign, not something out of 'The Office of the 45th President of the United States', I mean it's trailer trash talk dolled-up as an official statement from some bloke who once held some highfalutin position.

Ireland's Covid-19 death toll has surpassed 4,000, following confirmation of a further 57 deaths from the Department of Health. Also today an additional 650 cases of infection reported.

The total number of deaths now 4,036, while the cumulative total of cases since the pandemic began is at 211,751.

Currently 831 patients in hospitals with the virus, 154 in intensive care.

A further 6 people have died of Covid-related issues in Northern Ireland and a further 297 people have tested positive for the virus. 434 people hospitalized with the disease in the North right now, 53 in intensive care, 45 of whom are on ventilators.

Therefore, altogether, 321,536 confirmed cases of infection on the island of Ireland and, to date, 6,051 Covid-related deaths (although over 6,750 deaths in reality because Northern Ireland has a restricted way of counting what is and is not a Covid-related death — which is to say, death from covid-related issues within 28 days of testing positive for the virus, otherwise it is not counted as a Covid death in the Department for Health count).

Latest figures show a total of 271,942 vaccine doses have been administered in the Republic so far, 180,192 first doses and 91,750 seconds.

Northern Ireland has administered 447,685 coronavirus vaccines, 418,209 first doses and 29,476 seconds.

Saturday, 20 February

Forgot to record that this day last week I met Betty Chapple in the church grounds and she told me that Pat Hughes intends packing it in with the Ilen River Playschool at the end of this school year (end of June) and relocating to Australia where her two sons are (Pat and the husband split-up at Christmas). Pat gets her OAP this year apparently and she's put the house on the market, which, in fairness, in terms of the small world of Abbeystrewry, is a fairly big piece of news for she's been a staple here since the 1990s.

Apparently top level pandemic restrictions to stay in place until Easter at least — Easter's at the beginning of April this year — and maybe all the way into May too. Not just in this country but in neighbouring countries also. Authorities got so badly burned with the opening up they did at Christmastime followed by the almost impossible-to-manage spikes in January they do not want to take any risk of repeating the experience. In addition to which these new variants are so much more transmissible compared to what we were dealing with (or what we believed we were dealing with) for most of 2020 — nowadays 92% of new cases in Ireland are that UK variant apparently. If it was just the original strain we could probably be opening up again in April but not with this UK (B117) variant. They will want to get at least a third (or maybe as much as a half) of the population vaccinated before they start opening up again. At the rate they're going they'll be lucky to get everyone done before the end of the summer. And then, presumably, they'll need to start all over again with an updated version of the vaccines — edited to deal with new variants. And then, presumably, it'll be like that each year afterwards for a few years anyhow and maybe forever for vulnerable groups.

People with underlying health conditions are set to be moved up the vaccination priority list under a plan being worked on by Government this weekend.

More than 370,000 people aged between 18 and 64 were ranked at number seven in the initial vaccination allocation list announced late last year.

However, there is a view in Government that this needs to change given that thousands of people in this group have not left their homes in almost a year amid fears that they could get the virus.

Minister for Health, Stephen Donnelly, has now received updated advice on the matter from the National Immunisation Advisory Committee. A memo is now being drafted and is likely to go to a meeting of Cabinet on Tuesday.

While work on the revised list is still ongoing there are indications that those with health issues could be listed as the next priority group after the over 70s have been vaccinated.

These health conditions include diabetes, cancer, and heart, kidney, neurological and respiratory diseases.

Tuesday, 23 February

One thing I ought to have noted is the fact that yesterday the US passed the half a million mark in relation to coronavirus deaths (500,071), along with just over 28 million lab-confirmed cases of infection, and possibly as many more again undetected. (It was just over 400,000 deaths a month ago when Joe Biden was sworn into office, 420,000, something like that, so nearly 100,000 deaths in one month! Three and four thousand a day dying by the time Trump left office, that is, to be clear, between three and four thousand people dying each and every day! *Over* 4,000 several days.) People modelling these things say that although all the indicator numbers are beginning to fall now we can still expect another 100,000 to die before the end of June, by which time they expect deaths to be down at (or below) 500 a day.

That said, although the top level numbers look really bad for the US, it's interesting to note that as far as deaths per 100,000 of population go the US is not the worst country at all — still quite bad but not the worst — it's 9th in that undesirable listing, behind the UK and Italy for instance — the UK on 182 per 100k pop, Italy 158 and the US 152.

Still, half a million deaths is a shocker, worse than any war the US has been involved in aside from the US Civil War, but, once it gets up to 600,000, it'll be up in that territory too.

Here, and especially in the UK, all the talk is of opening up again. Yesterday Boris Johnson outlined a 4-step roadmap to full unlockdown which (all going well) they hope to achieve by June. Schools and colleges reopening next month — 8 March — also, at the end of the month (next month), outdoor sporting facilities; from early April all shops will reopen along with close contact services such as hairdressing, beautiques and the like — pubs and restaurants too as long as they can serve people outdoors — and then, assuming all going well, May will see indoor serving for pubs and restaurants as well as music and sporting venues reopening, only to half-capacity to begin with, which is to say, social distancing protocols will still apply, also hotels and all other leisure and heritage facilities, and then, finally, on mid-summer's day all remaining legal restrictions to be removed. That's the plan anyhow. Obviously things subject to revision if the numbers spike upwards again, however with the rate at which the vaccine rollout is going in Britain that's less likely than with previous unlockdowns.

Meanwhile here at home — nudged forward by the cascade of British PR, I believe — all of a sudden they're talking about reopening schools next week, i.e., the beginning of March. Only for Leaving Cert students in secondary schools to begin with, and for junior and senior infants in primary schools. The pace of reopening here cannot be as fast as in the UK because while they [in the UK] have very nearly 20 million vaccine doses administered, nearly a third of its population, we have only about 300,000 administered, about 5% of the population. At the rate we're going we're not going to have a third of the population done until about May or June. (I'm presuming that in the UK they'll be within striking distance of having half the population done by April — with one dose at least: they're administering about half a million doses a day at the minute so they ought to have another 15 million vaccinated by the end of March, which'll mean well over 30 million people vaccinated to some extent even if not fully vaccinated.)

In any event all the noise now is about the end of the coronavirus campaign. At the beginning of this month it felt like they were conditioning us to be prepared for the for the long haul, how all of this — the present full-on lockdown — would go on past Easter and into May at the very least, now the messaging has changed. It feels Orwellian. Today again — and it's been like this so many days already — every front page of every national newspaper has a picture of Boris on the front of it. I've never seen a prime minister dominate the front pages of newspapers so much as he has in the past 12/18 months. I find it horrifying; I'm so sick of his piggy face and the surrounding boosterish stories — we've even had *front page* stories about his fucking dog! I'm sure everyone involved in this PR drive believe they're doing a wonderful job but it's having an opposite effect on me, although, of course, I'm not a voter, obviously, nevertheless it's alienating me, and I feel sure it must be doing so for many in the UK too because I'm sure there are many in the UK like me in terms of outlook/worldview.

Sunday, 28 February

Beautiful spring day today. No rain in the forecast at all, all the way to next weekend. Cold in the nights, somewhere between minus 2 and plus 2, mostly towards the upper end of that range (around here anyhow), and then daytime highs somewhere between 8 and 12. Today, for example, it actually felt a little colder than 8 to 12 because there was an easterly wind — not too strong, somewhere between 10 and 20 mph — but it made for wonderful conditions for pottering about in the garden, for example — cut the lawn (my own little lawn) and strimmed the mossy meadow bank. I'm just acknowledging what a beautiful day it's been.

	Population	Infections	Deaths	Tests/1m pop
1. USA	330,806,424	28,605,661	513,091	1,071,639
2. India	1,378,604,014	11,112,241	157,157	154,555
3. Brazil	212,405,664	10,587,001	255,720	133,925
4. Russia	145,928,315	4,257,650	86,455	754,920
5. UK	67,859,075	4,176,554	122,849	1,308,897
6. France	65,259,187	3,755,968	86,454	793,250
7. Spain	46,752,999	3,204,531	69,609	823,054
8. Italy	60,470,472	2,925,265	97,699	654,813
9. Turkey	84,244,944	2,711,479	28,638	387,827
10. Germany	83,757,235	2,447,068	70,105	523,463

11. Columbia	50,919,972	2,255,260	59,866	222,129
12. Argentina	45,244,432	2,111,972	52,077	162,000
13. Mexico	128,844,230	2,089,281	186,152	41,477
14. Poland	37,833,389	1,711,772	43,793	258,269
15. Iran	83,921,387	1,631,169	60,073	125,350
16. S. Africa	59,316,193	1,512,225	49,941	150,975
17. Ukraine	43,649,444	1,352,134	26,050	157,161
18. Indonesia	274,219,048	1,334,634	36,166	38,880
19. Peru	32,932,217	1,332,939	46,685	225,084
20. Czechia	10,715,215	1,240,051	20,469	733,915
21. Netherlands	17,146,915	1,091,056	15,565	406,205
22. Canada	37,872,563	870,033	22,017	637,666
23. Chile	19,105,644	829,770	20,660	481,601
24. Portugal	10,180,572	804,956	16,351	802,601
25. Romania	19,188,803	804,090	20,403	304,123
26. Israel	9,197,590	778,172	5,758	1,297,604
27. Belgium	11,605,601	772,875	22,111	803,882
28. Iraq	40,417,268	695,489	13,406	165,987
29. Sweden	10,132,390	666,270	12,845	583,533
30. Pakistan	220,673,722	581,365	12,896	39,670

MARCH 2021

Friday, 5 March

Latest figures from the Northern Ireland Statistics and Research Agency (NISRA) indicate that 44 Covid-19-linked deaths occurred in the week ending 26 February, so for NISRA the total coronavirus-related deaths in Northern Ireland up to 26 February is 2,816.

On 26 February the health department's deaths total was 2,054 — 762 the difference.

Meanwhile, here in the Republic, the Department of Health has been notified of another nine coronavirus-related deaths today along with 522 new cases of infection.

It brings the number of coronavirus-related deaths here to 4,405 and the total number of cases to 222,169.

The 14-day incidence rate of the virus per 100,000 population is now 185 — it was 369 four weeks ago.

426 Covid-patients in hospitals at the minute, 102 of whom are in intensive care units.

Two deaths reported in Northern Ireland today along with 166 new cases of infection.

Therefore, altogether, 335,504 confirmed cases of infection on the island of Ireland and, to date, 6,473 Covid-related deaths (although, as the above makes clear, nearly 7,250 deaths in reality because Northern Ireland has a restricted way of counting what is and is not a Covid-related death — which is to say, death from covid-related issues within 28 days of testing positive for the virus, otherwise it is not counted as a Covid-death in the Department for Health count).

513,322 doses of Covid vaccine have been administered in the Republic so far, 363,601 first doses and 149,721 seconds.

631,654 vaccine doses administered in Northern Ireland, 588,803 first doses and 42,851 seconds.

Monday, 8 March

Ilen River Playschool returned today, as indeed did junior and senior infants in primary schools and Leaving Cert students in secondary schools. These are the first steps in unlockdown #3, the third and final instalment of same, hopefully.

Although, as I'm sure I've made clear in these diaries, I've quite enjoyed these lockdowns, enjoying the peace and quiet here in Abbeystrewry particularly (also the freedom from being obliged to go anywhere or have folks calling on me), lots of people beginning to grumble because at this stage it's been a long winter. Angela in Cork going particularly lockdown-antsy, for example. I've a good few things to attend to myself, however, lockdown or no lockdown I feel I've enough of what it takes to get me to the end of April at least. I don't intend going anywhere until I'm vaccinated and at the rate they're going that may not be until May or June, so, like I said to Angela when she called to grumble the other day, hold your horses cause we may be kept in our stables a good while yet. I'm pretty sure most people will hold the line until Easter at least — Easter's the first weekend in April this year — but there will be no holding them after that, and I'm sure the government will recognise this too. Anyway, whether they do or not people are going to bolt that weekend and they'll continue to do so from then onwards, unless of course the infection numbers spike back up again, obviously.

All the data beginning to look good now: only 8 cases of infection in this electoral area in the past 14 days apparently.

> There is sustained and "perhaps even accelerated progress" in suppressing transmission of Covid-19, a briefing by the National Public Health Emergency Team has heard.

Professor Philip Nolan, chair of NPHET's Irish Epidemiological Modelling Advisory Group, made the comments after the Department of Health reported 437 new cases of Covid-19, taking the total to 223,651.

No deaths have been recorded today, meaning the toll remains at 4,422.

Over the past 10 days the reproduction number has stabilised at around 0.7 to 0.8, he said, and this is reflected in all indicators of the disease.

He said the transmission rate is reducing by 20% per week, or 3% a day, and if this continues for the next 2-3 weeks, cases should reduce by 70-100 per week.

Friday, 12 March

Things beginning to go well in the United States with respect to the coronavirus campaign: the numbers of new cases and deaths per day has more than halved compared to a month ago; yesterday was the anniversary of the day on which the virus was declared a global pandemic, and, marking that anniversary, on what was his 50th day in office, Joe Biden did a televised address to the nation. Before being inaugurated he pledged his administration would get at least 100 million vaccine shots into the arms of Americans in his first 100 days in office. They've very nearly achieved this — 95 million already, apparently, 75 million since Biden took office; 33 million people fully vaccinated.

Biden's address also came on the day he signed into law the $1.9 trillion dollar American Rescue stimulus package, legislation which does a whole clutch of things — provide money for reopening schools and running catch-up programmes, funding for vaccine distribution, extends unemployment benefits — the existing funds for which were about to run out — alleviation of child poverty provisions, and then the headline $1,400 cheque for everyone (I believe) such that in a household of 5 you're looking at a cheque for $7,000! My understanding is that it's income-capped so that you don't get a cheque if you earn over $150,000, something like that.

The Biden people believe the Obama administration didn't sell the rescue package they did for the economy during the financial meltdown a decade ago — I mean really go out there and fanfare it politically — Obama didn't want to be seen 'taking a victory lap' as he characterized it, and as a consequence they suffered in the 2010 mid-terms, taking a 'shellacking.' Biden learned the lesson and they're sure making a song and dance about what they're doing this time, and hopefully it'll work such that they'll strengthen their grip on the House and Senate in 2022, which is their initial political objective. This American Rescue package is popular, understandably, enjoying 75% support in polls (even popular with significant numbers of Republicans) and Biden's popularity is holding up well, up in the mid-50s which is less than many other presidents have enjoyed at this point but it's significantly better than anything ever achieved by Trump, yet not one Republican law-maker voted for the American Rescue Plan legislation, despite the fact that back home in their districts they'll seek to take credit for the federal bounty you may be sure; like I say, these people do brazen more brazenly than Billy Brazenhead.

Biden is not going to do that thing Trumpolini did of making sure his signature is prominent on the face of the government cheques (as though the money came from Trump's checking account) but he sure is promoting his administration's achievements as he goes along, and in fairness they're doing it in a classy way. As I say, yesterday's address to the nation was delivered on the anniversary of coronavirus/Covid being declared a global pandemic — a pandemic in which 30 million citizens have been infected and 530,000 Americans have perished, more than died in the two World Wars and the Vietnam War combined — but, as I say, it was also the day in which Biden signed the American Rescue Plan into law and, without the silk bow & fancy wrapping paper, this was the real subject of last night's address.

Altogether, combined, the relief measures by the Trump administration — Trump twice helicoptered money to Americans, a $1,200 dollar cheque early in the crisis and another $600 cheque just before the election — and the Biden administration, total at $5 Trillion. In today's money the whole of the Second World War cost the American government $4 Trillion.

In his address yesterday evening Biden spoke of having everyone in America vaccinated by July 4th, Independence Day, the national holiday, everyone who wants to be vaccinated that is because about 30% of Americans are unwilling to be vaccinated for various reasons — many of them believing that the whole coronavirus thing is a Democrat hoax — but, if he does manage to vaccinate everyone willing to be vaccinated and by way of this American Rescue Plan the economy kick-starts again — which it will do, I'm sure, indeed economists are concerned that the ARP might over-stimulate the economic eco-system — then I believe Biden and the Democrats ought to be set fair for 2022.

Meanwhile Trump and his people are at war with the Republican Party establishment. Trump's legal representatives sent out a cease-and-desist communication aimed at preventing the party from using Trump's name or image in their fundraising campaigns. Trump has his own Political Action Committee and he wants any money people want to donate because of their support for Trump and Trumpism to come to his PAC, not to PACs controlled by Mitch McConnell & Co (who Trump identifies as RINOs — Republicans in Name Only). While Trump will undoubtedly harvest most of the low-dollar donations from gun-toting rubes and backwater clownsticks, GOP-friendly corporate donors are going to stick with McConnell & Co, and at the end of the day that's where the serious action is.

Wednesday, 17 March, St Patrick's Day

Lovely summery day today again, as was yesterday — sunny and 16 or 17 degrees, I'd say, maybe even more than that: caught out unexpectedly by this flash of warmth, everyone (myself included) walking around with pullovers or jackets laid over their arms, and about 40% of people wearing sunglasses all of a sudden, all more noticeable yesterday because we were caught unawares by the lovely summeryness, whereas today (because of yesterday) people expecting it so better outfitted.

It may be that yesterday, like me, people heard/saw the forecast for warm sunny day but after a long North Atlantic winter what they heard/saw was 'blah-blah-blah…Bloody Foreland, Malin Head, Roches Point, Fiddlers Green…' — at this time of year we really only listen to forecasts to hear if there's going to be rain or frost or floods or storms — and, as happened in my case, went out as per normal only to end up perspiring after about 500 yards of walking about. I became conscious of my wardrobe malfunction going through Fields carpark on my way to Drinagh Hardware — dis-robing before hitting the 1,000 yards mark — I made it to DH but did an outfit adjustment in the shade down there before launching into the return leg. Aside from cycling round the church and going to Kalbo's once a week and the like, this — going to Drinagh Hardware — is my first outdoors adventure this year; I don't think I've been so far from the house & grounds since September!; and it was on the return leg of yesterday's pioneering trek I noticed that similarly just about everyone else had a jacket or pullover draped over their arms, and so many sporting sunglasses all of a sudden; drivers without sunglasses hunched over their steering wheels squinting through their windshields, blinded by the light of spring.

I've even seen butterflies today and yesterday; well, I've seen *one* — I'm fairly sure it's the same fellow, extraordinarily beautifully coloured (shroud brown wings with dark blue and dull red circles, one circle inside the other) which I've seen in the Old Schoolyard sunning him/herself on the gable-end wall of the PH.

Got a load of things done yesterday too, too many to mention, but scores of little things like washing and gardening and shopping and cleaning and accounts and (in addition to food prep and rounds of cycling &c) I don't know how much more but I was going from early morning to suppertime yesterday evening.

I opened the blinds and curtains in the kitchen yesterday morning as the 7 AM news was on and I closed them again this evening as I was get-ting my evening meal together which was after 6, maybe 6:30. Sunny all day, from 7 AM until at least 6 o'clock in the evening. Ditto this morning; indeed, I opened up blinds and curtains this morning at about 6:50.

Monday, 29 March

That Promoting the Union unit in Downing Street, which was set up by the PM — which is really a Conservative Party anti-SNP unit dressed up as government business — has ordered that the Union flag be flown from all government buildings all year this year, i.e., not just on national holidays and other special occasions but all year round, and the benefits of the British Union are to be relentlessly promoted going forward, especially in Scotland and Northern Ireland, not least of which, of course, is that every Briton will be fully vaccinated before July while across the channel Frau Ursula von der Leyen is still struggling to get into her complicated Hanseatic knickers and start in on the mountain of tasks that face her and the Tower of Babel union she's at the pinnacle of.

And indeed it's true to say that there's a growing sense of crisis in the EU with respect to this whole mess of the European Commission's vaccine procurement policy — undertaken to prevent EU states from competing with one another — and the resulting vaccine rollout (or lack thereof to be more precise), which the administrations in the individual states are (unfairly) taking the hit for, Merkel's CDU tanking in the polls at the minute, for instance, and Macron beginning to look like he'll do really well to get himself re-elected next year — the smiley mannequin was already struggling to stay above water before this pandemic! If he fails to do so we may be looking at a President Marine le Pen, someone who is not only a racist-xenophobe but a Eurosceptic nationalist — Mail on Sunday with a heavy French accent.

Marine le Pen in the Élysée Palace would be a huge fillip to the sort of populist right-wing nationalist movements which appear to have all the political momentum at the minute — Trumpism in the US, Orban in Hungary, Erdogan in Turkey, Putin in Russia, Bolsonaro in Brazil and so on (Donald Trump may have lost the recent US election but he got more votes than any Republican presidential candidate ever[5] so while Trump himself may have been bested at the polling places — for the moment being anyhow — *Trumpism* is still a virulent force to be reckoned with).

---

[5] Indeed in last November's election Trump garnered 30 million more votes than Ronald Reagan did in his 1984 landslide win, a landslide in which the Republican candidate won 49 of the 50 states, an Electoral College victory of 525 to 13.

This quarter we're heading into is going to be critical: ramp-up vaccine rollouts all across the EU such that we're within striking range of the halfway mark by June (then get everything completed in Q3 such that at least 90% of people are vaccinated, which is to say, everyone willing to be vaccinated is vaccinated) and it may be all the rumbling & grumblings sounding now will be behind us and (for many) forgotten; get things going again so we begin to bounce-back in the final quarter, and 2022 a proper bounce-back year, and everything may be OK; but if things go on the way they appear to be going right now — and the way things appear to be going right now is that we appear to be heading into a third spike of this thing — and everyone who wants to be vaccinated is still not vaccinated by the time we get to the middle of Q4, then it'll be bad for a lot of people politically, which'll just add to our stockpile of problems.

In the UK they're already talking about arrangements for a second round of vaccinations using vaccines edited to deal with some of the new variants that've evolved — i.e., booster shots for the 2021/22 winter — and of course there's no such talk in EU territories as yet because it would appear laughably absurd to do so when no EU territory has yet managed to achieve even 20% coverage with the first round of jabs (meanwhile the UK has gone past the 50% mark, albeit that's just with the first of two jabs, up at around 57% at the minute I believe, however now they're really focusing on getting those second jabs done such that soon the UK will have more second jabs administered than the average EU territory has managed with the 1st). But even in the UK where they expect to have everyone willing to be vaccinated vaccinated before August — both 1st and 2nd shots — what with all these new variants, and having to do it all all over again between September and December it means we will all need to continue to be careful throughout next winter too, especially the most vulnerable and the medically compromised, wearing facemasks and being mindful of where one goes who one mixes with and so on.

We've got yet another long winter of this coronavirus thing ahead of us is what I'm saying.

APRIL 2021

Thursday, 1 April

Cycling round the church this morning at the foot of the sycamore tree I noticed some bluebells blooming; first time I've noticed them, which is to say, they may have been in bloom for one or two days already but only this morning did I notice them. There's a whole carpet of bluebell bulbs there and only maybe 8 or 10 of them flowering as yet so, clearly, they're new to this year's scene, a welcome addition to the garden's colour palette.

A beginning to the easing of full lockdown restrictions announced earlier this week, a modest beginning — from Monday, 12 April we'll be able to travel within the bounds of the county (or, for people living in border areas, within 20km of one's dwelling place), and some construction work can resume, house-building in particular. And then, from Monday, 26 April, non-contact sports training for under-18s can resume, along with golf and tennis for everyone, activities where it's easier to practice physical distancing.

And then — the plan is — every two weeks after that, activity areas under restriction will be released, the impact of each release-tranche monitored. A cautious reopening: the government wants to be seen to be doing something to get us back to normalcy without doing so much the numbers begin to spike upwards again because the new coronavirus variants are so much more transmissible than the variant we've been dealing with for most of last year. We only need to look over to mainland Europe to see what'll happen if we fail to get this vaccine roll-out and unlockdown in harmonic tandem where they're experiencing what must surely been seen as a third wave of this thing.

There's confusion about wave terminology, some speaking of a '4th wave' building at present in Germany and Poland and France and Italy and elsewhere and some speak of a '3rd wave'; I'm in the latter grouping: people who speak of a '4th wave' mean that the first wave was February to May last year — the initial wave — however the '4th wavers' then count September to November 2020 as a second wave because at that time the numbers went up, countries went back into lockdown — late October and all through November — and then in most places anyhow numbers came back down again — in Ireland, for example, numbers came back down to near 200 and 300 new cases a day, down from over a thousand a day at the height of the surge; and then there was the Christmas and New Year spike, the biggest spike of all, which we've been coming down from since middle-to-late January, and this they count as the '3rd' wave. However I'm of the view that everything that happened between September-October 2020 to now is all one wave; that unlockdown in December ought not to have happened, it was done mostly for the benefit of retailers, that weakness on the part of the authorities resulting directly in the enormity of the spike over Christmas and into the new year — which, let me be clear, would have happened anyway, and it would have been quite bad anyway, much worse than anything we'd experienced earlier in 2020, but I believe it would have been nowhere near as bad had we kept a firm lid on things from the end of November onwards. And this is not just the wisdom of hindsight, I said so at the time: we had an opportunity to make a virtue of a necessity and for once have a non-hyper-commercialized Christmas, a non-materialized Christmas experience, an opportunity never even considered (so far as I'm aware). It would have been refreshing.

The reaction to this little bit of PR from the government is mixed, people welcome talk of a return to normalcy at last because there's no doubt that people have had a bellyful of all these restrictions — although, so far as I can judge anyhow, they're not really blaming the government for the restrictions, they're just fed-up with the restrictions themselves, which is to say, most people recognise that no matter who's in power it would be the same or very similar, and of course it's the same all across Europe — but at the same time they can see that what's being offered is nothing but a super-sized mug of steam, nothing at all really, pleasant-sounding guff. However, I think people understand there can be no substantial and sustained reopening until at least 40 or 50% of the population is vaccinated and that's not going to be achieved until circa June. What people certainly do not want is for a third wave of this thing to build on this island like we're seeing all across Europe (France going back into a one-month national lockdown this week, for instance), the UK excepted where they have nearly half the adult population vaccinated — one shot vaccinated anyhow. People would be prepared to endure a slower unlockdown if it really was the last coronavirus lockdown rather than have a rush-job now only to have to begin restricting things yet again later on.

Monday, 5 April

One thing I haven't mentioned in the past couple of weeks is the outbreaks of violence on the streets of British cities (or at least potentially violent disturbances) — Bristol, Belfast, London but in other places too. At present all these have various proximate causes — a lot of the trouble in Bristol and Birmingham and in other urban centres have had to do with activist opposition to new crime and policing legislation which is before parliament right now which among other things impacts on public order issues including rights and freedoms to do with mounting demonstrations (the Police, Crime, Sentencing and Courts Bill, which would give police in England and Wales more power to impose conditions on non-violent protests — including those deemed too noisy or a nuisance [looking at you Extinction Rebellion], with those convicted liable to fines or jail terms). I have not been following the business too closely but the street level opposition to the legislation is marshalled under a 'Kill the Bill' umbrella and there have been fairly serious levels of riotous disturbances to do with it, particularly in Bristol for some reason. But as I say there's been 'Kill the Bill' demos leading to disturbances in other places too, cat & mouse running scuffles in Parliament Square in London for instance.

Troubles in Belfast are mostly in Loyalist areas where there have been DUP-sponsored demos against the Irish Protocol element of the Brexit Withdrawal Agreement with the EU. I say 'DUP-sponsored' because

that's exactly how all this has come about, the DUP in particular gin-
ning-up much of this trouble as part of their campaign to have the Irish
Protocol provisions of the Brexit Agreement ditched. And if they cannot
be ditched then they need to be ignored or otherwise trashed and/or
side-stepped.

Back in February DUP politicians were saying that staff at the ports
detailed to do the Irish Protocol checks on goods coming into NI had
ceased to come to work because of threats and intimidation, and when
these allegations were looked into they were found to have no or sparse
actual foundations. However within the space of a week the workers who
were supposed to be conducting these Protocol-mandated checks had
ceased to show up for work because of threats and intimidation and graffiti type anti-Protocol statements began appearing on walls and windows
in all the relevant neighbourhoods, which is to say, DUP politicians called
for displays of hostility/intimidation and they duly got the responses
sought.

After that (around the same time) they corralled most of the unionist
groupings in Northern Ireland to join in on their legal moves against
the Protocol, i.e., actions in the courts challenging the constitutionality
of the Protocol. And basically the First Minister and all her (unionist)
ministers in the government of Northern Ireland have begun a campaign
of non-cooperation with respect to anything to do with facilitating the
operation of the Protocol; for fear of legal exposure they've not actually
come out and made it explicit what they're at, because as ministers they
have certain obligations they'll be expected to fulfil, and if they say 'I'm
not going to do this or that' then they leave themselves legally exposed,
but if one knows how to read these plays it's clear enough there's a widespread campaign afoot to make the provisions of the Protocol inoperable
with a view to having it renegotiated if not totally scrapped.

In addition to which a Sinn Fein/IRA guy called Bobby Storey died
last year and his funeral was held in Belfast while coronavirus restrictions were still in force. Thousands turned up at the funeral, lining the
streets through which the funeral cortege passed and behind the Mafia-
like funeral procession (at the head of the mourners, coming before the
widow and her children) was Gerry Adams flanked left and right by his
deputies Michelle O'Neill (deputy FM in the NI administration) and

Mary Lou Macdonald, Sinn Fein president and member of parliament in the Republic of Ireland, indeed she's leader of the opposition in the Dublin parliament.

It was clear to see why the images would upset Unionists. And, in fairness, it wasn't only Unionists: I remember seeing the pictures myself and being upset because at the time we were giving Boris Johnson and Dominic Cummings righteous stick about their one-rule-for-them-but-no-rules-for-us-because-we're-part-of-the-governing-elite attitude, and this from the Sinn Fein/IRA elite was in essence the very same thing (except the 'We're above and beyond the law' attitude of SF/IRA is even more offensive because they think they're above the law even when it comes to planting bombs in pubs and buses and abducting people and putting them through sham 'trials' in isolated farmhouses and afterwards murdering them in military style executions and so on, and even if Mary Lou herself has never had any part in such activities she continues to defend those who have, or at least she refuses to condemn the like, even the killers of members of the police force of the state she seeks to become prime minister of, so thinking that they're above coronavirus regulations is the least of SF/IRA's offenses).

What I also found offensive about it was the clearly choreographed nature of this procession, it was a Sinn Fein/IRA parade, political theatre. Mary Lou and Michelle O'Neill wearing clearly coordinated outfits (Mafia widow outfits) and carrying black umbrellas; they flanked Gerry Adams left and right but they were also half a step behind his step (the message being — at least as I read the image-messaging — Gerry is still our leader, regardless of what offices we formally occupy, which, at least as I read it, gestures to another message which is that being president of Sinn Fein is not what's important, nor is being Deputy FM, what's really important is your place in the SF/IRA hierarchy and that's a hierarchy that's populated by people whose names you won't find written down on any sheet of paper or on any website because you don't need to know them, and you don't need to know them because if you don't know who's who then you shouldn't know, if you know what I mean…). And then of course the message that Crown regulations don't apply to us because the Crown and its regulations represent forces of occupation on this island

271

and we recognise no one except our own Army Council and associated organisations, not even the Vichy government down South.

The PSNI and the Crown Prosecution Service took no action with respect to anyone attending this parade (at which there were scores of elected representatives), however it took a long time 'looking into' it all before making this determination, months indeed, which is ridiculous; had I been in authority I would have initiated sample prosecutorial proceedings the following week, the evidence was as clear as could be, there was no need for any 'investigating' other than writing up what was plain to see — it was on the evening news broadcasts, for fuck sake.

In the wake of this decision not to go after anyone to do with this parade of SF/IRA power and togetherness and above-the-lawness — because of this mass contravention of coronavirus regulations [and remember at this time thousands of people North and South had already had to not go to the funerals of loved ones, uncles, aunts, mothers, fathers, grandparents and great-grandparents, husbands, wives and partners; I myself, for example, have had to pass on 4 family funerals in the past year] — Arlene Foster appears to have chosen not to make anyone at the CPS her target but to go after the Chief Constable of the PSNI, Simon Byrne, for some reason (after all it's the CPS who decide to prosecute or not to do so, albeit the police make recommendations, even if only implicitly, by virtue of the way the evidence is presented, but, at the end of all, it's the CPS who actually decide).

I'm not sure what her issue with the Chief Constable is but she's certainly going after him, and going after him in a way that (I believe) will make it impossible for him to remain in office. Ultimately he answers to the Policing Board of Northern Ireland which is a multi-party Good Friday Agreement type set-up so she doesn't have the power to sack or sanction him but certainly she can make life difficult for him, and this is what she's doing. She's called for his resignation, she's said she has no confidence in him, the DUP has come out and said the party has no confidence in him, and maybe other Unionist groups have done so too at this stage. She's totally politicized the issue such that the rioting we've seen in Belfast over the weekend and in Newtownabbey and elsewhere is anti-Protocol *and* anti-police.

It's really unforgivable what she's done, goddamn reckless. I can understand her upset about the Bobby Storey funeral parade — as I've said I felt the same way when I saw that SF/IRA procession — but, in fairness, the police were in a difficult situation. It would have been absurd to have moved in on the event at the time and dispersed the gathering; although perhaps with good intelligence something could have been done beforehand to prevent the gathering, however in Ireland funerals are tricky things and sometimes the smarter thing is to stand back and let matters proceed; although as I say the ante could have been upped and the police could have let it be known that prosecutions would follow for anyone violating the public health regulations, and then you'd actually follow through with a few selected prosecutions — certainly go after Mary Lou, Michelle O'Neill and Gerry Adams.

And so I share Mrs Foster's irritation that the police and the CPS decided to take no action with respect to that funeral procession, or the folks who organised it, after all during the lockdowns Orthodox Jewish weddings in North London have been raided, a Catholic mass in Tooting was broken up on Good Friday, and scores of house parties and illegal raves have been dispersed and the organisers of same prosecuted and even imprisoned.

I can understand letting it slide on the day but I think it bad politics (and poor policing) not to take sample action after the event. Doing so would have had support North and South.

Anyhow the upshot of Arlene's campaign against the Protocol is as I say a weekend of rioting in a number of areas. The situation in Northern Ireland is devolving, and the devolution is sponsored by Arlene Foster and the DUP. They led the way with all this and now, as I say, it's self-fuelling, feeding on itself.

Ultimately what the DUP and their allies want (but especially the DUP) is to force the EU to man the Six Counties border themselves: if the EU wants to protect its Single Market let it put officials and border guards on the border between the Republic of Ireland and the Six Counties of Northern Ireland which of course is now an EU/non-EU border. Why should the British Army or the security forces of Northern Ireland be exposed to IRA snipers and bomb-makers on isolated country lanes, let the fucking EU and/or those crafty hoors down in Dublin do so, see how they fucking like it.

And indeed ultimately the EU will have to do so — even over the objections of the authorities in Dublin who really do not want a checkpoint border on the island of Ireland again — or else the whole island of Ireland will need to be treated as suspect territory and we in the south lose fully open access to the Single Market (even if it's unofficial) because we happen to share an island with a bunch of Union Jackeens, backwoodsmen who want to return to the 1950s and 40s and 30s, back when things were good [from their pov anyhow] and people knew where they stood.

I don't want to get sucked into the insoluble quagmire of Northern Ireland politics right now, my point here is about rioting and disaffection in general in the UK in the wake of Brexit. I don't know if I recorded this in these diaries at the time but I certainly felt it and said it to several people but, basically, I predict a riot, lots of rioting and disturbances. It may be a policing issue in Hackney, it may be the Arlene Foster inspired disturbances in Northern Ireland, it may be supporters of Celtic and Rangers on the streets of Glasgow, maybe when Boris Johnson's government refuses the SNP demand for a second independence referendum, despite the fact that the SNP have swept the boards in the Westminster elections and in the Holyrood elections, and grievance piles upon grievance during a long hot summer, or it may be that in an effort to balance the books in the wake of this pandemic another bout of austerity measures will need to be instituted which almost always means cutting services for the have-nots… it may be lots of things in lots of areas but I believe ultimately it will be one thing which is dissatisfaction with the general direction of travel.

Recently, for example, there were disturbances in London to do with the policing of a vigil for a woman who was murdered by a police officer (not a police officer acting in the course of his duties, this was a crime of passion, a sex crime or whatever it was, he killed the woman and buried her body in some woodland in Kent). Women saw it was a crime against women (the victim, Sarah Everard, was abducted off the street near her home in South London) and when women activists attempted to hold a candle-light vigil in her memory on Clapham Common one evening, heavy-handedly the police moved in to break-up and disperse the gathering because it contravened coronavirus regulations.

First of all, if they had any sense, they would have let it slide: the kind of women gathering on Clapham Common did not need policing at all (more sensible, well-informed, self-policing people it would be hard to find) and secondly if you did want to have a police presence there make sure all the police were women police officers, even if that meant bussing WPCs in from surrounding forces, because the last thing you'd want is photos on the front pages of newspapers and news websites of male police officers policing women demonstrating about the killing of a woman by a male police officer, which is exactly what happened! The cops moved in to disperse the gathered women, the women took umbrage at being ordered about by male police officers scuffles broke out arrests were made and you can imagine the sorts of photos that were front and centre on news broadcasts and on newspaper front pages.

And all this with Cressida Dick as Met Commissioner! And several of her top team women too. Easiest thing in the world to spool through the various ways that whole thing could play out, yet somehow Cressida and her high-flying associates failed to do so. Again I do not want to get sucked into the specifics of this, the point is it's another disturbance flashpoint. And I believe we'll see more of the like, BLM type stuff to do with statues and archways and other forms of chiselled symbolism, for instance. Seen it already with the Edward Coltson statue in Bristol, and (I'm saying) we'll see a lot more of the like because (my point is) what and who Britain is is up for grabs right now, another of the unintended consequences of undermining the status quo that is/was leaving the EU. A bunch of Union Jack clutching older people decide we're no longer EU citizens and all that came with that status (a status cherished by millions) is now null and void, now we're just British and we're loud and proud about this happy fact, so let's fly the Union flag from all government buildings all year round and sing Rule Britannia, what could possibly go wrong with such a happy and harmonious demonstration of our patriotism, our shared values, our history and heritage?

What I'm predicting here may not happen this summer, and it may not be next summer either, but I feel sure it's coming. Probably it'll be later this decade, just when the impact of the Brexit swindle becomes clear and obvious and at the same time the pressure for a border poll in Northern Ireland and a second independence referendum in Scotland build to fever pitch. All of these coming at the same time will make it seem like the UK is coming apart at the seams, and it'll seem like that because it really will be.

And when it happens all of it can be directly related to what we've lived through in the last decade or so, beginning with the financial crash and the massive bailouts of them that caused it, then the austerity that taxed the poor to pay for bailing out the corrupt rich, the swindle of Brexit (and the abysmal failure by the anti-Brexit groupings to defend what was our shared inheritance, because that was our commonwealth too), and then, to make Brexit happen, Johnson, Gove & Co jumping into bed with the DUP, people who are as crazy and extreme as the Jim Jordans and Michelle Bachmanns and the Marjorie Taylor Greenes & Lauren Boeberts of the GOP in the US. And then finally all this business to do with the pandemic which you may be full sure working people will be made to pay for one way or another.

I'm predicting a decade as troubled and troublesome as the troubled decade the UK experienced in 1970s. The European project took the UK away from all that but they're going to find themselves right back in the same mess, or something similar to it.

Saturday, 10 April

A week of rioting in various areas in Northern Ireland, DUP-sponsored riots it ought to be said (and emphasised), except that now it isn't just Loyalist communities versus the police it's the two sides at one another (and both sides against the police) as in the Before Times. Scenes like we haven't seen for a generation and hoped we might never see again.

Thanks a lot, Arlene. And the like, once it gets going, feeds off itself, night upon night, such that a vicious self-sustaining momentum develops. The 99-year-old Duke of Edinburgh (the Queen's consort of 70 years) died yesterday morning and all political campaigning for the local government elections due to take place in May suspended for the weekend as a mark of respect; Unionist leaders asked their teenage rioters to show some respect and stay at home for the duration, and of course their doing so is simply a provocation to the other side, practically an invite to come out and show some corresponding disrespect, which of course they duly did which in turn brought out the Loyalist rioters again to defend their neighbourhoods and their heritage and so ding-dong it starts all over again, another cycle of it.

To clear the streets last night the police used water cannons (60 or so cops on the injured list, albeit that's a very easy list to get onto — not just in NI, this is how it is in all police districts, coppers as easy to 'injure' as Neymar); as I say, years and years since we've seen such scenes in Northern Ireland, water-cannon jets, buses aflame, burnt-out cars, peace wall gates on fire because of the petrol bombs being lobbed at the scum on the other side, topless 13 and 14 year olds in balaclavas and cheap, off-brand jogging bottoms giddy with the most toxic type of adrenaline as they lob their burning missiles into the sub-zero night sky.

On a brighter note, saw two swallows today, darting about above the old apple tree in the back garden of one of the Bridge Street houses. Happy harbingers of summer.

Sunday, 25 April

Contacted the Medical Centre this week asking Dr Creagh for a repeat prescription for Beclazone inhalers [for my COPD condition]. Sent an email, and in so doing asked to be informed as to whether I will be among the 'at risk' priority cohorts for vaccination. That was Wednesday afternoon; have not heard anything back as yet. If I haven't heard anything by the middle of this coming week I will get back in contact with them again.

Daniel down at the gate told me he's already had his first shot. His immune system is compromised as a result of the meds he's on, however he told me that it was he who first got in contact with the Medical Centre seeking vaccination because of his compromised situation (i.e., as opposed to them approaching him) and then about a week later he was scheduled for his first jab. He'll be getting his second on 19 May, he told me.

So far people I know who've been jabbed include June Collins, Tim Macey, and Don McCarthy, all of whom have been done because they're in the 70s or 80s. And Martin Condon's mum.

Then Tim and Abina (Abina because she has had a kidney transplant fairly recently so she was certainly done as a high priority case, however Tim's been jabbed too, I think), Liam because he suffers from diabetes and Mary, his partner, because she works in Bantry Hospital, and, as I say, Daniel down in the Sexton's Lodge.

And Martin Condon who got done by the family GP the same time as his mum was done.

The point is, it's clearly increasingly common to encounter people who've had at least one shot, which is encouraging. We're getting there. Here in the Republic 25% of people have had at least one shot (10% fully vaccinated).

Tuesday, 27 April

Most UK newspapers have front-page headlines saying stuff like 'PM tainted by sleaze, say voters' (the i), 'Slurry of Sleaze' (Metro), 'Boris on the Ropes' (Mail), 'Johnson 'said he would let Covid rip' in lockdown row' (Times), 'Pressure on Johnson after claim of slur on Covid dead' (Guardian), 'Boris denies 'let bodies pile high' outburst' (Express) and so on.

There are several stories on the go at the minute and I'm not going to spend time reflecting on all of them but there's one I want to pick out because it's something that's been a thread in these diaries over the course of the past 12 months.

During the time the Covid numbers were getting worse and worse in autumn last year and medical experts (and the leader of the Labour Party) were calling for a circuit-breaker lockdown, fearful of the impact on his Brexited economy Boris Johnson set himself against ordering a second lockdown. As the days and weeks went by it became more and more obvious that whether he wanted to or not he would have to reverse his position, but the more the numbers went against him the more defiant he became, and, at one point, the allegation goes, in an outburst he said 'Let the corpses pile high in their thousands, I will *not* authorize a second lockdown!'

Of course he did do so — order a second lockdown — his position was unsustainable.

My point here is that in these diaries I wrote about all this at the time and the way I characterized Johnson would easily have him saying something along such lines. I've been rereading these virus diaries in recent weeks (the 2020 diaries) so I'm intimately mindful of these events and it may be that had someone read my diaries before this story emerged they might say 'That's just Perry being OTT and hyperbolic — he hates Johnson and all those Brexiteers with a passion so he would say the like, wouldn't he?' but, in fact, no, it looks like I got it spot on. If the allegation proves true he really *was* saying 'Let the corpses pile high, fuck em, nothing matters more to me than the economy and the success of the Brexit project.'

I should also add that the prime minister denies he said this — flat-out denials 'No, I never said that, nor anything like it,' he's said. He and his spokespeople couldn't be clearer in their refutation of this story. Yesterday in the House of Commons Michael Gove was indignant at the suggestion, spittle flying from his lie-hole as he indignantly refuted the idea that the wonderful member for Uxbridge would ever utter anything of the kind. '*I* was in that meeting,' he said, 'and nothing of the like was said. Not alone that but the prime minister did actually order a second lockdown, as the House will recall', he added. 'And a third one after that! So the whole suggestion is absurd. Moreover he himself nearly died from Covid, so the idea that such a good man would say such a dreadful thing is offensive to me and to God and to all the people of this country who voted for Brexit.' (I'm paraphrasing, obviously, but he did make a fulsome defence of the Plump Controller along such rhetorical lines in a spittle-spraying fit of indignancy and phoney self-righteousness.)

Trouble is several outlets (including the slavishly Tory-supporting Daily Mail) have sources confirming that Johnson *did* say precisely what he's accused of saying. The BBC say they have 'sources' confirming the story (i.e., multiple sources). And there's talk of an audio recording of the outburst, which if there is it'll really impact. Johnson might get away with it if they'd not been so all-out aggressive in saying he never said such a thing — the prime minister was frustrated, he uses colourful language, he works hard, he was seeking to keep the economy afloat and so on, in short he was frustrated and under pressure and over-worked and in exasperation he misspoke — but given the way they've wholly denied it — including the PM himself — if an audio recording should emerge if nothing else it'll establish that these people would lie at the drop of a cap, and they'd do so without shuttering an eyelid. They'd lie right to your face. (And of course, as I've recorded previously, Johnson's career is latticed with instances of him brazenly lying, he's lost jobs and houses and marriages and access to his offspring because of his casual relationship with the truth, his total disregard for whether he's telling the truth or an untruth. The thing he'll be forever remembered for — Brexit — wholly based on misdirection and deliberate misrepresentation.)

I know Johnson and his people would lie right to your face without batting an eyelid, it's perfectly clear to see as far as I'm concerned, and I'm sure it's clear to millions of others also, but while all sorts of indicators of the actual character of Boris Johnson do not cut through to the man on the Uxbridge omnibus, this — 'Let the corpses pile high in their thousands'— will (or at least is more likely to do so because he's actually saying I don't really care for these people — British people remember — ultimately they mean nothing to me). The story itself as it stands may not do so but if an audio recording exists and it emerges that will clean punch through, surely.

I wouldn't bet too much on it, however, because, like Trump in the US, it's quite astonishing what Johnson gets away with. Stuff that would sink any other politician seems only to add to his charming lustre as far as an electoral majority in the UK are concerned (and abroad too, for he plays well in foreign markets also, bad cess to him).

I saw a Channel 4 News report last night which was recorded and edited at the end of last week (so before this 'Let the bodies pile high' story) and people on the streets of Uxbridge didn't give a flying fuck about any of these sleaze stories (Johnson's the MP for Uxbridge). Most people weren't aware of any of these inside-the-beltway stories concerning corruption and cronyism, which is to say, none of them had any cut-through whatsoever, and, even when people had heard of one or two of them, they didn't give a toss, they felt it was media shit-stirring to sell newspapers or to get eyeballs onto news websites, or else they felt it was all part of the noise and dust-up of the present elections cycle (local elections ongoing at present, elections postponed from May of last year). Most people thought 'Boris' was doing a great job and the media ought to get off his case. The way they spoke reminded me of the way Trump supporters spoke about Trump during the Trump presidency, no matter the outrage: denial, deflection and/or whataboutism.

> *He didn't say that. He didn't do that. And if he did, he was only kidding. And if he wasn't, then you just don't understand. And if you do, it's not a big deal anyway. And if it is, it's for the best. And if it's not, I still don't care.*

And there are many scandals: billions of dollars of contracts have been handed out to Tory party donors and supporters (all under cover of this emergency — i.e., the virus crisis — which is to say, clear corruption and cronyism wrapped in Union flaggery), the guy responsible for overseeing the implementation of the ministerial code has resigned because he wrote a report concluding that that poisoned dwarf Priti Patel is a workplace bully and Johnson said thanks very much for doing this report for me as he threw it into the trash-can. The bloke resigned in protest and no one has been appointed to replace him.

And, despite all this (and more besides), the Tories are 8 to 10 points ahead in the polls. Keir Starmer and Labour drew level with the Tories for a little while last year, even pulling ahead of the Tories at one point for a couple of months in the autumn, but getting Brexit done as he said he would and securing a no-tariffs trade deal with the EU like he said he would combined with the clear success of the vaccine rollout — especially when contrasted with the mess in the EU — has revived and re-inflated Johnson's fortunes in popular opinion.

We shall see how all this impacts at the actual polls next week (i.e., actual ballot papers in actual ballot boxes), as I say, this 'Let the corpses pile high' story is bound to have some impact, even without an audio recording. If there is a recording it'll surely emerge this coming weekend, i.e., the weekend just before people go to the voting places.

There's one other element to these sleaze stories I want to mention and that's the refurbishment of the prime minister's Downing Street flat.

Johnson and his ladyfriend do not actually occupy the apartment above 10 Downing Street; like Tony Blair before him, and the Camerons too, I believe, he and Carrie Symonds have ensconced themselves in the larger (4-bedroomed) flat above 11 Downing Street, the flat traditionally going to the Chancellor. The prime minister gets an allowance of £30,000 to make whatever alterations he (or she) may wish to make to refurbish the grace & favour apartment to their liking. Johnson and his ladyfriend have blown through this (not an insignificant allowance of money) and spent an additional £58,000. (Some accounts say altogether up to £200,000 has been spent on these renovations and alterations, however by means of clever accounting they've media-managed the story so that only the £58,000 figure is mentioned for the most part. But like I say, even with that it's actually £58,000 on top of the £30,000 allowance, if I understand matters rightly.)

Upmarket designer Lulu Lytle is on the job apparently so we're talking about hand-crafted wallpaper (£850 per roll according to reports) and sofas and carpets that cost more than the vehicles most people can afford and so on. £3,000 for a coffee table!

This became a story when it emerged the Conservative Party were ringing around in search of Conservative Party donors willing to fund these excesses, one donor apparently writing a cheque for the whole £58,000. (This is how we know it actually cost more because £58,000 wasn't enough to cover all the costs involved.)

However now the story coming out of the Downing Street lie-machine is that nobody ever paid for any of it, Boris Johnson paid for all the excess out of his own pocket and there were no donors and no search for donors. However we know for sure this is not true because, aside from the fact that we know some of the people who were contacted in search of people willing to help out under this head, one of the intermediate lies was that the Conservative Party HQ paid the excess. Then for a while the story was that the excess was paid for by Tory HQ (or whoever) and that Johnson had undertaken to repay whoever it was that stumped up for doing the work. But now, as I say, the line is that BJ himself paid for everything and there were no donors and no loans, and just to clear matters up the prime minister has ordered the Cabinet Secretary to do a review of all the business relating to the refurbishments just to ensure everything is above board and in accordance with the rules and regulations. (And of course I can tell you right now that the Cabinet Secretary's review is going to find everything's perfectly kosher; and, even if he doesn't, whatever report he submits will be put into the trash can to sit alongside the report on Priti Patel's monstering of people she doesn't like or trust. The purpose of the review is to take the story away from the media because now we'll be told we must wait until the Cabinet Secretary completes his review so that the facts of the matter are established, a standard kick-it-into-the-long-grass tactic.)

As indicated, in all there's been about 5 different stories about how this work was paid for, and, as I say, reporters have had trouble even establishing the basic facts of the matter such that it's still unclear whether these renovations and refurbishments cost £58,000, £88,000 or even twice that (latter) amount.

The latest line is that voters don't care about Whitehall village tittle-tattle, they don't care at all who paid for what as long as the taxpayer didn't pay — and indeed this was the line taken by many on the High Street in Uxbridge in the Channel 4 News report.

As a matter of practical politics it appears this is true: the country has just elected Johnson (and they've given him an enormous 80-seat majority) and the people who voted him in are in no mood to hear any guff about him at the minute. They think (and if you'll ask them they'll tell you) all this stuff about so-called 'sleaze' and cronyism and so on is just 'Remoaners' still sore about Brexit attempting to stir shit up.

And, as with Trump, they knew the bloke was no saint when they selected & elected him so that, if Boris fucked Miss UK on the cabinet table while Carrie was upstairs breast-feeding his latest seminal legacy, they wouldn't give a tu'penny fuck, so fuck off with your reports.

One thing I haven't mentioned in all this is the (alleged) Dominic Cummings aspect of it. Lots of people (including the people who lie and savage on behalf of Boris Johnson and Carrie Symonds in Downing Street) believe the evil genius of Dominic Cummings is behind several of these stories. It is he who is leaking WhatsApp messages to and from the PM, and he is the person behind the 'Let the corpses pile high' story too. However at the end of last week DC put up a statement on his blog denying he's behind any of these stories, however, he says he is due to appear before a parliamentary select committee in May and at that time he will be willing to answer any questions the committee members may have about these matters (meaning any of the matters referred to in his blog post).

Wednesday, 28 April

So much going on at present I don't have time for it all: I want to get on with editing the Virus Diaries and if I was to attempt to keep abreast of all that's going on right now I'd be at it all day.

However I have to mention that in a surprise move it looks like the DUP are going to topple Arlene Foster for not being Brexity and hard-line enough on the Protocol! Jesus Christ! I thought she was appallingly intransigent as it was! However apparently she's not nearly right-wing and ultra-Unionist enough for the DUP rank and file. According to reports last night and this morning over half the DUP MPs and three-quarters of the DUP Stormont Assembly members have put their names to a 'No Confidence' document. If this is true she cannot possibly survive. Everyone concerned has gone dark in the way only Ulster Protestants can do so it's not yet clear what's happening, however clearly something's afoot, and the fact that everyone's been taken by surprise by this (including Mrs Foster herself apparently) suggests that it's serious — a move which has been in the works for weeks — and she's finished.

The DUP have now tangoed themselves into a position of outright opposition to the Irish Protocol, no tinkering or foot-dragging will please them now it seems, it must go in toto or we'll burn the fucking place to the ground.

After the story about the DUP ambush first surfaced yesterday, Mrs Foster posted a quote from the Book of Psalms on her Facebook page: 'It is God who arms me with strength and keeps my way secure.' This is the kind of cornhole culture we're dealing with here.[6]

Since writing the above this morning Arlene Foster has fallen on her sword, resigning as DUP leader and as First Minister this afternoon (she will continue to serve as party leader until the end of May and as FM until the end of June). As I said if the reports proved true her position would be untenable, and the reports have proved true: more than 20 of her 27 colleagues in the Stormont Assembly put their names to the 'No Confidence' document and over half the party's MPs at Westminster.

She made her stepping-down announcement at about 4 o'clock this afternoon and in it she got all femmy about how her achievement in becoming party leader and First Minister broke through partitions for women and how she hoped her career achievements would be an inspiration for other young women blah blah blah — although, in fairness, there's no doubt but that she *is* surrounded by some seriously misogynistic characters, she even referred to them as such, calling them out as 'misogynistic' in her resignation statement, which is strong poteen for someone so conservative, I mean this is not the language of conservatives, especially the sort of Ballymena type conservativism she embodies.

More surprisingly in her stepping-down statement she sought to portray herself as a unifier, someone who sought to bring together all the people who are privileged to call this part of the world home to build a better future blah blah blah (devil the bit of this did I see from her over the course of the past 5 or so years), nevertheless I suppose she's attempting to distinguish herself from the ultras to come who certainly want more division and hostility, who thrive on it (the frontrunners to

---

6 It's the Pharisee-like virtue-signaling on Facebook I'm objecting to here, not that someone might be inspired & bolstered by scripture & faith. If you depend on a Higher Power for strength and security then do so in silence and stillness and humility, don't be letting everyone know that this is what you're doing on Facebook in hopes that they might think well of you for it. This is what I regard as cornhole culture. And I think Arlene Foster is full of it.

replace her are the loathsome Jeffrey Donaldson, who apprenticed in politics with the Euro-phobic and race-baiting Enoch Powell, and the Creationist Edwin Poots, the NI Agriculture minister, the lad who last year said that about 80% of the cases of Covid in Northern Ireland came from Catholics — presumably implying that RCs didn't wash properly and they live like rats in rat-holes and so on — so this is what we have to look forward to).

Lots of people being really nice about Arlene, in London and in Dublin, so I suppose she'll get a peerage and get her ass onto worthy commissions and promotional sinecures and what have you. She'll be fine, you needn't worry, she won't struggle to put a Sunday roast on the table nor to pay her electricity bills you may be sure. She lost her position mostly because of Boris Johnson's lies: he promised there wouldn't be any kind of trade barrier down the Irish Sea and then he went and signed up to an agreement that had a trade barrier down the Irish Sea, just another Johnsonian lie to add to the lie-pile. So he owes her, Lady Foster of some part of Fermanagh is the least she can expect, I imagine. That's what the House of Lords is for — a gilded trash can.

MAY 2021

Sunday, 9 May

[My sister] Angela got vaccinated today, first shot (AstraZeneca), at City Hall.

From tomorrow museums, galleries, libraries and so on (lots of the heritage sector) can reopen in the latest tranche of unlockdown. Libraries can lend and receive returned books but there will be no reader services or access to public access computer facilities or anything else of the like.

Also inter-county travel — including for non-essential reasons — can resume from tomorrow, people from up to 3 households (up to a max of 6 people, not including children, so 6 adults plus children) free to inter-mingle, although such meetings are still supposed to take place outdoors — however fully vaccinated people are free to meet up with other fully vaccinated people indoors — hairdressers and beauticians and all such like services free to resume (albeit by appointment only for now, i.e., no walk-ins), and public transport can operate with up to 50% capacity — it was down at 30%, i.e., most of the seats on the buses were taped out of bounds, however from tomorrow only 50% will be out of commission.

And religious services can resume from tomorrow, albeit with a limit of 50 people for now; communion services still not authorized, prayer services only.

Monday, 10 May

Local and devolved elections in the UK at the end of last week and because of the pandemic restrictions it took longer than usual to get all the results, the last of which have been coming in over the weekend.

The Scottish National Party has been returned to power in Scotland where they've been in power now for 14 years, albeit sometimes in minority governments, supported by the Greens usually. The SNP needed 65 seats in the Holyrood parliament to have an overall majority, it achieved 64 of them.

However the Greens returned with 8 seats so it'll be status quo resumed.

Both the SNP and the Greens pro-independence so a clear majority in parliament for progressing towards independence. This was so in the previous parliament too but the difference is that in this election whether or not to move forward with a second referendum on independence was one of the central issues in the campaign. No reasonable doubt about it, a vote for SNP or for the Green Party was a vote for progression towards a second referendum.

The Scots had a referendum on independence in 2014 and the pro-independence proposition was rejected 55-45, an unambiguous margin in favour of continuing with the union.

However since then the Tory government in London has taken the UK out of the EU — and did so on a 52-48 margin nationally (i.e., all of the UK totalled up) — despite the fact that the Scots voted 62-38 to remain in the EU.

The 2014 referendum was supposed to be a once-in-a-generation thing and this is what all unionists push back at those wanting a second referendum. But the people wanting a second referendum say that Brexit represents a fundamental alteration in our constitutional status, something done against our express will and over the top of our clear and strenuous objections, so that a second referendum would be about whether Scotland wants to continue to be part of *this* union — the UK of the 2020s — which is not at all the union at issue 7 years ago. Now, in the wake of Brexit, effectively, the question will be do you want to be part of the British union or the European Union?

The union of the kingdoms of England and Scotland is supposed to be a union of consent and if in the Westminster elections — the parliament of the United Kingdom — and in the Holyrood elections [for the Scottish parliament] the pro-independence Scottish National Party sweeps the boards, which they undoubtedly have done, which is to say, the people of Scotland continually and consistently vote for pro-Independence parties, London cannot continue to deny a second referendum on independence and still maintain that the union is one of consent. Quite clearly the Scots — at least a majority of them — no longer consent to the union.

For now London is determined to hold the line that we had a once-in-a-generation referendum on independence for Scotland in 2014 so the issue is now settled for a generation at the very least.

In Scotland people have two votes: one is a constituency vote — one MSP per constituency in a first-past-the-post system — and the other a party-list vote which is done on a regional basis so as to achieve proportionality in the results, the country divided into 8 regions.

There are 129 seats in the Scottish parliament. 73 of these are constituency seats and the remaining 56 are party-list, or regional seats. Almost all the Greens come in on the party-list, for example, because the Green vote is significant in Scotland but it's not geographically concentrated so as to be able to prosper in first-past-the-post contests.

In the elections last week as I say the SNP ended up with 64 seats
Conservatives 31
Labour 22
Greens 8
Lib Dems 4
So, in terms of seats in parliament the pro-independence parties ended up winning the election 72:57, a very respectable performance.

Nicola Sturgeon and the SNP take this as a mandate to push ahead with preparations for #indyref2 — as the second referendum is hash-tagged. The SNP is pledged to do so in this parliament, so at some point in the next 5 years — so 2023 or 2024, probably the latter if I had to guess, 10 years after the 2014 referendum and 5 years into the unwanted Brexit.

In 2014 the SNP government in Edinburgh applied to the authorities in London for permission to stage an independence referendum which, with polling showing that it was not too much of a gamble, the Cameron government eventually granted. That's how matters were then understood. In the devolution Act of 1998 certain powers were designated as 'reserve powers', i.e., powers reserved to the UK government in London and nothing the Edinburgh authorities could do could transgress onto what were set out as reserved matters — defence, foreign affairs, stuff to do with the crown and with the union of the two kingdoms and so on.

However since then SNP thinking has evolved. SNP legal heads now believe that in fact the authorities in Edinburgh would have the power to stage a referendum on independence legally without seeking permission from London because staging a referendum on independence does not affect the union of the two kingdoms because after all a referendum is but a glorified opinion poll, so the SNP say that acting as the lawful government in Scotland they will stage their own independence referendum which will be lawful because commissioning an opinion poll does not transgress onto areas that are reserved as the legislation is currently drafted.

London disputes this reading of the legislation so it's likely that the two sides will end up in the courts.

The SNP want to achieve independence and then their policy is to apply to re-join the European Union. So they cannot simply declare independence like we here in the Republic did a century ago, nor can they run the risk of staging what might be deemed an illegal ballot as the Catalonians did a few years back because if they do so Spain — and maybe a few other EU states also — will veto their re-entry into the EU for fear of inspiring and fertilizing their own separatists. So the Scots want to proceed lawfully.

In any event they want to proceed lawfully because they'll want to achieve a negotiated settlement with the UK when they leave — a Withdrawal Agreement — a divorce settlement with divorce settlement type division of assets and liabilities so they don't go over a cliff-edge in terms of pension liabilities and other fiscal matters, which is to say, go fucking bankrupt and be a basket case like Greece (or like this country was for 50 or 60 years after breaking away from the UK).

They need to do everything by the book because with EU backing they have a good chance of securing a reasonably equitable divorce settlement with the UK — or with what will then be the Rump UK — especially as the UK and the EU still have many matters to settle — the UK-EU trade deal concluded at the end of last year only dealt with goods, they still need to settle matters in relation to services and finance and data interoperability and in several other subject areas, so what the Scots want is to be part of these negotiations (even if only unofficially) in which, clearly, they will have far more negotiating leverage than if they were attempting to deal with the embittered English on their own; and, of course, conversely, what the English/Tories want is the exact opposite: they want to delay the business with Scotland for as long as they can, they want to conclude their dealings with the EU and then they'll turn around and deal with the isolated Scots.

So the game's afoot.

I'm not going to get into the business of Northern Ireland right now but with elections for the Northern Ireland Assembly next year NI will be part of this whole tangled mudball too, as if matters not tangled and muddied enough.

In the wake of these elections it is not difficult to envision a scenario in which the First Minister in Northern Ireland is not a Unionist, and if the FM not a Unionist then she/he is most likely to be an SF person. If that happens almost certainly there will be an application for a border poll and it will be much trickier for London to say no because all the stuff to do with this is detailed in legislation and in the Good Friday Agreement and in international treaties and elsewise.

Northern Ireland also voted against Brexit (56:44) so all of these things are direct results from Brexit. At the time Johnson & Co were warned this is how it would play out but selfishly and recklessly they powered ahead with their Brexit project anyway because Johnson's primary interest was getting himself into Downing Street, not the best interests of the United Kingdom.

And, as I reported at the end of April, Arlene Foster has been ejected as leader of the Democratic Unionist Party for not being thuggish enough in her opposition to the Irish Protocol — which is to say, for being too trusting with respect to Boris Johnson who's clearly pulled a fast one on Unionists, betraying the union for his own political success in England — and the DUP is now having a contest to replace her with the doolally Creationist Edwin Poots in the red-white-and-blue corner and the repulsive Sir Jeffrey Donaldson in the redder, whiter and bluer corner, a man who apprenticed in politics with the outcast Enoch Powell, someone who was considered beyond-the-pale racist in the *1970s*, a time when there was undisguised racism on prime-time television seven nights a week. The contest is quite literally a contest about which of them is capable of being more offensive and repulsive and non-cooperative.

Both the DUP and the Ulster Unionist Party are catching heat from an outfit called Traditional Unionist Voice,[7] who, like the MAGA folks in the US, want to return to simpler days, people who look back fondly to the 1950s and 40s, a time before we had all these LBGQIRA types and blacks and Chinamen and Muslims and Hindus and Sikhs and basically non-Protestants on our high streets and in our hospitals and GP surgeries and on our wirelesses. And that's not even to mention the disgusting fem-libbers who are also unnatural sinners and pagans bound for never-ending hellfire and damnation upon the terrifying return of The One Who Was Promised.

The DUP fear that if they don't toughen-up and get smart they're going to get it in the you know where from the TUV in the elections next year (and in other elections in other years after that) — i.e., that the TUV will do to the DUP what the DUP did to the UUP — and that between the jigs and the reels the whole unionist project falls to the floor between 3 unionist stools and Northern Ireland ends up in the hands of Sinn Fein. So learning from the Tories with respect to UKIP and the Brexit Party they're moving to suck the blood and air from TUV by being at least as extreme as the TUV before it's too late and they feel they gotta move now if they want to have the masquerade ready for those elections next year.

Indeed, now as I write these lines it occurs to me that there's some chance the unionists will bring down the whole system of government in Northern Ireland rather than run the risk of handing the reins of government over to SF-IRA, which is to say, collapse the Stormont Executive,

---

[7] Indeed over the weekend Steve Aiken stood down as the leader of the Ulster Unionist Party, Aiken doing the walk of shame for the same reason Mrs Foster was sent home to do the dishes by the hardcore DUP guys, which is to say, heat from the Monster Raving TUV.

which they have the power to do by refusing to make it work, in which event NI reverts to direct rule from London via the Northern Ireland Office.

I can see both referendums — Scotland's and Northern Ireland's — happening in the 2020s, maybe even happening at the same time, although I doubt if London would want this; but even with them happening at different times it would still be impactful because one would impact on the other, maybe sparking one another off, or maybe having a dampening effect one on the other; you may be sure there's a team of people somewhere in England's Home Counties war-gaming all this right now.

In Wales where the Welsh Labour Party is in power Labour (and in particular its leader Mark Drakeford) did really well, ending up with more seats in the Welsh Senedd.

Meanwhile in England — in the local council elections in particular — the Labour Party did terribly, losing about 250 seats while the Conservative Party picked up over 300: Tories now have 2,345 council seats in England to Labour's 1,345; the Tories now control 63 councils — a net gain of 13 — to Labour's 44.

In addition to which there was a by-election in Hartlepool — which has been a Labour stronghold for as long as anyone can remember (the parliamentary seat once held by Peter Mandelson) — and the Conservatives won it, winning with a majority of something like 7,000.

It's a crisis for Keir Starmer, there's even talk of a leadership challenge.

Labour has been destroyed in Scotland (where once they were kings — well, shop stewards anyhow), although in fairness this not Keir Starmer's fault as the SNP had gobbled up the most of what used to be the Labour vote in Scotland before Starmer was first elected to parliament, but Labour in England now appears to be going the same road, and it's the same phenomenon in both countries essentially: Scottish Nationalism north of the border and English Nationalism in the form of Tory-sponsored Buchaneering Brexitology south of it.

In terms of local government, with the exception of London and the urban areas dominated by Liverpool and Manchester the map of England is now Tory blue from Northumberland to Cornwall.

But the story is complicated by the fact that Andy Burnham's done well in Manchester where's he's been elected for a second term as mayor of Greater Manchester — retuned with an increased majority — and Sadiq Khan has been re-elected in London.

So, clearly, looking at Khan in London, Burnham in Greater Manchester and Mark Drakeford in Wales, regionalism works (look also at the SNP in Scotland) however the Labour Party as a whole, as a UK entity, looks like it's finished.

Political parties are the ossified remains of previous movements and that's precisely what the Labour Party looks like right now, something ossified, the remains of something from another age, a time of rickets and polio and Bovril and Butlins and Blackpool and Bennie Hill and Dad's Army and Rising Damp.

The Tory party is a fluid, moving thing, fleet-of-foot, it became a radical Thatcherite party in the 1980s, then under Cameron and Osbourne it switched to being a Conservative version of Tony Blair and the Blairite Labour Party, and then it dumped Cameron and Osbourne and stole the costumes and songs of UKIP and the Brexit Party which is still the biggest crowd-pleaser in England. It's almost like the Tories have been 3 distinct parties in the space of two generations.

Meanwhile the Labour Party is the same old fucking ding-dong: I see no future for it at all with their cumbersome conference architecture and 'National Executive' and their thousands of committees and composite resolutions, and characters like Len McCluskey speaking on behalf of 'the Labour movement,' fuck off the lot of you because you're really only talking to yourselves.

Don't get me wrong, I believe (and feel strongly) that we need something like the Labour Party, we need a party that does the job the Labour Party ought to be doing. And indeed I like Keir Starmer. I think he's a good bloke, I wish he was successful.

But if you did hear the way the people on the high street and on the seafront in Hartlepool were speaking — saying that 'Boris' is a good man, he's batting for Britain and he's going to do good for the people of Hartlepool and all the rest of it, and the fact that he spent £840 per wallpaper roll for the refurbishment of his grace & favour apartment is none of our concern, only shit-stirring people attempting to do a good man down, and so what if the head of Carphone Warehouse paid for his £15,000 holiday in Mustique, what business is that of anyone's and so on, and this from tatted lads wearing Aldi leisurewear eating chip-suppers off plastic-trays outside a miserable looking chipper in Hartlepool — you'd realised what a total failure the whole Labour Party project is. What an enormous and fabulous swindle Boris Johnson and Michael Gove and Jacob Rees-Mogg and all the rest of these shameless posh school toffs have pulled off. And the Labour Party not able to land a glove on any of em. "Let the corpses pile high in their thousands," yet posh-boy Boris is the champion of the plain people of England — Eton and Oxford-educated Alexander Boris de Pfeffel Johnson, pro demos champion of the little folk of the shires of Middle England! You're havin a bleedin larf, ain't ya?

Tuesday, 11 May

Just registered for vaccination at a vaccination centre. Don't know where or when as yet.

Website is good, in fairness, clean, simple, no glitches or any kind of bullshit. Even looks nice. I'm impressed. (Just goes to show, the authorities can do things well when it's really important; even from a copy-editing pov everything flawless. Lots of good quality information provided too, and well-presented.)

Took about 5 minutes; I'd read all the info beforehand so I had every-thing I needed prepared.

Tim Macey has offered to take me to whichever vaccination centre I'm sent to. We can travel with the windows open. It'll be fine.

Angela got vaxed on Sunday (AZ vax) and apparently they said that she wouldn't get second dose until 12 weeks after, which is end of July/early August.

Daniel down at the gate will get his second dose 4 weeks after his first. Mark McCarthy also 4 weeks. (Both Pfizer.) Which is to say, if it's 12 weeks before I get second dose it could be end of August or even into

September for me because I might not get an appointment for my first shot until sometime in June: they say they'll get back to me with date for first shot within 3 weeks. 3 weeks from now is the end of May, so my guess is I'm not going to get my first shot until June at the earliest.

Friday, 14 May

Ransomware attack on the HSE overnight which means the health service has had to shut down all systems and networks. The following is the report on the RTE News website this morning.

> The Health Service Executive has said some health services have been impacted since it was forced to shut down all of its IT systems after a major cyberattack.
>
> The ransomware attack is focused on accessing data stored on central servers.
>
> The health body said it has taken the precaution of shutting down its systems to further protect them, and to allow it to assess the situation.
>
> The Covid-19 vaccination programme is not affected by the cyberattack and is going ahead as planned.
>
> There was an immediate shutdown of the HSE's national IT system early this morning after it emerged it had been subjected to a ransomware attack overnight.
>
> Health service providers around the country have been left to assess the impact while continuing to care for patients.
>
> Many hospitals have described situations of being compromised without access to their electronic systems and records, and having to rely on contingency measures such as paper-based systems.
>
> In some cases, hospitals have warned of significant disruption with routine appointments cancelled today, including maternity check-ups and scans.

With delays expected to some patient services, health providers are also warning this IT outage could pose difficulties in accessing patient results.

The HSE has said it is working to resolve this serious issue with the support of cyber security experts and gardaí.

The following also taken from the RTE News website, another report posted later in the day.

A previously unseen version of the existing "Conti" ransomware appears to have done the damage.

[Conti] was first detected in May of 2020 and according to anti-virus provider Sophos is similar to some other ransomware families.

But it has also "undergone rapid development since its discovery and is known for the speed at which it encrypts and deploys across a target system," Sophos said.

The original Conti is also a human-operated virus, meaning that rather than automatically worming its way into a system, it can be manipulated by humans.

This may mean that it has been placed in locations that will make it harder for the HSE, hospitals and services to track down and remove.

It also points to the HSE having been targeted this time, making the attack different to the Wannacry ransomware in 2017.

On that occasion, pre-emptive action by the HSE as the virus randomly swept the globe led to a similar precautionary and disruptive shutdown of systems for several days to prevent infection.

This time round though, the HSE has acknowledged that Conti has managed to infect some systems.

Conti is also different because it is a "double-extortion" ransomware.

In other words, whereas traditional ransomware encrypts files on a computer or system and only unlocks them when a ransom is paid, Conti can also do this and steal them.

Consequently, the data can then also be used to extract an additional ransom from the subject, or the organisation from where it was taken.

"A year ago, a back-up system was seen as a reasonable security measure against these incidents – but the blackmail situations surrounding the threat to leak information is a completely different scenario and one that is extremely difficult to tackle," said Ronan Murphy, founder and CEO of Smarttech247.

The HSE claims there was a ransom demand displayed on the screens of the encrypted computers, but it won't be paying it because of the message it would send out.

Resolving the situation won't be easy or quick.

Experts think that despite the disruption it has caused, the HSE has taken the correct initial approach in rapidly shutting down its systems to prevent the further spread of the ransomware.

Opening it back up though will take longer, with every sub-system and in some cases individual machines having to be checked one at a time.

Only then can those networks be booted back up again, with the final step being their connection to each other.

In the meantime, hundreds if not thousands of appointments will be cancelled, test results stalled, diagnoses and treatments delayed and widespread disruption caused to an already under pressure health system.

One can only imagine what impact it might have had if this attack had taken place in January at the height of the current wave of the pandemic.

It all begs the question, who would do something like this?

The answer, most likely (though we don't yet know and possibly never will), is international cybercriminal gangs who prey on large organisations, especially those where reliability of service is literally a matter of life or death.

According to Sophos, 34% of healthcare organisations say they were hit by ransomware in the last 12 months, and one in three paid a ransom.

Of those that escaped a direct hit, 41% say it is only a matter of time before they're a target, mainly because ransomware attacks are becoming too sophisticated to stop.

Which goes to underline just how vulnerable organisations and individuals are.

Paul Donegan, Palo Alto Networks country manager for Ireland, said the average cyber ransom paid in 2020 at $312,493 was more than double the figure for a year earlier.

"So far in 2021, the average payment has nearly tripled compared to the previous year – to about $850,000," he said.

"The highest demand we've seen in the last four months was for $50 million."

Saturday, 15 May

Department of Health has said there will be no daily Covid-19 figures update provided today due to the ransomware attack.

Backdated figures will be published 'when possible.'

The HSE has said it will take a number of days before its systems, which were shut down early yesterday morning, are restored.

Vaccinations and testing for coronavirus/Covid continuing as scheduled however.

Northern Ireland no longer provides virus updates at weekends.

Monday, 17 May

Things beginning to fully open up again in the UK: from this week on cinemas, theatres, heritage venues, indoor dining, pubs and so on can resume business, although they'll still need to follow some health and safety protocols. Over the weekend, for instance, 20,000 people at Wembley for the FA Cup final (Leicester defeating Chelsea 1-0), and quarter capacity crowds due to be allowed in grounds for the remaining rounds of Premiership fixtures, soccer and rugby premierships.

Over 55 million first doses of the vaccine administered in the UK now, and nearly 20 million people fully vaccinated.

However there's growing concern about a new variant of Covid, the so-called Indian variant (B.1.617.2), which is highly transmissible — believed to be 50% more transmissible than the Kent variant (B117), which itself was much more transmissible than the original form of the virus with which we were engaged for most of 2020; over the course of this week it appears to have tripled its presence in the UK, now over 1,300 cases identified.

Authorities say the approved vaccines are effective against this variant however there doesn't appear to be consensus on this.

Travel from India banned towards the end of April but critics saying government too slow in putting India on the so-called Red List of travel-banned countries because they're too keen to progress trade deal talks for which they have great hopes.

The final stage of unlockdown in the UK due to happen in June — 21 June — midsummer's day, in England anyhow — the devolved administrations in Wales, Scotland and Northern Ireland might move at slightly differing rates, however all are expected to lift all restrictions by the end of June, assuming there aren't upsurges of infections between now and then.

268 million first doses administered in the US so far, where 120 million are now fully vaccinated. In light of which the Centers for Disease Control and Prevention eased mask-wearing guidance for fully vaccinated people on Thursday, allowing them to stop wearing masks outdoors in crowds and in most indoor settings too.

Here in Ireland — in the Republic — because of this ransomware attack the last day we have figures for vaccinations is Tuesday: 1,922,913 doses administered up to the close of business on Tuesday, 11 May, 1,408,105 first shots and 514,808 seconds.

Apparently vaccinations have continued since then — people with appointments have been told to turn up for their appointments, and presumably they have appointments scheduled up to the end of the month at least — and, so far as I'm aware, at present they're vaccinating about 30,000 people a day — anywhere between 25,000 and 30,000 a day according to the figures I've seen recently, although whether they'll be able to sustain this with this ransomware situation I do not know.

The portal for registering for vaccination was down for a day or two but it's up and running now again.

Similarly with testing: there was disruption for 24 or 36 hours but they have a system up and running now again, even if not the system as was.

Naturally enough after all the expense and effort, everything Covid-related is being given top priority and the authorities are clearly keen to stress that everything Covid-related is back online again and we should all proceed as per schedule. Whether that's the full truth or not we shall find out. Nevertheless, one way or another I believe they will have things sorted out fairly quickly — even if that means paying the ransom, which of course they will never admit to doing.

Meanwhile in Northern Ireland 1,548,255 vaccine doses administered in total (that's up to yesterday, Sunday, 16 May), 995,904 first doses and 552,351 seconds. (1,893,700 people in Northern Ireland in 2019 according to Wikipedia — this the census estimate for 2019.)

According to the Our World in Data website the Top 10 countries for vaccinations (vaccinations per 100 people) are — there are lots of farty little places like Gibraltar, Jersey, Falkland and Cayman islands, San Marino, Bermuda and so on which have very high numbers because very small populations, however this (below) is a list of the main countries, which is to say, substantially sized countries so as to provide a sense of where things are at globally. (Hungary and Serbia using the Russian Sputnik vaccine, well they're using the Russian vaccine plus the western ones, presumably.)

Israel[8]	121.62
Chile	86.15
Bahrain	85.1
UK	81.66
USA	80.26
Hungary	74.65
Uruguay	64.69
Serbia	57.55
Germany	47.04
Denmark	44.59

Still no figures being given out because of this ransomware attack. The Department of Health has tweeted out that up to midnight last night

---

[8] People need to get two doses of vaccine so 200 a top score. Ireland on 38.94 in this table.

there were 360 additional cases of infection and over the weekend I saw a report that said that up to midnight on Saturday night there were an additional 802 new cases.

The only other thing the Dept of Health says is that presently there are 110 people in hospitals with Covid-related issues, 42 of whom are in ICUs.

Therefore, altogether, 377,642 confirmed cases of infection on the island of Ireland and, to date, 7,091 Covid-related deaths (although over 8,000 deaths in reality because Northern Ireland has a restricted way of counting what is and is not a Covid-related death — which is to say, death from covid-related issues within 28 days of testing positive for the virus, otherwise it is not counted as a Covid-death in the Department for Health count; indeed, according to the Office of National Statistics, as of the end of February, the difference between the Department for Health count and the NISRA count is 762 — see RTE News report in Friday, 5 March, diary-entry; and NISRA says counting up to 2 April the difference is 803).

Wednesday, 19 May

Yesterday evening got a text message giving me an appointment for vaccination: this Saturday, 22 May @ 10:15am at the Primary Care Centre (CVC) in Bantry. (Text came in late, around 9:15pm.)

Janssen vaccine (Janssen is a Johnson & Johnson subsidiary)

Janssen is a one-shot deal, which is good, however it has an effectivity score of only 66% to 70%, depending on which study group results one looks at, whereas the Pfizer and Moderna vaccines, for instance, are up in the 90s, and up into the mid-90s too.

At the bottom of the text message it says 'If you need to reschedule your appointment, reply "New" to this text.'

I'm wondering whether if I did do so I'd get not only a new appointment date & time but maybe also another vaccine, a different vaccine, I mean, because if I had a choice I'd choose one the of the mRNA ones, i.e., Pfizer or Moderna.

Even as I write these lines I'm conscious of what First World over-privileged nonsense this is: I'm being offered a vaccine (free of charge) before mid-summer's day less than 6 months after it's been approved for use and I'm saying 'It's a pity I cannot have one of the ones I believe to be better'!

In any event I might well end up getting another appointment and get the same vaccine offered to me. And I might get another appointment date & time a couple of weeks from now because having turned down the appointment date & time I was first offered they'd hardly make an effort to squeeze me in next week, I'd go to the back of the queue is my guess, which is to say, I'd be treated as if I'd only just registered.

Or it may be I get another appointment date & time a couple of weeks from now and I'm offered the AstraZeneca vaccine, which isn't that much more effective, and I'd have to go for two shots of that before I'd be fully vaccinated which would mean I wouldn't be fully vaccinated until August or September.

Because of course it's not like a one-in-four shot — like I'm playing some form of one-arm bandit and I just give the fruit-wheels another whirl and see if I can land on a three-cherry Pfizer or Moderna — because at these CVCs (which I presume means Community Vaccination Centre, or maybe it's Covid Vaccination Centre?) may only stock the AstraZeneca and Janssen vaccines; although I suppose they'd also have limited provisions of one or both of the mRNA ones too in case there was any reason it was advisable not to administer someone a viral vector vaccine.

In other words I could reset the appointment several times and still not get anything other than Janssen or AZ, and in the process I'd waste weeks, *months*.

With the Janssen vaccine I'd be good to go 14 days after I get the shot, which would be the end of the first week in June (Saturday, 5 June), although apparently one ought not to consider oneself fully protected until 28 days afterwards, which would be mid-June (Saturday, 19 June), which is still really good, in fairness.

Actually, no, I must be nuts! This is a great result: get vaccinated on Saturday (with a one-shot deal) and then I'm free to move about from mid-June onwards (well, freer anyhow — one is still supposed to practice physical distancing and wear facemasks and wash hands frequently and all the rest of it), free to get to the opticians to get my eyes tested and get (much needed) new glasses, and free to get to the dentist and hygienist which I also need to do. In fact free to do everything I need to get out and do this summer because I will continue to be cautious in the coming winter months as well, i.e., again September through to April/May next year because so much is unknown about all this — they cannot even say how long one will be immune for after vaccination, and of course we don't know what we don't know about the hundreds of variants of the virus and so on.

I'm presuming we'll get booster shots in the autumn too. And, even if we don't, all the more reason to continue to be cautious from September through to April/May of next year. Hopefully I will have a reasonable amount of immunity for 6 months at least.

Sunday, 23 May

I got vaccinated yesterday at the newly-built Primary Care facility up near the new school in Bantry, opened just last year, apparently. Looks like a mini-hospital.

Tim Macey drove me. Just about 2 hours' worth (round trip). Left here at about 20 past 9 and was back in Skibbereen collecting my fruit Danish and focaccia from the Dunmanway Germans in the Farmers' Market in the Fairfield at 11:15.

Everything to do with the vaccination centre and the way all organised really good. Staff about every 10 or 20 metres, guiding you around every corner. Good quality personnel too, I felt — you know, confident, outgoing, smiley (but not false smiley), pleasant and good quality people in every respect. Even the kid in the carpark, good manners, good attitude, good at the function he was asked to perform — basically to ensure everyone driving into the place was masked.

My only criticism is that the room we were asked to sit in for 30 minutes afterwards (in case anyone had an adverse reaction to what they'd been injected with) seemed a bit on the small size. About the size of the Pink Room in the Parish Hall, maybe 10 or 20% larger, in it there were about 20 people, not counting the nurses/medical staff coming and going. Four rows of chairs longitudinally arranged exam-hall like (not quite 2 metres apart from one another) with about 6 or seven chairs in each row; when I was there, about 5 people seated in each row. To my way of thinking there ought to have been only 3 rows in such a room and no more than 5 chairs in each row. Put it this way: left to my own measures I would *not* have walked into such a room, a room with 20 or 22 people in it, in the midst of a respiratory pandemic, much less stay in there for 20 or 30 minutes!

I felt a pain in my arm as soon as I was injected. And this wasn't needle penetration pain, or any irritation relating thereto, this was more like 'a headache' in the top of my arm. Tim laughed at this characterization of it but I'm attempting to get across the type of pain it was, i.e., nothing to do with needle-penetration; the reaction seemed to be to the content of the injection, and astonishing how quick this reaction was. It came on almost immediately, even before I had my shirt buttoned up. I mentioned it to the vaccinator, adding that I have the flu vaccine every year and I'd never had anything like this. She said that while the Janssen vaccine was like the flu vaccine in a number of respects it was different too, the fluid being injected was thicker for one thing. (It certainly didn't look thicker.)

Aside from that I felt fine afterwards, and by the time I got back to Skibbereen even that pain was gone, although I was still aware that I'd had an injection a little while ago.

I continued to feel OK but felt tired in the afternoon such that I went to bed for a couple of hours, sleeping for about an hour and a half.

I went to bed a little after 2 o'clock and I got up before 4 to watch the European Champions Cup final (La Rochelle v Toulouse).

However during the course of watching that match the situation deteriorated; it came on over the course of the two or so hours I was watching the match and by the end of it I was feeling really grotty, feverish, fluey, and a little bit sick.

Symptoms included: a headache (an actual headache in my head) combined with a 'spaced-out' feeling (kinda like if you got a proper knock to the head and you were a little bit concussed), low-level muscle pain all over plus joint-pains and just general unhappiness in all my joints and limbs, as I say feverish chills (which involved being too hot and too cold — as soon as I put on a hat and cardigan I was too hot and as soon as I took them off I was too cold again), distinct coldness in my hands, especially my fingers which I couldn't warm up, not even when I put them on the heater (they would warm up when I put them on the heater but the heat would never stay in them, not even for one second after I removed them from the radiator), in addition to which I developed a sore throat, a little bit of a cough and I was sniffling a little too.

I went to bed at about 8:30 in the evening feeling really shit, I mean a full-blown fever (too hot one minute and too cold two minutes later), my whole body sore, couldn't sleep. In fact I did sleep in short snatches but it felt like a sleepless night — I woke up at least every 20 or 30 minutes — in any event it was a long, feverish night.

It was quite bad, especially between say 9pm last night and, say, 3 o'clock this morning, so bad I was a little bit panicked for a while.

As I was watching the rugby all the symptoms were quite mild (as I was watching the match I had a notebook and pencil and I scribbled down what I was feeling as I became aware of each on-setting symptom), on a scale of one to ten I would say 3 or 4 (by half time I was suffering all of the symptoms at the same time) but they continued to get worse and worse. So, for example, during the first half I would say that on a scale of one to ten most of the symptoms were 2 or 3, however by the time we got to the post-match analysis it was more like 4 or 5. Indeed, the quality of my handwriting deteriorates significantly as you go down the pencilled notebook page, something which tells its own story, I think.

And then by the time I went to bed it was like 5 or 6 on said scale.

And last night for about 5 or 6 hours I'd say it was 6 or 7 on that scale. That was the worst of it.

As I say it was enough to make me a little panicked for a while, not so much because a whole army of things were attacking me from all sides and I felt like I might be overwhelmed, but because I was aware of the way the situation was getting progressively worse and I feared that 6 or 7 might become 7 or 8, and for me 7 to 8 would be panic stations.

Another thing: I felt quite hungry yesterday evening but the idea of food made me feel nauseous. In fact I started to prepare some supper yesterday evening and abandoned the project halfway through and, surrendering to the siege-assault I was enduring, went to bed instead, literally curling up in a foetal scrunch and just enduring the long dark night of the thing.

It was impossible to get comfortable, no position, no arrangement of bedding or the bed clothes I wore which included a snood which I had on and off and on again every 2 or 3 minutes the whole night through. And then aside from the fever, all-over muscle pain and a rising sense of fear and panic, I had to go to the loo about 6 times during the night. And *god* that was so awful: as soon as I got out of bed (which, because of muscle and joint aches, was painful to do) I was *freezing*, I mean Labrador-in-February cold, Straits of Magellan cold, Elephant Island cold; and even though I had a heater on in the room I was shivering with freezing cold before I could get the dressing gown on, literally shaking and teeth chattering with cold. And I feel sure the amount of piss I pissed all those 6 times combined wouldn't fill a brandy glass. It was such torture to feel like you absolutely had to get up and go to the loo and at the same time know it was a complete waste of time, yet the feeling that you had to go was so strong you still had to get up and make the pointless trip, despite the ball-breaking discomfort and cold.

O and by the way, I took a couple of paracetamol like I was told to do, so it's not like I didn't follow all the guidance I was given.

Anyhow the whole experience was just awful. And I'm still not right, I still have muscle and joint pains, I still have a sore throat, I still have that spaced-out feeling in my brain, and my fingers are still icy cold (such that I have to stop every half a dozen words or so as I'm writing this now and rub my hands together and blow on my freezing fingers, and I have the heating on in this room so it's not like this room is cold, and, trousers and underwear aside, I'm wearing 4 layers of garments, including lambswool pullover and cardigan, and a wool beanie up top). I mean I would not go outside the house right now, not even to walk around the grounds. In any event it's raining today so even if I felt 100% I wouldn't venture forth this morning, it's shit-looking.

Everyone I know who has been vaccinated so far has said it was no problem at all, no reactions, no difficulties whatsoever.

Liam and Angela have had the AstraZeneca and both said they had zero aftereffects.

Tim Macey, June Collins, Martin Condon, Mark McCarthy, Daniel Jackson, John Ardis, Betty Chapple… all have had the Pfizer vaccine and all have said they suffered no adverse reaction whatever. Zero, nada, zilch, nothing.

Now it may be that they're telling the truth and it is and was exactly as they say, however it may also be that they don't want to discourage others from getting vaccinated and so whatever mild reaction symptoms they may have had aren't worth mentioning.

And it may even be that six months from now I'll have forgotten much of the horrors I endured yesterday evening and last night and I will also say 'No, it was absolutely fine. No problems.' (And I'd be even more likely to say this to someone who has not been vaccinated and is inquiring about how it was for me. I would probably lie — although, in fairness, I'd probably acknowledge that I felt 'a bit grotty' for 24 hours — but I'd be reluctant to go into too much detail for fear of putting them off getting vaccinated.)

However, all that said, let me also say this: unless I'm mistaken, one *ought* to have a reaction to getting vaccinated, to some extent anyhow, surely; I mean after all you're injected with something that has all the characteristics of a foreign and hostile body (in this instance Covid/coronavirus), even though the viral vector has been disarmed, nevertheless your immune system *ought* to go to Defcon 3 or 4 in reaction to this perceived invasion/intrusion, surely (although like I say I feel like my system went very near to 'severe threat' yesterday evening and last night). So it may be that everyone is telling little white lies with respect to having zero reaction.

That said, Tim told me yesterday that he really had no discernible reaction whatsoever and he felt a bit of a fraud because Laurence made a huge fuss of him after getting his shots, and I believe him. I believe Tim would tell me the truth about something like this, even if he expressed it in deadpan, low-key terms, which is to say, he wouldn't speak a direct untruth, I believe.

Now that I'm vaccinated I'll ask all of them about how it was for them again (i.e., all the above mentioned), see if I get slightly different accounts of their experience now that I'm vaccinated.

I think if I'd heard at least one or two stories of a night of shakes and shivers I might have been more prepared but as it is I feel like I've been caught unawares with a right hook from someone experienced at throwing sucker punches.

Anyhow this is an account of my experience of getting vaccinated. Hopefully I'll be back to normal (or very nearly to normal) tomorrow. This is how I'm feeling right now; it feels like it will take at least another 24 hours to get better from where I am at the minute. Right now, in fact, I feel like I felt during the first half of the match yesterday. I'm up about 3 or 4 hours now and for a little while I felt like I was getting better with each hour, however now I'm not so sure. My headache is worse than it was an hour ago, I feel, and the muscle pains are worse too (my back and shoulder blades and thighs especially).

And also, just to mention, there's some cognitive impairment too: I've misspelled about one in every five words I've written here — really frustrating — and, worse, I cannot think what the correct spelling is, or at least I'm having trouble correcting my misspellings even when I recognise them or when the word-processor highlights the misspellings for me (writing this I've used the spellcheck more than I have for the past 5 or 6 days combined, and I've been word processing all day every day this whole week). It seems to be partly cognitive (I cannot spell) and partly coordinative, I'm having trouble getting my fingers to do what I want them to do so they keep hitting the wrong keys.

Similarly, my concentration is shot, I find it difficult to follow stories and reports; for example, I'll watch a video on YouTube and simply not be able to provide a coherent synopsis of what I've just watched (I've done this just now and by the time the 3 or 4 minute video ends I'm thinking 'What was that about again?', like I've got Alzheimer's or something).

Indeed, I'm very likely to go back to bed this afternoon because I feel exhausted and fucked-up.

It's 3 o'clock in the afternoon now. I did go to bed for a couple of hours, however I didn't sleep, at least I don't think I did (I may have done for one or two short snatches but mostly it seemed to me to be me *attempting* to get off to blessed sleep rather than actually sleeping). In any event I'm feeling much better. It has even stopped raining — turned into a lovely sunny afternoon — so my mood and outlook altogether better now.

Monday, 24 May

OK, glad to report I feel great this morning. I had a really good night's sleep (well, fairly good anyhow, woke up two or three times, in any event it was restful and restorative). What a weekend! I really feel like it was an event, a substantial trip-like event. I'm so glad it's over; even though I read the leaflets and website info which warned of side-effects including tiredness, headache, muscle pain, chills, fever and nausea what I'd actually read was blah blah blah blah blah. That might be a bit of an exaggeration, I did actually read the words printed, I just didn't take on-board their full import, and I certainly didn't expect to experience *all* of them, and all of them so intensely. In fairness nausea wasn't so intense, nor the head-ache especially in the normal sense of 'headache', what I had more than headache per se was that 'spaced-out' sense in my brain, which was quite pronounced, the kind of feeling or sense you get when you experience whiplash, or if you go up or down in an elevator faster than you were expecting, that disorientating thing. The fever and chills and muscle and joint pains were the worst however.

I was actually quite sick yesterday too, something I recognise more clearly today than I may have done yesterday. I felt 'OK' yesterday mostly because I didn't feel anywhere near as bad as I felt the night before — and I was clearly recovering — but looking back at yesterday from where I am now I can see I was quite sick yesterday too. I went to bed for a couple of hours yesterday afternoon and, even though I didn't really sleep, I felt much better for it such that I was able to get up and follow the climax of the 2020-21 Premiership season (and enjoy it) and afterwards cook myself a big meal and eat it — well, eat 80% of it anyhow.

And I went to bed early last night as well, at about 9pm.

The one thing they don't mention in their list of possible side effects, which I think they ought to, is the cognitive impairment and deterioration

of coordinative ability which I found quite pronounced, so pronounced
that it really ought to merit up-front mention. I know typing at a laptop
keyboard requires quite a lot of coordinative ability but (total non-expert
as I am) I would strongly urge the manufacturers to advise people not to
drive (or operate machinery) for 24 or even for 48 hours after vaccination,
even if they're feeling perfectly fine: my attack came on in quite a stealthy
fashion and I was in quite a poor way before I fully realised I was in the
midst of it.

And indeed my coordinative skills still aren't quite what they ought
to be this morning, I feel, I'm still hitting the wrong keys quite often, for
example, more than normal I mean because I do hit the wrong keys quite
often — maybe once every 3 lines, whereas now it's a lot more than that,
and yesterday it was once every 3 words.

And I would advise people to get well provisioned in terms of food
supplies and the like, enough for 48 hours at least (so as to be able to
remain housebound if needs be), which, happily, I was able to do.

And I'd give this advisory about not driving or operating machinery
even though maybe only one in 50 has the kind of reaction I've had. I had
a telephone conversation with Liam earlier and he tells me that Tim in
Gortanure also had a night of fever and chills and other unpleasantnesses
following his first shot (AstraZeneca). Pity Liam didn't inform me of this
before now because Tim had his first vaccine shot about a month ago
so plenty of time for him to flag this up for me. Like I say, it's the way
the whole thing caught me so wholly unprepared for the experience that
really knocked me for 6.

And this morning Liam also told me of a fellow from near Bandon
he knows who went on a car journey the day he got vaccinated — the
bloke felt perfectly fine for a few hours afterwards — [the trip was
something to do with greyhounds] and the attack came on him in the
course of that trip so much so he had to abandon the greyhound mission. Whether the abandonment happened on the outward journey or
the return journey Liam didn't say (or at least I cannot recall) but the
bloke and his vehicle and the greyhound had to be rescued from the side
of the road apparently.

Even if the authorities gave the advisory quite a few people would
quite likely ignore it, of course, but at least if the warning is given as the

thing is coming on you'd give people a chance to recognise it for what it is and maybe the person would abandon what s/he'd embarked upon half an hour or an hour earlier than s/he might do otherwise, and that hour/half an hour might make all the difference.

Muscle and joint pains all gone now, however I still do have a very slight sore throat (on a scale of one to ten about 0.5) and similarly I do still have a slight bit of that spaced-out sense in my brain. And my whole body (but especially my brain) knows that it's been through something, some kind of traumatic experience, if you know what I mean, the aftereffects of a trauma or impact.

However there's no significant pain or discomfort anywhere, I'm happy to say, and my spirits are good. The sun is shining and has been since 6 this morning and I'm in a really good mood. Feeling optimistic.

All the talk everywhere is about opening up and post-pandemic stuff of one sort or another. Not theoretical either, practical day-to-day stuff.

Northern Ireland reopening pubs and restaurants from today and these two weekends past we've had crowds in sports stadiums, rugby and soccer particularly, albeit at about 20% capacity.

The Republic of Ireland is about 6 weeks behind where the UK is in terms of vaccination rollout (at present, for example, people aged 30 to 34 can register for vaccination in the UK while here in the RoI we're presently registering 45 to 49 year olds) but what I mean here is that I've been vaccinated at just about the perfect time I feel. Getting vaccinated now just as everything is genuinely opening up — and the reopening they're doing now is nothing like the re-openings done previously, none of which felt convincing — gives me a sense of being in tune with the zeitgeist, if you know what I mean.

Things won't really be fully reopened here in Ireland until next month at least, even though, aside from pubs and restaurants, if you walk up the high street here in Skibbereen today (or any day last week), or if you look at the Farmers' Market in terms of the numbers of stalls and the crowds milling about, it looks like any other summer so far as I can see, however this level of reopening has only come about in the past couple of weeks (since about the second week in May).

All that said, on the RTE News website today I see the health minister warning that in all likelihood we'll be wearing masks right into the autumn and winter months, a good thing in my view because like I say I intend to continue being cautious right through the coming autumn, winter and spring, whatever the authorities recommend, and I'd hate it if I looked like a mad lad in so doing (however I'd be prepared to go it alone if it came to it).

Also several local council areas in England moved back into restrictive regimes again, partly because certain communities reluctant to get vaccinated and partly because of this super-transmissible Indian variant which is super-spreading in these districts.

And on news websites today I read that India has just gone past the 300,000 dead mark, for example, and these are just the official figures, the actual situation on the ground is far worse. And there's lots of countries far worse off than India — i.e., in terms of economic power and capacity to respond to the situation. And, for another example, the virus is surging again in Japan, so much so that 75% of people in Japan do not want the Olympics to go ahead this summer despite the fact that all they're planning to do is have empty stadia run-offs of all the events, just to get it over and done with; however the structure of the IOC is such that when a country is 'hosting' as Japan are this time round it's not up to the Japanese authorities, the IOC is effectively a sovereign body which you invite into/onto your territory — IOC members are immune from prosecution under Japanese laws and they and their commercial partners are exempt from all sorts of levies and normal regulations and so on — and the IOC seem determined to push on with the show this summer, even if it means staging events in total lockdown conditions while the corpses pile high in surrounding morgues and in outlying cities. So, what I'm saying is, while I'm conscious of the fact that the story of this pandemic is far from over, I'm beginning to feel that I and we — i.e., we here in Ireland, particularly towns & villages out here in the west side of Ireland — really are at the beginning of the end-stretch of it now.

It'll take a long time before we're fully out of the woods with all this, of course, maybe even a decade before everyone everywhere is vaccinated, and then there's the ball-breaking economic impact of it all. It looks like Ireland is going to end up with higher levels of unemployment because of this pandemic than we experienced during the financial meltdown a decade ago, at which time the state was literally bankrupted. The public finances won't be in the right of all this for a decade at least, especially when combined with the impact of Brexit, the climate crisis targets Eamon Ryan is setting, and ought to set (which need to be significant) and the fact that the super-low multinational corporate tax rates that've underpinned Ireland's economic success since the 1990s looks like it might need to come to an end (Ireland's corporate rate is 12.5% which is why the European headquarters of so many of the top Big Tech firms are located here — Google, Facebook, Twitter, Apple, Microsoft, Adobe, Intel… — along with several Big Pharma facilities) because now the US and the EU (and the UK too) want everyone to move to a flat rate of 21% in multilateral coordination because such firms are organising their business so that these Trillion dollar operations are actually paying almost no tax at all, crowd-surfing on the multitude of competing nation states; and if all these big guys do get their corporate tax ducks in a row then Ireland will need to fall in line because it doesn't have the power to resist if the US and the EU &c are really determined to make corporate tax rates uniform across the piste, which it looks like they are, although I suppose Ireland will be able to negotiate an off-ramp type deal so we're not cliff-edged with this change.

300,000 vaccines administered in the Republic of Ireland last week apparently, the most in any one week so far. And, of course, I'm a data-point somewhere in that 300,000.

Tuesday, 25 May

Spoke with Tim & Laurence today (on the phone) and learned that Laurence is due to get vaccinated on Thursday, the day after tomorrow (at about lunchtime), also at that new Primary Health Care facility where I was vaccinated, and also to get the Janssen jab. It'll be interesting to see how it goes for her.

Having heard my account of my experience she certainly won't get caught unawares, that's for sure. I kept my account of my experience fairly well reigned-in — i.e., nothing like all the detail recorded in these pages — because I didn't want to put her off getting vaccinated altogether (even though Laurence is keen to get vaccinated because she's had quite enough of lockdown at this stage and, for example, she's keen to get over to Belgium to see her mum who's in her 80s and on her own in the Belgian countryside). I'd say I gave her just the headlines. Enough so she's properly prepared for what may happen but not so much that she's frightened or put off.

When I'm speaking on the phone — Tim & Laurence usually have me on speaker so I'm speaking to the both of them at once — I can feel (or sense) the intensity with which she's listening to what I say about my experience of being vaccinated with Janssen, which is not at all surprising, of course, I'd be the same if it was the other way round.

In addition to which she's quite diligent about all such like anyhow so she's done all sorts of investigating on all sorts of (creditworthy) websites. For example, yesterday she was telling me about one trials report she read on the Janssen website which said that about half of the people given the vaccine (the Janssen vaccine) had side effects. *Half* of em! I wish the vaccinator had flagged this up for me, i.e., the fact that at least one in every two people will experience at least some of these here side effects. The way my vaccinator spoke about side effect made them sound like remote possibilities. She brushed aside my anxieties (I don't think I was especially anxious, it's fair to say), what I'm saying is she minimized them too much I now feel. Clearly side effects genuinely not an issue with Pfizer, and they don't appear to be with the AZ jab either, not so much anyhow going by the hearsay I've heard, even though one does hear of a few instances with AZ (Tim in Gortanure, for example), but with Janssen side effects *are* an issue, no question about it, and they should be upfront about it. 9 times out of 10 it'll not be a bother, which is to say, it'll be fairly low level stuff, you just need to be prepared for it, however in my case the situation was quite strong; I cannot know if it would've been less impactful if I'd been prepared for it. I suspect it would, my guess is it would've reduced the situation by about 10% or 15%, and, of course, it would have taken a good measure of the panic and anxiety out of it — and panic and anxiety are always worse after midnight, especially when you're on your own.

Indeed, I can even see a situation in which, if one is properly prepared, you could go through the physical experience I went through and experience it as the medicine working, which is to say, in a somewhat positive way, which I tried to make myself do at the time, but, like I've reported, there was enough semi-panic and anxiety in the mix to nullify the rational and the positive.

Anyhow, we'll see how Laurence fares on Thursday, hopefully she won't have anything like the experience I had. Indeed I'd be willing to bet she won't, partly because she's well prepared in all sorts of ways, they've even got their catering for Thursday and Friday and into the weekend sorted already (they're great planners). So my guess is that even if she suffers some of the side effects she'll be able to cope perfectly well. Additionally Tim's there and he's more than capable of doing a good job of nursing her if needs be.

Dan and Pika are due to get jabbed too. They're registered but I don't think they've had jab-dates as yet.

Wednesday, 26 May

Dominic Cummings appearing before a joint session of the Science & Technology Select Committee and the committee for Health & Social Care today. He's confirmed that, in the early part of the run-in to the first lockdown last year, 'herd immunity' was 'Plan A' in Downing Street.

At the time (and ever since) Downing Street denied this was so — because of course it would have been politically unacceptable to have a policy that let the thing rip, let it do its worst and we'll have herd immunity before the end of the summer, even at the cost of mountain of corpses, most of them will be ancients anyway so fuck em — but everyone (including me in these diaries) suspected that this was so, however, when it became clear they might be looking at up to half a million corpses, and maybe more than that, they lost their nerve and began scrambling to attempt to mitigate the escalating situation.

The plan was not just to let it rip and do its worst but even to drive it along so it went through the population before September — before the winter set in when demands on the NHS increase by an order of magnitude even without a pandemic — i.e., have the peak of it in the summer months. They even discussed ways in which they could drive it, you know, do things like they used to do with chickenpox parties years ago, accidently on purpose infect people, which is to say, nudge things so people infected one another. However, morality aside — in fact, morality never came into their calculations at all, it seems — they lost their nerve not only because modelling suggested that this weakest-to-the-wall strategy could result in a politically catastrophic corpse-pile but that, even in best case scenarios, even in the summer months doing the like would crash the NHS.

Cummings may be an embittered ex-advisor — and of course this is the spin coming from the Downing Street media management machine (they're handling this situation using the same playbook the Trump admin used against anyone who left the Trump admin and told damaging stories about what was really going on behind the scenes there) — but there's no denying he was in the rooms where it happened and when it happened and the picture he portrays of the chaos and incompetence (and of the character of Boris Johnson) is devastating.

Cummings says that Johnson used to refer to it as the 'Kung Flu' and for a long while refused to take it seriously. Well into March he said Johnson was still saying it was all just media nonsense, nothing more than Swine flu reheated and re-presented — i.e., no need to turn the world upside down on account of it. Staff in Downing Street had to almost stand in his way to prevent him doing his weekly (in person) audience with the queen, a woman in her 90s, eventually getting the palace on-board with doing the prime ministerial briefings by telephone for the duration. Johnson thought their concerns all tosh and piffle. And of course all of this bolstered by the fact that Johnson got infected with the virus by shaking hands with infected people in a hospital, presumably in an attempt to show there was nothing to worry about with this damn 'Kung Flu' nonsense.

At one point Johnson even proposed doing a live television event in which he was infected with the virus to show that it was basically harmless, there were actual discussions about this piece of medico-political theatre, with Professor Chris Whitty, the chief medical officer supposed to do the necessary to infect him — as I've written before, like Trump, Boris is a politics-as-reality-television type figure so that when he thinks about being prime minister he thinks of himself doing his Oxford Union type performances at the Dispatch Box during PMQs and doing photo-ops in front of a captive press corps, because for him, as it was for Trump, the whole thing's a show, it's all about charisma and entertainment and ratings, which is why we see Boris doing photo-op stuff on the front page of newspapers more than I've ever seen from any other prime minister, even a media-whore wannabe pop star like Blair.

And at one point in the autumn of last year, back when he was determined not to do another lockdown — especially after Keir Starmer had come out and formally called for one in support of the SAGE advisory committee which had recommended going back into lockdown to reset the dial on the second wave which was building at the time — Johnson's supposed to have said 'Look, only fucking 80-year-olds are dying from this thing, I'm not going to shut down the economy because of the risk to them.' This is not a direct quote but it's the gist of it, which of course chimes with that other quote he's supposed to have come out with: 'Let the corpses pile high in their thousands, I will not order a second lockdown!'

In fact, not surprisingly, Cummings was asked about this 'Let the bodies pile high' quote and his response was that the BBC got it correct in the way it reported it — which I think was a Laura Kuenssberg story — but other news outlets, particularly The Times' version of it, not accurate, which is basically a confirmation that Johnson did say it, something to that effect anyhow. One of the select committee members did a follow-up to clarify and, yes, he said it, according to Cummings, which, by the bye, I totally believe, I mean it's so on-brand. According to Cummings, Johnson said it in his study but that wasn't the only time he said it or something in the same vein. However, what Cummings testified to having heard him say was 'Let the bodies pile high', i.e., not 'Let the bodies pile high in their thousands.' His saying it in the first place is not going to be the problem, it's his categorical denial that he said it, which is to lie to the House of Commons if nothing else for at PMQs he categorically denied he said it or anything of the like.

And pile high in their thousands they did, 83,000 people over the age of 80 perished in the pandemic in the UK. 127,000 perished altogether, 83,000 of them 80 and older. A genocide of the ancients, and Boris' attitude was 'Fuck em, to me they're not worth 2 points of GDP.'

Told ya, the guy's a real bad dude. Might be fine to have such a character as a newspaperman or a TV host (or even a backbench shire knight) — and of course he'd be good fun if you were on the tear with him for a stag-do or some such — but he's not the kind of person you want in the captain's quarters, at any time but especially not in a time of national peril.

Cummings tells of one day back in March where they realised they had to do a complete U-turn and go to national lockdown but they didn't have any kind of lockdown plan or roadmap for managing anything of the kind so they were attempting to roadmap the lockdown and healthcare strategy on whiteboards and Princess Nuts Nuts was upstairs 'going crackers' about a story in the Times about her new dog, Dilyn, some kind of unfair coverage as far as she was concerned, and she wanted the Downing Street press office to get into gear and do something about it. Meanwhile at the same time Trump wanted the UK to be part of a bombing mission in the Middle East. It was chaotic and Armando Iannucci farcical, and, according to Cummings, Johnson was at least as concerned about her upstairs going crackers about the dog-story as he was about the lockdown roadmap or the invitational demands coming out of Washington.

Cummings has really put the boot in on Boris, on Carrie Symonds (Princess Nuts Nuts), and especially on Matt Hancock, the health secretary who he obviously has unlimited contempt for. Cummings says Hancock knowingly let people with Covid — confirmed cases of infection — go back into care homes with no provisions made to quarantine them there, and lied about doing so to cabinet and in other meetings and to the public at those press conferences he so frequently fronted; Cummings says Hancock did about 15 or 20 things for which he ought to have been sacked; he also said that several people, including the head of the civil service, wanted Johnson to dismiss Hancock, and that while Johnson appreciated the case for doing so, he kept him in place so that he [Hancock] could serve as the fall guy when the inquiry report determined that mistakes were made.

Cummings started testifying this morning at about 9:30 and so far as I know he's still at it, I haven't watched it live, just seen some headlines and read one or two reports as I was having lunch, I'll see YouTube clips and news broadcast reports of it later on.   ,

Thursday, 27 May

Spoke to Fintan O'Connell this morning (on phone), he was also vaccinated in Bantry on Saturday — also getting the Janssen jab — and he had an experience similar to mine (fever, chills and pains all over &c), except he had two shit nights of it apparently.

But the really odd thing is that his wife also vaccinated, also getting the Janssen vaccine, and she had no problems at all, nothing other than an awareness that she'd been injected in the upper arm.

Friday, 28 May

Having been given the Janssen jab yesterday (at around lunchtime), Laurence Macey has had a perfectly good night of it last night, she tells me. Some muscle pain and fatigue and a little bit nauseous for about an hour yesterday evening but otherwise fine. She even had a good night's sleep; woke up once, she said, and she was quite sweaty & clammy, however she went back to sleep and slept soundly until getting-up time this morning.

I'm delighted for her. Lovely sunny day today too (it rained all day yesterday).

Dan Ballard's brother has also been vaccinated with the Janssen vaccine and he also had a terrible night of it one night this week. Fintan, myself and Dan's brother all got it bad and Rita and Laurence no after-effects whatsoever, could it be something to do with men v women?

467 new coronavirus cases reported today.
99 Covid-patients in Irish hospitals, 38 in intensive care units.
75 new cases of infection reported on in Northern Ireland today.
No new deaths.

Saturday, 29 May

Weather's been broken these past two weeks, not disastrous by any means but, by comparison with the long dry spell we had between mid-March and mid-May, we've had quite a bit of rain, including whole days of it (Thursday of this week, for example). Other days have been raining in the morning, say, and mottled or even fine in the afternoon, or the other way round — sunny from 6am to circa noon then clouding over and then rain from mid-afternoon onwards — and then others showery, untrustworthy.

The British press have been bitching about the weather this month non-stop (and the east coast media on this island too), and not without good cause apparently because I heard on the radio this week that it's been one of the wettest Mays on record in Wales, however here in the southwest corner of this island it's not been too bad at all, a perfectly lovely May in my opinion, even though as I say since mid-May it's been noticeably wetter (but I don't think it's been disastrous at all, nor anywhere near it, for us anyhow, I can't speak for Wales or Wiltshire or Wicklow, and I've no desire to do so).

Heading into this weekend (according to all the weather apps) we're heading into a glorious patch, full suns from 5 in the mornings to 9 at night as far as the eye can see. And that's not just down here in southwest Ireland, it's the whole of Britain and Ireland — cooler down on these coasts with the likelihood of lingering sea-mists in the morning hours. Even so we're set to hit 20 on the thermometer; I don't know if it's the first time this year we've hit the 20 mark, however I suspect it is.

Although 20 and 21 June is the crown of the year on the calendar and in terms of our revolution around our local star this right now — the way things are this morning and this whole weekend — would have a very good claim on that honour too. Everything just so full, things haven't grown to their fullest extent as yet — they're still heading up towards their fullest reach of full summeriness — but because of the rain we've had everything is flourishing with such vigour, however it's still so early in the year very little had been cut back as yet, everything busting out and overflowing. Full of promise; full as a love-bird's nest, as Dylan Thomas has it in a line about mid-morning in Under Milkwood.

France re-introducing tighter rules on arrivals from UK who are not French residents to curb the spread of Covid, notably the Indian variant. Britons and other non-EU arrivals will again have to prove that they have a "compelling reason" to enter France.

In addition those visitors — those with compelling reasons — will have to self-isolate for seven days on arrival.

In these diaries, particularly in recent weeks, I've been writing as though this coronavirus story is coming to an end but increasingly it's clear we're far from that. Even though in the UK 70% of adults have had at least one vaccine jab and something like 40% have had both shots, they're still getting over 4,000 new cases of infection a day (4,182 yesterday, for example).

That's bad enough but the real worry is the fact that the so-called Indian variant is now the dominant strain in the cases being reported each day. Now over 7,000 cases of this variant identified in the UK. A few weeks ago the total was in the hundreds but back then they were worried because it was doubling each week. Well, despite the on-going restrictions and despite the vaccine rollout, the figures for this variant are still doubling each week and now they're at over 7,000 identified cases.

The Indian variant is twice as transmissible as the so-called Kent variant which itself was twice as transmissible as the original form of the virus (and the super-transmissibility of the Kent variant was what powered the unprecedented explosion of cases we saw in January, which was the very worst of the pandemic so far, many times worse than all of 2020 combined).

And, more concerning still, is that the approved vaccines are not as effective against the Indian variant as they are against the Kent variant. The AstraZeneca vaccine, for example, is believed to be up to 60%

effective against this Indian variant when a person has had both shots. However this full 60% is not achieved until a couple of weeks after the second dose, which is to say the Indian variant is spreading faster than the vaccine rollout can counter.

Too many people have had their second shot too recently to have good levels of protection from this Indian variant, which, as I say, is continuing to double each week, and which, if they cannot get on top of this upsurge is going to explode very soon, in June and July very likely.

Boris Johnson and his government have said that all restrictions will be lifted by 21 June but, if things continue on as they are, what with the Indian variant being as transmissible as it is and the vaccine rollout not being fast enough to prevent it's spread and Johnson politically committed to liberating his country from all restrictions by midsummer's day, it's potentially an explosive cocktail.

The Select Committee testimony of Dominic Cummings earlier this week gives us an insight into the mindset in Downing Street, and if that's how things were in March and in September-October last year how much worse is it likely to be now after a lockdown of 5 months' duration and what is supposed to be a world-beating vaccine rollout? (one which is constantly trumpeted as being 'second to none' despite the fact that it is second to the vaccine rollout in several states).

Johnson will want to stick to his roadmap to liberation (or whatever catchphrase title they have for it) however the Cummings' testimony will make it harder for him if he sticks to his unlockdown schedule and the whole thing blows up again such that they need to re-impose lockdowns in the autumn; they will only do localized lockdowns from now on, of that you may be sure, there will not be another national lockdown during this pandemic, I believe.

Johnson will be accused of having learned nothing, even after 15 or 16 or 18 months of it, and, equally credibly, of being scandalously indifferent to the mountain of corpses (not to say cavalier with respect to the death and suffering of so many), which he could possibly survive politically — in the short term anyhow — but he's committed to having a public inquiry into all this pandemic stuff beginning next year and presumably — between one thing and another — that'll run right into the next general election's battlefields — presumably the inquiry will take evidence for 6 months or so at least and then another few months to write-up the report which takes it up to the end of 2022.

Right now, as things stand, because of the relative success of the vaccine rollout — especially vis-a-vis the rollout in the EU — it looks like Boris is away out of this pandemic largely unscathed, but by the autumn of this year most people in most EU countries will be fully vaccinated so this relative superiority won't feel so pronounced, but if there's another wave of this thing and despite the warnings — right now people urging him to delay full unlockdown until August at least — he continues to open up (because of some boosterish political commitment) he'll get the blame for it good and proper no mistake.

Israel didn't beginning its unlockdown until 70% of its people were fully vaccinated with the result that the unlockdown there has been a success. However, as I say, Johnson is pushing for unlockdown with less than half the population fully vaccinated. He really is a reckless fool.

So far about 100 cases of the Indian variant of the virus have been identified in the Republic of Ireland (I'm not sure what the state of play is in Northern Ireland, although I know cases of it have been identified up there too) so how things are going over in Britain ought to be a forewarning for us. The government here appears to be as committed to reopening for the summer as Johnson, however with us a month or 6 weeks behind where the UK are at with respect to the vaccine rollout, it has always been the case that Ireland would not be fully reopened before midsummer's day.

That said, if you walk around the streets of Skibbereen right now — with the exception of pubs and restaurants — it sure looks like everything is back to normal again. Lots of people about, it's as busy right now as in July most other years — presumably because people either cannot go abroad because they would need to quarantine, or they're reluctant to go to the places we're allowed to travel to without quarantining, therefore most people holidaying at home again this year.

		Population	Infections	Deaths	Tests/1m pop
1.	USA	330,806,424	33,259,571	594,431	1,433,937
2.	India	1,378,604,014	28,047,534	329,100	242,035
3.	Brazil	212,405,664	16,471,600	461,057	229,413
4.	France	65,259,187	5,666,113	109,431	1,277,300
5.	Turkey	84,244,944	5,242,911	47,405	625,411
6.	Russia	145,928,315	5,071,917	121,501	937,044
7.	UK	67,859,075	4,484,056	127,781	2,644,246
8.	Italy	60,470,472	4,216,003	126,046	1,083,504
9.	Argentina	45,244,432	3,781,721	78,093	297,822
10.	Germany	83,757,235	3,681,126	88,442	704,517
11.	Spain	46,752,999	3,678,390	79,953	1,062,810
12.	Columbia	50,919,972	3,406,456	88,774	325,304
13.	Iran	83,921,387	2,893,218	79,741	228,696
14.	Poland	37,833,389	2,872,283	73,745	416,964
15.	Mexico	128,844,230	2,413,742	223,568	53,655
16.	Ukraine	43,649,444	2,202,494	50,536	232,341
17.	Peru	32,932,217	1,955,469	69,342	379,680
18.	Indonesia	274,219,048	1,816,041	50,404	59,370
19.	S. Africa	59,316,193	1,662,825	56,439	191,651
20.	Czechia	10,715,215	1,661,272	30,108	2,214,310
21.	Netherlands	17,146,915	1,647,329	17,601	803,616
22.	Chile	19,105,644	1,384,346	29,300	754,196
23.	Canada	37,872,563	1,381,582	25,547	905,601
24.	Philippines	109,902,061	1,223,627	20,860	119,009
25.	Iraq	40,417,268	1,197,082	16,351	250,904
26.	Romania	19,188,803	1,077,737	30,312	469,235
27.	Sweden	10,132,390	1,068,473	14,451	961,251
28.	Belgium	11,605,601	1,062,373	24,955	1,180,378
29.	Pakistan	220,673,722	921,053	20,779	57,871
30.	Portugal	10,180,572	849,093	17,025	1,140,195

AFTERWORDS

Now — at the end of summer — the Republic of Ireland has 77% of its adult population fully vaccinated and 89% one-shot vaccinated. Last week the 6 millionth dose of Covid vaccine was administered here.

Similar figures for Northern Ireland: 75% of adults fully vaccinated and just over 84% partially vaccinated (75% and 89% for the UK as a whole).

North and south vaccination centres now offering walk-in vaccination services.

From here the focus is on vaccinating schoolchildren before schools restart: 16 to 18 years olds already done — most of them anyhow — so now the focus is on 12 to 15 year olds.

Bualadh bos, in fairness, I really didn't think they'd manage to get it all done before September. I believed they'd get it done but I thought they'd still be at it well into September and maybe even October too, especially in the wake of the cyberattack on the health service computer networks in May.

And the uptake is and has been really good, looks like we're going to be up in the 90s, which is about as good as could reasonably be expected, *better* than expected.[9]

---

[9] Fintan O'Toole had an article in the Irish Times a couple of weeks ago — 27 July — about variations in vaccine scepticism/hesitancy and vaccine uptake: Ireland has one of the lowest levels of vaccine scepticism/hesitancy and correspondingly one of the highest levels of uptake in Europe, something he links to attitudes toward the state, which I think correct to do because at the end of all it must come down to a question of trust and confidence in the system: while we might bitch and whine and moan and legitimately dispute with Leo Varadkar, Micheál Martin, Eamon Ryan, Stephen Donnelly, Simon Harris and all the rest of them under scores of policy headings, something like this — this pandemic and

Most everything's reopened now — everything's reopened so far as I know — however some restrictions still in force: pubs and cafés still doing outdoor service mostly, for example, although one can go indoors if fully vaccinated and you have your Vaccine Certificate to prove it, and only 50 people permitted in cinemas and theatres, large gatherings still restricted, even outdoor events, and we're still required to wear facemasks in indoor settings, shops and shopping malls and on public transport and so on because the authorities would prefer to err on the side of caution.

And with good cause too because, as we've seen in the UK, when restrictions are totally swept away in a boosterish "Freedom Day" act of bravado cases of infection shoot up again — the UK going from 3,000 to 4,000 new cases a day at the end of May up to 40,000 to 50,000 in mid-July.

It's levelled off somewhat since, nevertheless at the minute the UK still getting between 20,000 and 30,000 new cases a day, but the important point is these diagnosed cases are not resulting in massive upsurges in hospitalizations and deaths.

In January, at the height of the pandemic, when 50,000 to 60,000 cases a day were being diagnosed, there were circa 40,000 people in UK hospitals with Covid-related issues, today it's somewhere between 5,000 and 6,000.

Same here — except we haven't swept away all government-mandated restrictions like they did in the UK — we're getting between 1,000 and 1,500 new cases a day and at the minute we've about 200 Covid-patients in our hospitals, 28 or 30 of whom are in critical care units. Manageable.

Back in January for every 1,000 cases of infection 80 or so were hospitalized, now it's something like 20 hospitalizations for the same number of infections.

---

our way out of it — is where the rubber meets the road and, as can be seen, when it comes to it, clearly we have confidence in the authorities which these individuals represent because (indisputably) they've been elected to do so. Compare and contrast with Russia where even now they've only just over 20% of people vaccinated, despite having a vaccine available since the end of last year — the Russians began their vaccine rollout in Q4 of 2020 — or the United States where they've only just over 50% of people fully vaccinated, and there's a direct correlation between states that voted for Biden in the presidential election — good to reasonably high levels of vaccine uptake — and states that voted for Trump — disappointing to poor levels of uptake.

Being vaccinated doesn't mean you won't get infected, you can do and you probably will do (eventually), however vaccination provides you with the wherewithal to protect yourself from the worst effects of Covid if you do happen to get infected. I'm not sure what the precise figure is but something like 90% of the people getting sick and being hospitalized are people who for one reason or another are unvaccinated, or are only partially vaccinated; which is to say, there *are* instances of people who are fully vaccinated getting infected and getting sick and suffering such that they need hospitalization. Vaccines do not offer 100% protection, they never promised to.

Ireland's deputy chief medical officer Dr Ronan Glynn compares it to wearing safety belts: wearing a safety belt won't prevent road accidents but nine times out of ten people wearing safety belts are going to have better outcomes in the unfortunate event of a road accident as compared with those not safety-belted.

Vaccines are 80% to 85% effective against symptomatic disease, Dr Glynn says, and 95% effective against hospitalisation.

From September attention will turn to rolling out booster-shots for the coming winter cycle, which they're planning to do at the same time as they administer the winter flu jab this year.

The authorities want most people to get a flu shot this autumn because it is feared flu strains and other respiratory bugs are going to be serious issues in the coming winter. Virtually no flu strains circulating in the 2020-21 season as most of us were living in fairly strict lockdown regimes, therefore our protective systems will have run low for lack of match fitness, so to say.

Moreover, from here onwards the Republic's moving over to using only mRNA vaccines, i.e., discontinuing supplies of the Janssen and AstraZeneca vaccines, neither of which are as effective or flexible as the mRNA vaccines, something I'm really pleased about because until I'm vaccinated with an mRNA vaccine I'm not going to feel as secure as I'm going to need to feel in order to fully function again.

One final note on the pandemic in Ireland — just to bring the story up to date — altogether (so far), there have been 320,711 confirmed cases of infection in the Republic of Ireland and just over 5,000 Covid-related deaths (5,035).

172,866 confirmed cases of infection in Northern Ireland and 2,238 deaths. Therefore, altogether, 493,577 confirmed cases of infection on the island of Ireland and, to date, 7,273 Covid-related deaths, although probably over 8,000 deaths in reality because the UK's Department for Health (including the health service in Northern Ireland) has a restricted way of counting what is and is not a Covid-related death — which is to say, death from Covid-related issues within 28 days of testing positive for the virus, otherwise it's not counted as a Covid-death in the Department for Health count; indeed, according to the Office of National Statistics in Northern Ireland, as of mid-July the difference between the health department's count and the statistics agency's count is 829.

As I write the town still echoes the cheers for two local rowing club members, Paul O'Donovan and Fintan McCarthy, who took gold in the lightweight double sculls in the Olympics in Tokyo, which — having been postponed from last summer — were finally staged over the course of the past couple of weeks. No small matter considering this is just the 10th gold medal Ireland's won since Ireland first sent a national team to the Olympics in Paris in 1924.

And then atop that in a small town like Skibbereen you can imagine the added excitement. The final was at about 2 or 3 o'clock in the morning (Irish time) and about half the people in the town and surrounds stayed up to watch it. I didn't because I'm working flat out getting these diaries ready for typesetting but I caught up with the excitement at 6AM — when I woke first thing I did was check see how they'd fared.

Later in the day I went up to Fields to fetch some groceries and lit-erally *every* conversation I overheard was about rowing (albeit I caught only snippets of conversation, words and phrases), not just *in* Fields, also on the way to Fields and on the way home again. I had one conversation on that outing and that was with the cashier at the checkout: first thing she says was to ask whether I stayed up 'to watch it.' The whole town's buzzing with it, despite the fact that most of us wouldn't know one end of a rowing boat from the other. However, isn't this what the Olympics is supposed to be about, isn't this what athletes work so hard for? — to make your hometown/neighbourhood thrill in just this way — more so than the medal itself, I mean, or the RTE interview or the grip & grin with the Taoiseach in front of a sponsor's logo.

Another Skibbereen Rowing Club member won a medal at Tokyo too, Emily Hegarty, one of a women's four who took bronze behind Australia and the Netherlands. I thought this race more exciting to be honest because the two guys were sure-fire medal prospects, after all they're the reigning European and World champions, and they won fairly easily in the end, whereas the women really had to battle for what they won, winning it right on the line.

Weather's been astonishingly good this summer, must be one of the best summers ever in Ireland — all of July excellent (every day between 22 and 28 degrees) and the latter half of June really good too (between 20 and 24) — and what with all the pubs and cafés and restaurants turned inside out (chairs and tables out onto the street everywhere) the town has had a real summer holiday vibe to it.

No big homecoming parade for the Olympians because of the ongoing pandemic restrictions but an informal show of appreciation happened when they got back to Skibbereen on the August bank holiday weekend, people coming out to their front doors to applaud and cheer them. Doing a block of cycles round the church I heard the cheering and clapping out on Bridge Street and deduced what was going on.

In any event a spontaneous show of appreciation is so much better than anything organized, more authentic, as opposed to a lorry-trailer for a stage in the Fairfield and grotesquely amplified music and some local radio 'personality' shouting into the microphone like he's a Big Fight Night announcer in Madison Square Gardens.

The 2020 Euros also finally staged — in June and July. It was a good tournament, a success, particularly for Italy playing a really attractive brand of football.

And this weekend the Premiership starts up again which will have full stadia so we're almost back to normality.

That said, I'm not sure we'll ever be going back to what once we thought of as 'normality' because the planet (our homeland) is on fire — huge fires in Turkey and Greece this summer, serious square miles of uncontainable wildfires akin to what's happening in California and Oregon, so serious that several Greek islands have had to be evacuated in scenes like you'd see only in disaster movies, nothing but deserts of grey ash left in the fires' wake.

47 degrees of Celsius recorded in Spain this summer and a 48 in Sicily.

All this in the same summer as we've seen shocking flooding and deluges in Belgium and Germany, washing away not only bridges and walls and vehicles but whole houses, streets and villages, leaving behind deep water-sculpted gouges where once your neighbours dwelled. Hundreds dead. Thousands bewildered.

Hundreds also dead in Canada and all up and down the Pacific Northwest because of a so-called 'heat dome' — 49.6 degrees recorded in Canada. In *Canada*, for goodness sakes, where moose and elk live! And several places in California, Nevada and New Mexico recording temps of over 50 degrees, making this summer the hottest ever in North America.

'Climate Change' is not something that may happen if we don't drastically cut polluting emissions, it's something we're already experiencing because of a century and more of unsustainable pollution and wanton destruction.

We've been poor stewards of our inheritance and there's going to be a tsunami of reckoning for it. We've totally wasted these last 21 years of opportunity with bullshit wars, stupid smartphones and tosser apps.

The Creationist Edwin Poots was elected to succeed Arlene Foster as leader of Democratic Unionist Party in Northern Ireland, however he lasted but a month.

Having been elected on a promise to listen to the party membership as opposed to dictating policy and strategy from on high — as he accused Mrs Foster of doing back when he was conspiring to topple her — in his first play as party leader he arrogantly refused to listen to his Assembly colleagues with the predictable result that the people who put him in office voted no confidence in him before the new business cards he'd ordered were printed and delivered. 33 days Loony Poots lasted; it was a comic turn, a clown on a unicycle juggling firesticks.

The loathsome Jeffrey Donaldson is leader now, he was elected unopposed once Poots flushed himself down the loo.

I haven't heard much from any of em since. And why not seeing as the UK government is now carrying their water: on 21 July UK Brexit negotiator and Cabinet Office minister David Frost announced the UK's new position on the Irish Protocol: they want to reopen all documents relating to it and start negotiating it again — i.e., renegotiate it into non-existence — which is to say, the British government's horse is now pulling the DUP's cart.

It was obvious enough at the time but in light of these developments it's now perfectly obvious that the Brits negotiated in bad faith all through the Brexit negotiations. They simply wanted to get matters to where they could go to the country and win an election then they'd brazenly renege on what they agreed to, knead that bruise in the north of Ireland until the Irish capitulated — Dublin needs to have good trading relations with the UK more than the EU as a whole does — and then, with a cowed Dublin onside, return to the EU offering a new settlement proposition which basically amounts to 'Hey, Hans, we have Paddy here in a headlock, so fuck you, and fuck your Single Market.'

The following is part of the RTE News report on Frost's long-awaited 'Command Paper' on the Irish Protocol:

> The British government has indicated it is seeking a "standstill period" to negotiate major changes to the Northern Ireland Protocol, the element of the Brexit trade agreement intended to avoid the return to a hard border on the island of Ireland.

> The British minister with responsibility for relations with the EU, David Frost, has said that the protocol is not sustainable and that the UK government is seeking for existing [Northern Irish] grace periods to be maintained.

> Mr Frost said: "At the same time (as discussions) we must provide certainty and stability for businesses as we do so.

"So we believe that we and the EU should also quickly agree a standstill period, as it were, including maintaining the operation of grace periods in force and a freeze on existing legal actions and processes.

"This is to ensure there is room to negotiate and provide a genuine signal of good intent to find ways forward.

"These proposals will require a significant change to the Northern Ireland Protocol, we do not shy away from that. We believe such change is necessary to deal with the situation we now face. We look to open a discussion on these proposals urgently.

"We urge the EU to look at [our proposals] with fresh eyes and to work with us to seize this opportunity and to put our relationships onto a better footing. We stand ready to work with them to deliver the brighter future which is in reach."

In the wake of which, unsurprisingly, the loathsome Jeffrey Donaldson — happy as a cat with two dicks — simpered "This is a significant step in the right direction by the government, an acceptance that the Protocol is not sustainable."

"The Prime Minister must continue at pace to remove the Irish Sea Border, which is fracturing the economic and constitutional integrity of the United Kingdom.

"The rigid refusal by Brussels to even consider renegotiation of the Protocol is symptomatic of how we reached this point."

In response European Commission vice-president Maroš Šefcovic said the EU will seek "creative solutions" to difficulties in relation to trade between Britain and Northern Ireland caused by Brexit, but will not renegotiate the Brexit deal on Northern Ireland.

The UK negotiated the protocol line-by-line so knew precisely what was involved in the agreement they signed up to and so recently ratified; the difficulties that have arisen directly result from the UK choosing the hardest form of Brexit.

Foreign Affairs minister Simon Coveney said Ireland will closely analyse British proposals to reduce trade frictions between Britain and Northern Ireland, but any solution must remain within the terms of the deal agreed with the EU last year.

And so matters remain for now as parliaments are in recess and everyone's off on August holidays but in my view there's nothing but trouble ahead the way the Brits seem determined to corral and shepherd us.

Meanwhile Arlene Foster has a new job: she now appears alongside Nigel Farage on a GB News politics show because she says she wants 'to bring Northern Ireland into the mainstream of UK politics' — because, you see, for Arlene, appearing right alongside Nigel Farage on GB News is how you bring something 'into the mainstream', that's where the UK mainstream is, she thinks, right there beside Nigel on a wannabe British version of the divisive, repulsive and utterly toxic Fox News.

Speaking of matters divisive and repulsive, Tucker Carlson, one of Fox News' leading hosts, is doing his prime-time show from Hungary at the minute because Hungary, according to Tucker, offers the US a vision of what it could be if it had the will to go for it. Taken to view Hungary's 175km high-tech, razor-wire border fence with Serbia this week, Tucker liked what he saw, praising the fence for being so 'clean and orderly', in contrast to the 'chaos' on the US-Mexican border: "It doesn't require a GDP the size of the US," he told his viewers "it doesn't require high-tech walls, guns, or surveillance equipment. All it requires is the will to do it."

Which is to say, the right in America now openly embrace populist authoritarian regimes like Orban's in Hungary, promoting them as models for what could be accomplished in the US. I regard him as a preposterous little dingleberry but, fact is, right now Tucker Carlson is seen as one of those best placed to inherit Trumpolini's fan base if the former president decides not to put himself forward again in the 2024 election cycle.

Not heard too much from the Prince of Bronze these past few months — I haven't anyhow, even though he's been the keynote speaker at CPAC and he's done a few other events, but such appearances simply aren't getting the coverage they once did. However the Trump Organisation — its CFO Allen Weisselberg in particular — have been indicted on tax fraud and false accounting charges at the state and local level (New York state and New York City), which, no doubt, are the opening salvos in the coming war on Trump and the Trump family organisation.

What prosecutors really want is for Weisselberg to plea-bargain and walk the prosecution through how business is (and was) conducted at Trump HQ. They have all the paperwork necessary to dismantle the organisation, they just need someone well-informed and credible to go into the witness box to walk a jury through the forest of paperwork — dense financials, tax returns, accounting practices, legal documents.

Weisselberg appears to be remaining loyal for now but — dollars to donuts — he either ends up dead (one way or another) or else Donald flips on Weisselberg and says 'It was all Weisselberg; I didn't know anything about that stuff. I'd no idea the guy was such a crook!'

Meanwhile Congress has set up a Select Committee to investigate into and report on the events leading up to the riotous invasion of Congress on January 6th, which as the emerging evidence makes clear was indeed a full-on attempted coup d'état. The Department of Justice has waived 'Executive Privilege' in relation to the documentation the committee has asked for — something it wouldn't do normally without a fight in the courts, however the charges are so serious it merits the waiver (as I say we're talking about a full scale coup d'état, it doesn't get more serious than that) — so the whole story will be fully fleshed out between now and next January, all of which puts me in mind of Sir John Harington's celebrated Elizabethan epigram: 'Treason doth never prosper. What's the reason? Why if it prosper, none dare call it treason.'

Meanwhile although things went really well for Biden for six months or so, it looks like he's headed into some mosquito- and gator-infested swamplands at the minute. The trouble is that even with prize-giving incentives (literally paying people to get vaccinated) the US cannot get itself up much above 50% fully Covid-vaccinated, which is simply not good enough — in order to have any fair chance of being effective it needs to be up above 70% and there's a whole bunch of states which have hopeless levels of vaccine uptake. No prizes for guessing which states have seen reasonably good uptake and which have poor to middling uptake — it correlates almost precisely with the way the states voted in the election last November. Indeed overall uptake is so poor the US is in danger of seeing another wave of this thing; they *are* into another wave of it in fact — right now they're back up to getting nearly 100,000 cases of infection a day and they're on their way back up to a thousand deaths a day. And it's all politics, toxic politics.

'No Masks & No Mandates' is the Republican rallying cry; they're encouraging infection (by discouraging mitigation measures) so that when the numbers surge again this winter they'll blame Biden for it, and then they'll run on the fact of the resurge in the mid-terms, saying Biden failed to protect us like he promised he would. As I write Biden's approval ratings are still above 50% — however, at 50.2%, only just — but the overall trend is clearly downwards so he'll be sub-50 before too long more, I expect (7 points the gap between approval and disapproval at the minute, down from 18- and 19-point differentials earlier this year).

Worldwide, just over 200 million confirmed Covid cases so far, and coming up on 4.5 million deaths.

And, finally, just for the sake of completeness, the following are the up-to-date[10] figures for the top 30 countries in terms of the numbers of confirmed cases of infection.

	Population	Infections	Deaths	Vaccinations[11]
1. USA	330,806,424	36,681,559	621,636	50.26/59.2%
2. India	1,378,604,014	32,225,513	431,642	8.79/30.62%
3. Brazil	212,405,664	20,364,099	569,058	23.19/54.63%
4. Russia	145,928,315	6,600,836	170,499	22.1/27.85%
5. France	65,259,187	6,471,035	112,702	52.51/68.43%
6. UK	67,859,075	6,267,437	130,953	59.77/69.68%
7. Turkey	84,244,944	6,059,806	53,005	38.59/51.91%
8. Argentina	45,244,432	5,088,271	109,105	21.73/58.78%
9. Columbia	50,919,972	4,870,922	123,580	27.02/40.62%
10. Spain	46,752,999	4,719,266	82,595	63.72/74.25%
11. Italy	60,470,472	4,440,669	128,432	57.05/67.29%
12. Iran	83,921,387	4,389,085	97,208	5.22/18.47%
13. Indonesia	274,219,048	3,854,354	117,588	10.25/19.59%
14. Germany	83,757,235	3,823,139	91,871	56.81/62.77%

[10] Saturday, 14 August 2021. Figures for infections and deaths taken from the European Centre for Disease Prevention and Control website.

[11] Vaccination figures taken from the Our World in Data website. By the bye, the percentages given in the OWD tables are percentages for the total population whereas the vaccination figures I gave at the top of this ('Afterwords') section are for the percentage of *adults* vaccinated. So, above I say 75% fully vaccinated in the UK, and 89% partially vaccinated (UK's Department for Health figures), whereas in the OWD presentation the figures for the UK are 59.77% and 69.68% respectively. Similarly, at the top I say the Republic of Ireland has 77% of its adult population fully vaccinated and 89% partially vaccinated, the corresponding OWD figures for Ireland are 62.36% and 70.84%.

15. Mexico	128,844,230	3,108,438	248,652	22.53/41.76%
16. Poland	37,833,389	2,885,461	75,299	47.97/49.74%
17. S. Africa	59,316,193	2,605,586	77,141	6.88/12.45%
18. Ukraine	43,649,444	2,266,329	53,269	6.22/10.73%
19. Peru	32,932,217	2,134,365	197,487	20.91/28.10%
20. Netherlands	17,146,915	1,901,827	17,909	61.47/69.49%
21. Iraq	40,417,268	1,775,764	19,672	1.23/2.05%
22. Philippines	109,902,061	1,741,616	30,340	11.47/17.07%
23. Czechia	10,715,215	1,676,297	30,375	49.60/54.34%
24. Chile	19,105,644	1,629,932	36,420	68.15/74.33%
25. Canada	37,872,563	1,455,973	26,704	63.66/72.54%
26. Bangladesh	164,802,127	1,418,902	24,175	3.17/9.36%
27. Malaysia	32,818,781	1,404,899	12,510	32.32/52.31%
28. Belgium	11,605,601	1,155,185	25,298	66.15/71.58%
29. Japan	126,052,492	1,128,382	15,400	37.34/49.55%
30. Sweden	10,132,390	1,111,177	14,659	48.60/65.00%